T0303859

Working Together

Working Together

Organizational Transactional Analysis and Business Performance

ANITA MOUNTAIN

CHRIS DAVIDSON

GOWER

© Anita Mountain and Chris Davidson 2011

First published in paperback 2015

All rights reserved. No part of this publication may be reproduced, stored in a retrieval system or transmitted in any form or by any means, electronic, mechanical, photocopying, recording or otherwise without the prior permission of the publisher.

Published by
Gower Publishing Limited
Wey Court East
Union Road
Farnham
Surrey, GU9 7PT
England

Gower Publishing Company
110 Cherry Street
Suite 3-1
Burlington, VT 05401-3818
USA

www.gowerpublishing.com

Anita Mountain and Chris Davidson have asserted their moral right under the Copyright, Designs and Patents Act, 1988, to be identified as the authors of this work.

British Library Cataloguing in Publication Data
Mountain, Anita.
 Working together : organizational transactional analysis
 and business performance.
 1. Transactional analysis. 2. Communication in
 organizations. 3. Communication in management.
 4. Psychology, Industrial. 5. Achievement motivation.
 I. Title II. Davidson, Chris.
 658.3'145-dc22

Library of Congress Cataloging-in-Publication Data
Mountain, Anita.
 Working together : organizational transactional analysis and business performance / Anita Mountain and Chris Davidson.
   p. cm.
 Includes index.
 ISBN 978-0-566-08846-9 (hardback) -- ISBN 978-1-4094-3156-5
(ebook) 1. Organizational behavior. 2. Business communication. 3. Psychology, Industrial. 4. Transactional analysis. I. Davidson, Chris. II. Title.
 HD58.7.M6888 2011
 650.1--dc22

2011008235

ISBN 9781472461599 (pbk)
ISBN 9781409431565 (ebk – PDF)
ISBN 9781409486671 (ebk – ePub)

MIX
Paper from
responsible sources
FSC® C004959

Printed and bound in Great Britain
by Printondemand-worldwide.com

Contents

List of Figures

List of Tables

Foreword – The Past is Prologue: The Relevance of TA Today

CARY L. COOPER, CBE
*Distinguished Professor of Organizational Psychology and Health,
University of Lancaster*

An American President once said that 'the past is prologue' historically if we are to understand what is happening today and tomorrow. The theory of transactional analysis was developed by Eric Berne in the beginning of the 1960s, with his book *Transactional Analysis in Psychotherapy*. His ideas were relevant for the time, particularly in a therapeutic context and latter in understanding personal relationships, dyadic[1] and group behaviour. There was also early work linking TA within organizational behaviour, but this did not develop as rapidly as it deserved.

This book, *Working Together*, is making up for the past failures in the field by providing the theoretical framework of TA to understand a range of dynamics of organizational behaviour. It starts with the use of the theory in self-understanding, why 'recognition' is important, the relationship between the individual and the organization, its significance in the context of leadership, organizational culture and the current work–life balance issues.

This is a very significant book in providing a framework for understanding a wide range of organizational issues and problems, and how they might be tackled. Before anyone can take action, they must have a clear vision of the issues. It is important, therefore, to have some conceptual framework to understand the dynamics of organizational behaviour – TA provides this and can help us plan our change programmes more effectively. As the old Japanese proverb goes, 'vision without action is a daydream but action without vision is a nightmare'.

---

1   Editor's note: dyadic – relating to or based on two.

Anita and Chris help us take a fresh look at common workplace frustrations, providing the framework and vocabulary to understand and prevent them. The exercises provided help us change our behaviour at home and in the workplace to help us get the successful outcomes we know we deserve. A 'must read' reference book for CEOs, managers, salespeople, trainers and anyone who has ever struggled to understand the human condition!

Nigel Dunand, Professional Development Director, Sandler Training

Anita and Chris appear on the surface to work a kind of magic – with ease and in a relaxed style. When they talk to people they can see and hear things that other people miss and get to the centre of issues easily and quickly. They have a unique style and approach. This book shows how you and I can take this approach and work that magic for ourselves.

Opening up the subject of TA and adding in some real experience and deep knowledge the authors have created a book that unfolds to give away the secret to becoming a great manager or motivator.

Julie Hanson, Owner - The One Company and Sloe Road

Working Together is one of those rare business books that is easy to read. The style adopted by the authors leads to an immediate understanding of the theory whilst the examples used turn on that light bulb for the reader. Particularly useful are the tasks, it is comforting to know and easy to see that the authors genuinely want to aid the reader in putting the theory into practice. I have found TA very useful in my business and shall be dipping in and out of this book regularly. It will not be in my bookcase but on my desk.

Mark Poultney, Managing Director, Imperial Catering Equipment Ltd/
Hatco Corporation

Preface

This book has been written for all those who would like to understand and improve the way in which they communicate. We are passionate about making the work environment a good place to be for the individual as well as a productive place for the organization.

Ultimately an organization is the people who work within it and the culture that exists between them. Many quality improvement methodologies focus on the systems and processes, but are ultimately ineffective because they lose the human focus. In this book we are starting with the people, and building on strengths rather than just focusing on weaknesses.

The approach we are using is called Transactional Analysis; however, it could be called common sense. Transactional Analysts give names to the ways we are and how we behave so that everyone can develop an understanding and change if they wish to; however, this is not just a book about the individual. Organizations have a life of their own and we also take a look at what happens in organizations, from their founding to the present-day activities and how these interrelate. In a way you could say that this book is all about change, but change to make the workplace life-enhancing as well as productive, all based on common sense.

TA is particularly accessible, and we believe effective, because every concept can be illustrated with diagrams which gives it an edge over many other methods, as it is not just words. When things are drawn they are much easier to understand and remember. The diagrams explain concepts in a way that promotes instant understanding.

Our challenge in writing this book has been to obtain a balance between academic theory and practical application without oversimplifying the approach. Talk to those who have heard about TA and they are likely to say that they had a day on it as part of their university course or within a course on such topics as careers or leadership. This has tended to discount TA as a body of knowledge with breadth and depth. Yet there is also merit in these short courses as they offer the opportunity for understanding and change for a variety of people of all ages and from all walks of life. This then can be its strength as well as a weakness.

This book is our interpretation of Transactional Analysis based on years of being trained and then applying this to organizations. The partners of Mountain Associates have a total over 40 years of experience enabling clients to gain exceptional perspective to promoting development and growth in organizations.

Even though this is a published work it will never be a final product. We are continuously questioning our own thinking so that we can go further. Other TA theorists will, no doubt, also be questioning and continuing debate which will develop the theory further. This is part of an evolving dynamic process and long may it continue.

And in summary:

First of all find the principle
Then believe the principle
Then practice it
Then become it.

(First Nation saying, author unknown)

Anita Mountain
Chris Davidson

Acknowledgements

We would like to thank Alison Skinner, Barry Baynes, Rob Davidson, Joyce Brand and Bill Garland for reading and commenting on the text. The way in which they each offered their constructive criticism reflects the very approach we write about. We also want particularly to thank Alan Davidson, who painstakingly read the whole final manuscript meticulously.

To Jonathan Norman, our editor, for his enthusiasm on receiving our proposal for the book and subsequently for his unerring patience and goodwill throughout this process. Thanks also go to all the staff at Gower for their helpfulness during the proof reading process.

We also wish to thank Julie Hay for her support and generosity during the trials and tribulations of book writing. Thanks too, to Peter and Glynis Harper, our dear friends, who maintained their interest in our endeavours and offered their support.

Anita Mountain
Chris Davidson

About the Authors

Anita Mountain, MSc CTA (O)(P) Teaching and Supervising Transactional Analyst (with Organizational and Psychotherapy specialties) has been working nationally and internationally since 1990. She has trained and coached a wide variety of professionals from Owner/MD's to Consultant Psychiatrists and other trainers, coaches and consultants. As a company, Mountain Associates have worked with multi-nationals to SME's as well as local authorities within the UK. Her training in two fields of Transactional Analysis and the way she uses these has meant that she has been called iconaclastic and her professional expertise is in demand both as a key-note speaker and as a consultant, coach and coach supervisor.

Chris Davidson, CTA (O) Provisional Teaching and Supervising Transactional Analyst (with Organizational specialty) joined Mountain Associates in 1999 after many years of experience in working in the public sector. His wealth of experience in groups and groupwork allied to his knowledge of human behaviour is of particular benefit when working in organizations. Chris Davidson also works internationally training others both in-house as well as in Mountain Associates open Developmental/ Organizational TA, and Official Introductory TA workshops. His considerable computing skills are also utilized in the company developing their own e-Learning modules.

Chris Davidson and Anita Mountain are business and life partners and so the title of this book – *Working Together* – also has relevance for them. They work as a team, each with their own areas of expertise which, when combined, add up to over 40 years of experience.

1 *Introduction*

Why You Should Read this Book

This book offers a different approach to the usual business books. We do not use techniques or gimmicks. The approach is pragmatic because it deals with the process of relationships and is about common sense. This book will provide everyone within the workforce – from the shop floor to the MD – with different options on how to relate. Whilst written for the workplace, those who read it will gain new insights that will also stand them in good stead in all areas of their lives.

The reader is offered an opportunity to expand their awareness of themselves and others in a matter-of-fact way so that relationships will be enhanced. Part of a larger model on the structure of organizations (see the concluding chapter), this book puts work relationships in a context. We offer a powerful combination of theory and application enabling the new MD, trainer, consultant or HR executive an opportunity to gain in-depth insight into using Organizational Transactional Analysis.

Transactional Analysis is a social psychology, a theory of human personality and a systematic approach for growth and personal change in individuals, groups and organizations. It promotes and improves communication, thereby enhancing relationships. We use clear explanations with diagrams to outline how to develop and maintain effective communication. Since its development in the 1950s, TA theory has developed and changed and is currently used worldwide in a range of organizations, both large and small.

With chapters on how to apply TA in the workplace this book is a down-to-earth yet intelligent read and a must for those who wish to improve the quality of relationships and improve productivity. It will be invaluable to individuals, leaders and managers at all levels. Therefore whether the issue is emotional intelligence or different departmental/regional perspectives, this book offers a toolkit of resources to support the people side of organizations. It offers up-to-date theory developed by the authors through their knowledge of TA and of the business world.

Organizational TA falls within the generic term 'Developmental TA', which covers educational, counselling and organizational specialties. This term was developed by a well-published organizational transactional analyst in order to differentiate these fields from that of psychotherapy (Hay, unpublished).

The Approach

We have kept the style as conversational as possible. Each chapter includes a small vignette or case illustration which is then explored using TA theory. These composite illustrations are based on our experience and are designed to enrich understanding.

At the end of each chapter there are exercises for the reader to undertake so that learning can be reinforced and enhanced.

Aim

We aim to:

1. Offer those in business an overall guide to increasing productivity through developing and enhancing workplace relationships.
2. Enable the reader to develop an understanding of themselves and others so that they can be aware of the processes involved in carrying out decisions and strategies.
3. Give some clear how-tos for those who require extra tools for developing effective communication.
4. Offer a way of understanding the relationship between people, processes and productivity.

How this Book could Specifically Help Organizations

Studies of work related absences through stress demonstrate that this is a major problem (MacKay et al., 2004). Since this study, the estimated number of days lost due to stress has increased with the Health and Safety Executive quoting 11.4 million working days lost with a further 19,000 people who reported 'work-related heart disease' due to work stress in 2008/09.

If people understood how to communicate effectively and relate to others, one major source of stress would be eased. Communication often goes awry due to assumptions and a lack of clear agreements about how to proceed. Get these things right and we enable workforces around the world to be clear about the task, feel good about themselves and others and be conflict-resolving rather than conflict-avoiding.

Further, self-understanding means that individuals are more likely to develop good relationships. They will be able to recognize when difficulties may be occurring and be able to deal with these early on, rather than waiting for things to fester.

Naturally, stress is not the only reason to read this book, but it is certainly a compelling one. Other factors include the need for effective leadership at all levels so that productivity is enhanced. When relationships are not working many people can become passive, and in the workplace these behaviours are counterproductive at best and destructive at worst.

This book offers a comprehensive look at a whole range of aspects that enhance and support relationships. It covers everything the reader might need to develop and maintain effective communication including practical 'how-tos'.

Implementation in Organizations

We, the authors, are implementing Transactional Analysis within organizations in a variety of ways; for example, working within one of the military services undertaking direct teaching of TA for their leadership instructors and trainers. We have also worked with an advertising company running management programmes and offering short seminars for the 200 staff on a variety of aspects of TA applied to their work in their own organization. Team development has been a major part of the work of Mountain Associates and we have undertaken programmes for a variety of different organizations including the NHS, a Pension Service and an IT department providing support for schools. We work nationally and internationally in a diverse range of organizations such as an international logistics company where we taught communication skills. We undertake coaching and supervision of coaches with a variety of organizations including non-departmental government bodies and other organizational development and coaching consultancies. It is this range of experience, as well as our expertise in TA, on which we draw to write this book.

This book is filled with practical ideas linked with sound theoretical information. It is not just a 'talk shop', nor is it about a 'quick fix'. Developing the use of TA throughout an organization can enable the improvement of the organizational culture – promoting a healthy environment in which to work, where people feel respected and valued, with the space to be creative as well as the skills to set and maintain boundaries and social control.

This unique balance between theory and practice gives TA a primary position in the development of organizations, offering as it does the ability to consider both the micro and the macro – the individual, team, department and the larger organization. It enables those who use and integrate the approach to consider themselves in relation to those with whom they work and develop the skills to communicate effectively. Further, these skills are underpinned with a philosophy and value base about the worth of ourselves and others.

As with any theory, TA can be applied mechanistically. This can occur if those who use it have not taken on board the holistic nature of the approach or perhaps are unable to use it to develop personal awareness. TA needs to be applied to self and others and undertaken with thoughtfulness and 'heart' without losing any of the structure and precision.

Transactional Analysis is used worldwide. Because of this there is greater opportunity for the development of international understanding as members regularly interact with each other and write articles for the Transactional Analysis Journal. This interaction offers the opportunity to develop greater understanding of different nationalities and how to deal with diversity as our frames of reference are frequently challenged and updated.

Many people, when exposed to the ideas in this book, find them immensely helpful. This includes an owner/MD of a family-owned company who wanted to develop a different leadership style, one which recognized the knowledge and skills of his workforce. This went against the approach traditionally used in the company but was one he wanted to adopt. Having learnt TA he recognized what he needed to do and how to do it and went on to increase productivity and profit. There have also been those who did not know how to make and set clear boundaries between themselves and certain members of their team, which created difficulties with other members. Again, having understood the issues their teams have improved communication and are now thriving.

Organizational TA

We use the term *Organizational TA* – not 'TA in organizations'. Whilst this might seem to be playing with language, there is an important distinction here. 'TA in organizations' implies that there is a single body of knowledge that you carry with you whether it be into a therapy room, a school or an organization. Organizational TA more accurately conveys the message that there are specialist branches of TA – of which organizational work represents one. Whilst there are concepts that the Organizational TA field shares with the other TA applications it also has a body of theory and practice which is particular to the Developmental fields of TA.

This is akin to specialisms within any profession. There is a common body of knowledge shared by all those specialisms, and the specific knowledge and practice particular to each field of application.

We hope that this book will promote awareness of Organizational TA and the breadth and depth of this approach for those who wish to develop themselves and others and take the organization on to greater heights.

The Underlying Principles and Values of Transactional Analysis

At work how often do you hear people saying that they don't trust someone because 'they say one thing and do another'? Such statements bring into question someone's value base and their lack of consistency. The development and congruence between the individual and organizational value base is crucial if productivity is to be maintained and increase. Trust needs to develop between people, supported by the organizational processes.

The principles and values of TA highlight the underpinning and foundations of the approach. We hope to encourage those of you who read this book to not only understand some of the TA theories but also to embody them in how you are, thus developing a greater congruency between what you say and what you do.

Organizationally, ethical behaviour relies on a congruity between philosophy, values and behaviour, without which there will be little trust and empathy or understanding between the workforce. Through adopting a human-based philosophy you will not only be able to think about the TA concepts and apply them, but that application will be congruent and therefore trust is more likely to be forthcoming.

TA is not just a set of techniques but a comprehensive structured set of concepts offering a holistic framework leading to development and change. It offers concepts for assessing and understanding organizations, situations which arise in them, as well as making sense at an individual level.

The development of an ethical organizational culture is to move away from the 'dog-eat-dog' mentality, and instead is a move toward a socially aware and responsible organization. This in itself instils pride and hope within the workforce. New employees coming into this environment are more likely to adopt positively the views and attitudes of the organization.

The specific philosophical bases of TA can be outlined as:

- We all have the ability to think
- We make decisions about ourselves and others as we grow up. Many of these decisions are not helpful to us as adults and these can be changed
- We all have the right to be in the world and to be treated well and should treat others well (or as TA puts it, 'people are OK')

The above philosophical points lead to the further basic principles of open communication and to a contractual method.

We All Have the Ability to Think

Organizations are susceptible to 'groupthink' which will influence the consideration of values. Groupthink was a term coined by Janis (1972) when he identified that in some groups people do not consider alternatives, thereby placing limits on decision-making. In such groups, he argued, there is pressure for everyone to agree with each other. This might mean that individuals are conflict-avoiding rather than conflict-resolving (Peck, 1987). When people are conflict-avoiding it means that the preservation of superficial harmony is given precedence over critical evaluation of ideas and values. This in turn might mean that an option is given the go-ahead even though the outcome might be the exploitation of others (for instance the use of child labour to produce garments for the clothing industry).

The value base of an organization runs through all aspects, from the product or service being offered to marketing, accounting and management style. These in turn affect the loyalty, honesty and integrity of the employees. For example, employees may be dismissed or have legal action taken against them for stealing. The other employees will take note of this and recognize that boundaries have been created and reinforced. These actions need to be congruent throughout the organization so that when a director has been dishonest and it is sufficiently serious, they do not get a 'golden handshake', but instead are similarly dismissed. This will engender a sense of fairness amongst the workforce and loyalty and commitment will be maintained.

Decisions are Made in Childhood and these Decisions can be Changed

Most people are able to develop sufficient thinking ability to be able to make decisions and in the workplace this translates into each individual's abilities being recognized. However, sometimes this is not always consistently carried out as each leader or manager has their own style and may believe that only they can make decisions.

New decisions can be made by updating old ways of thinking. Particular decisions made in childhood may need updating as the person may still be acting on some decisions as if they are facts, which often leads to complications in the work place. For example, a manager may have grown up with a parent who was particularly severe and punitive. That manager may then decide that, in order to have some control as a grown up, they themselves have to adopt the same behaviour. Alternatively, they may have become used to sorting out problems on their own and then, at work, instead of being a team player, they go off and make decisions without reference to anyone else, yet at the same time feel isolated and without support. These sorts of actions emanate from the early decisions they made about how to be with other people. Whilst it is not the job of the organizational consultant or manager to delve too deeply into why a person acts in a particular way, it is sometimes helpful to understand our own, and others' behaviour and explore if it is relevant and appropriate today.

People are OK

One of the basic tenets of TA is that we are all OK. OK in this instance is a basic philosophical stance meaning that everyone has the right to be in the world and be safe. The concept of OKness is therefore important in relation to diversity as well as personal growth and development. After all, it is a contradictory position to hold that others are OK but that we are not, or vice versa. Further, we cannot hold everyone to be OK and yet exploit others. This will have implications for those whom we work for (or with), as well as what we buy and from whom. We will look at the concept of OKness in more detail in Chapter 2.

At the philosophical level this statement is about everyone having the right to be in the world and be treated equally. Their behaviour may not be acceptable but their rights are nevertheless recognized. Alternatively, if someone has taken an action that annoys you and you believe that the person, rather than their behaviour, is the problem then it is unlikely that discussion will be possible in a way that moves to a resolution. In contrast, keeping the other person OK and concentrating on their *behaviour* will ensure that there are opportunities to understand all parties.

Open Communication

Open communication means that we believe in sharing as much information with others as we can. In the work place this means being open and not having unnecessary secrets. It also means dealing with conflict with the person or people concerned, rather than gossiping and not resolving issues. We teach people how to improve communication so that if there are conflicts they can be resolved.

Contractual

In the workplace there needs to be agreement about how people will work together and who is responsible for what. In TA we teach people how to make contracts that are specific and without assumptions. Often when things go wrong they can be traced back to a lack of clarity in the contracting process. For example, a meeting is held and a working group is set up to undertake some research into a particular issue and then report back. One of the team members, James, could not be at the meeting and is given a job to do because of his particular expertise. James is, however, on overload and is unable to take on this task. No one follows this up and the working group does not fully complete its task. Clear contracting entails clarifying assumptions and ensuring that everyone expected to carry out a task is involved in the decision-making process. This is an area we will explore further in Chapter 6.

Competency

In order to undertake anything we do, we need to ensure that we are competent, that we know the limits of our skill and knowledge and that we get supervision and perhaps coaching so that we are more able to undertake our work roles. Continuous professional development is still necessary even in times of global financial crisis, in order to develop and maintain competency.

Summary

The broad principles outlined in this chapter are arguably applicable in all cultures – it is the specific details – such as ethical considerations – which will vary according to the laws and policies of a particular country. Embracing these principles helps to develop a workplace which is more vibrant and creative, thereby increasing productivity. People will feel safe enough to voice opinions, set and maintain boundaries, receive and offer recognition, and share ideas together.

How to Use this Book

Each chapter of the book is structured in the same way. It is possible to read the book as a whole, or to dip into particular chapters of interest. We have cross-referenced related areas throughout, which should aid those who wish to follow up particular themes.

After this introduction and summary of the underlying principles and values of Transactional Analysis, the remainder of the book is divided into two main sections. The first covers some central Organizational TA concepts whilst the second section (Chapters 12 onwards) is an 'application' section where we explore the application of TA to countering conflict, bullying, stress and motivation. This gives the reader the opportunity to see the concepts covered earlier, applied and further developed in relation to a detailed example of resolving organizational issues. The theoretical, conceptual section is intended to link closely with the application section.

USE OF CAPITALS IN THIS BOOK

Some words with a specific meaning in Transactional Analysis also have an everyday meaning. Whilst this is usually connected to the TA term, it will usually have a more general meaning. In order to distinguish one from the other, the tradition in TA is to use a capital letter when the specific TA term is being used. Thus 'Parent' refers to the Ego State (see Chapter 3) where 'parent' refers to a real life parent.

2 *Context of People at Work*

Introduction

This chapter examines beliefs about self, others and the world. These beliefs have a large influence on what happens in relationships. From the shop floor to the board room, people need to relate effectively with each other, and the quality of their communication is an essential part of this. Communication will be most effective where people are respectful of each other. This will especially be the case where they disagree or dislike each other. Without such respect, more time is spent on defending or attacking, than on problem-solving.

One central concept in TA is *OKness*. This is to do with our relationship with ourselves, others and the world.

Examples

The following examples illustrate how our beliefs affect responses to different situations and how these in turn affect the final outcomes:

Miranda applied for a promotion she did not get. It took her a long time to decide to apply for the post because she was not at all sure she was good enough. When she failed to get the post it reinforced her belief that others are better than her.	*Miranda is unlikely to apply for further promotions unless she changes her beliefs about herself. Someone may employ her if they believe they can boss her around. They may pick up on her need to please others and her belief that others are more important than her. If this should happen it will just reinforce Miranda's beliefs.*
Nicky has been overlooked in terms of promotion. She experiences her boss as favouring Neil, who got the promotion instead of her. This experience reinforces her belief that she is not good enough. At the same time she believes that Neil sucks up to the boss and that was how he got the position. As for her boss, Nicky believes that he appoints people who will do as they are told.	*Nicky is unlikely to learn from experiences and may have difficulty moving on. Her perspective is that the world is an awful place and she just has to put up with it. She believes that she is not good enough and that others are also, in some way or other, not all right.*

John also applied for the position and did not get it. He is angry, as he believes he is the best one for the job. There was a presentation to do and he believes that others had an unfair advantage over him as he didn't have all the information. He has decided to look for another job and in the meantime is acting as if he is better than others, getting impatient if someone does not do something straight away or does something wrong.	*John may eventually obtain a promotion but he is likely to remain angry and when things don't go his way he will probably take it out on others and not look at what is his responsibility. He views himself as better than others and is likely to alienate other people.*
Frances also applied for the same post. She did not get it either but recognizes that the person from outside the organization who did get it had far more experience than she did. When Frances tells a colleague, Tina, that she was unsuccessful Tina responds by saying 'I'm not surprised'. Instead of immediately taking offence Frances clarifies what Tina means by this and Tina apologizes saying that she put that in a clumsy way but meant that she thought Frances needed more experience for that particular post. Frances is OK with Tina's response and is determined to develop her skills and experience so that when she applies for promotions in the future she has more likelihood of achieving them.	*Frances has the ability to recognize others skills and abilities without putting herself down. She learns from situations and can also hold her disappointment at the same time. When her colleague, Tina, makes an insensitive response Frances does not immediately withdraw or attack her but clarifies the situation and the relationship is maintained.*

Reflection on the Examples

These examples can be considered using the TA concepts of *Life Positions* and *OKness*. Your Life Position is the deep-rooted stance you take up in terms of the way you see yourself and others. For example, you may under stress consistently believe that you are wrong and become defensive. You may put others up on a pedestal and think that someone else would be able to do things better than you can. In this frame of mind, you want to get away from other people, leave the office, go home or even leave the job. In the vignettes above this would reflect Miranda's response to the interviews.

Alternatively, in response to a problem, you may believe that no one can do anything about it and that everything is hopeless. When you ask for help you can see no value in what the other person is suggesting and respond with 'Yes but I've tried that' or 'Yes, but you don't understand' and so on. From this stance you are more likely to be passive – and at your worst, resort to drink or drugs to solve problems. This at least eases the pain for a bit. From the vignettes, this would be Nicky's response.

A different response would be to believe that others are always wrong, and move into blaming. You are angry at these times and would like it if people left you to get on with the job – 'if a job is worth doing you need to do it yourself'– others can't be trusted to do it. You feel good about yourself only if you are putting other people down. If the other person were to be Miranda, then her stance and yours would reinforce each other, since they 'fit'. If you are someone who puts others down you may well have started life being put down by a member of your family. You may then have come to believe deep down that you are inferior, making others more important. However, since this is not a comfortable situation, you may have later reacted by reversing this – and in so doing, put yourself in the upper position. At least by Persecuting you can invite other people to be Victims, rather then feeling a Victim yourself. In the vignettes above, John has responded to the interviews in this way (see also the description of the Drama Triangle, Karpman, 1968, Chapter 9).

Ideally you need to believe that you are OK and that others are too. This means that when a mistake is made, either by you or by another person, you see it as just that – a mistake. You are able to separate out the behaviour from the person and find ways to learn from the situation. This would be Frances' stance in the vignettes above.

SO WHAT IS OKNESS?

Life Positions

Life positions are basic beliefs about self and others, which are then used to justify other decisions and behaviour. There are four Life Positions, based on the permutations of *I'm OK* or *I'm Not OK* and *You are OK* or *You are Not OK*.

During its time in the womb, providing nothing untoward happens, a child is waiting to emerge into the world once sufficiently grown to be able to survive outside this protective environment. In this case he or she is likely to perceive the world from the perspective of *I am OK and You are OK*. Given that at this stage the child has no language, this is a sensing, rather than a thought or belief. In this respect, it is not yet a Life Position.

Berne (1972) argued that where the mother had some traumatic experiences during pregnancy, or the birth was difficult or even life threatening, this experience would be likely to have an effect on the way the child experiences the world. In this case the sensing may be that life is scary. Subsequent life experiences might reinforce this initial impression, or contradict it. If the child were to be treated punitively, talked down to, and not held, they may begin to form the belief *I am Not OK and You are OK* or alternatively *I am Not OK and You are Not OK*. This might be the only sense they can make of their experiences.

Thirdly, let's take another situation, where someone was picked on and bullied as a child. They learnt that the way to get by was to bully others, and that way they felt stronger and in control. Their behaviour then comes into the *I am OK and You are Not OK* quadrant. However, this will be covering up their internal belief that they are Not OK. However, that internal belief will not usually be visible to others. In fact the child may have forgotten all about their negative feelings towards themselves as they successfully moved away from them by adopting this strategy.

These Life Positions are perceptions of the world. The reality is just *I am and You are*. How I view myself and others is just that – a view, not fact. However, we tend to act as if it were a fact. Just like when somebody says 'I can't do this, I'm useless', rather than 'I don't know how to do this. Will you show me?' The latter stays with facts – that they do not yet know how to do it, whilst the former links 'being useless' as a person with not being able to do something.

There are a number of ways of diagramming the Life Positions. Ernst (1971), the originator of the 'OK Corral', drew the four positions in a quadrant – though he was actually writing about the visible behaviours, not the underlying beliefs.

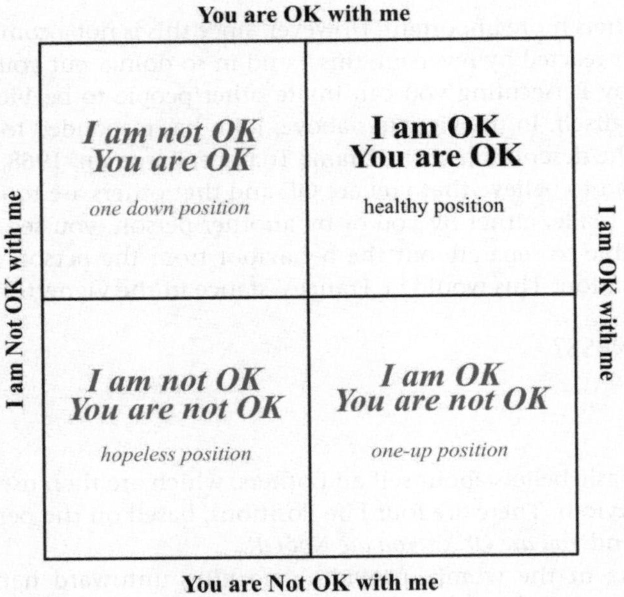

You are OK with me
I am not OK
You are OK
one down position
I am OK
You are OK
healthy position
I am not OK
You are not OK
hopeless position
I am OK
You are not OK
one-up position
You are Not OK with me
I am Not OK with me
I am OK with me

Figure 2.1 The OK Corral

In this book, we have used **bold black text** to signify the effective, and *italic grey text* to signify the ineffective, positions for communication and healthy relationships (in colour, as with traffic lights, these would respectively be green for go and red for stop).

By shading in the squares according to the amount of time you think you spend in each you can get an idea of the way you function.

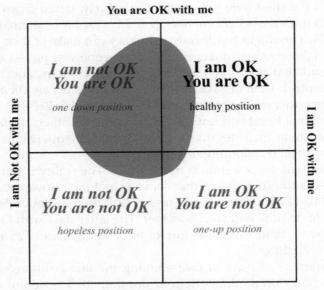

You are OK with me
I am not OK
You are OK
one down position
I am OK
You are OK
healthy position
I am not OK
You are not OK
hopeless position
I am OK
You are not OK
one-up position
You are Not OK with me
I am Not OK with me
I am OK with me

Figure 2.2 The OK Corral – shaded – Not OK

In this first example, the person spends a lot of time in the *I am Not OK, You're OK* position, less time in *I'm OK, You're OK*, and less still in the other two positions. In the second example, the person spends most of their time in the *I'm OK, You're OK* position.

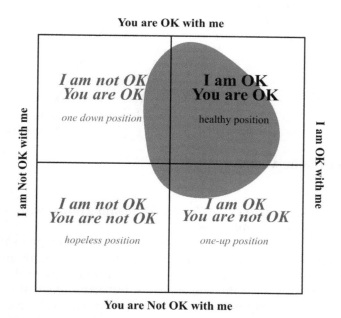

Figure 2.3   The OK Corral – shaded – OK

Whilst you might move around any or all of these positions during a typical day, there is likely to be one of the positions to which you are more likely to go to under stress. This is the Life Position, and this can change as you develop and grow. The difference between the behaviour and the underlying belief is important. The basic, 'existential', Life Position is particularly useful when working with people over time so that we can make sense of the patterns they are more likely to get stuck in. In this way we are more likely to find interventions which enable them to change to the *I'm OK, You're OK* quadrant. However, understanding the behaviours is important because it helps us make sense of the 'invitations' people constantly give each other (see the OKness Mix later in this chapter).

Jim Davis, a TA colleague, came up with the idea of using the word 'blame' as a way of considering OKness, particularly in relation to problem-solving. When a situation occurs which is problematic some people may blame themselves for the situation going wrong, they may blame the other person, blame both people, or blame neither. Of course, in the last position everyone just gets on to sort it out, rather than beat up on themselves or others.

Jim's diagram looks like this:

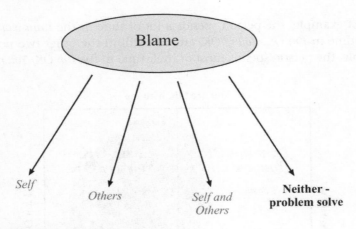

Figure 2.4   The Blame Model
Source: Davis (unpublished).

So here, blaming self equates with *I'm Not OK*, blaming others with *You're Not OK*, and blaming neither with *I'm OK, You're OK*.

It is possible to differ strongly from someone else, or be unhappy with what they are doing, and still hold them as being OK. In this way OKness represents an ethical position of treating others with respect and acceptance. You may not always live up to this goal, but it is arguably not only a worthwhile objective, but also a pragmatic one. People tend to respond to you more positively when you respect them. This does not necessarily equate with liking or agreeing with them.

We can see the existential Life Position as a frame of reference governing a person's whole outlook on life. However, in addition, you can move to any of the four positions as a response to what is going on around you in the moment, as Ernst (1971) argued. An example here could be:

Frank:	You stupid idiot!	*I'm OK, You're Not OK*
John:	How dare you say that to me!	*I'm OK, You're Not OK*
Frank:	Well you started this!	*I'm OK, You're Not OK*
John:	I'm sorry I feel bad now, I should have thought before I opened my mouth	*I'm Not OK, You're OK*
Frank:	Well it's fine to say sorry now – you started this	*I'm OK, You're Not OK*
John:	I don't know how to sort this out – I'm lost, and you're not helping	*I'm Not OK, You're Not OK*

However, there is likely to be one consistent position that you flip back to under stress – and this is the Life Position.

Ubuntu

The African philosophy of Ubuntu – 'humanity towards others' – fits well with OKness. Ubuntu philosophy speaks of our humanity existing only through other human beings. Despite the western view of people as independent individuals, in reality we need each other for our survival and well-being (Nabudere, 2007). At birth – when we are completely dependent – without the generosity of the adults around us we simply would not survive into childhood, let alone adulthood. As adults, we are still interdependent.

The Positions

I'M OK, YOU'RE OK

If you are in the position of *I'm OK, You're OK* then you will see both yourself and others in a positive and accepting way – which may or may not include agreeing with them. If this is your existential Life Position, it will represent your predominant way of being in the world. You are therefore likely to 'get on with' other people, even though you may not always like their behaviour. This is an important distinction, given the tendency for parents (and other caregivers) in white western society to fuse children's personalities with their behaviour (for instance 'You're a bad girl/boy' – rather than something like 'What you have just done is not acceptable').

By fusing personality with behaviour, we arguably create the kind of situation which sometimes happens in appraisal, where reference to minor 'issues for development' leads the appraisee to react out of all proportion to the feedback. Their experience has taught them that if there is a 'defect' in their behaviour, then that is equivalent to there being a defect in them as a person.

Very frequently, people's behaviour and interactions 'invite' others to move away from the OK–OK position – often with the apparent aim of rejection. Staying 'in there', keeping self and that person OK, is an important strategy to keep communication going.

I'M NOT OK, YOU'RE OK

If you are in the *I'm Not OK, You're OK* position, you will see yourself as less important or able than others, so that you are likely to give your power away to them and put them on a pedestal ('because you are so much better at ... than I am') and so on. You are likely to want to get away from them in embarrassment or discomfort.

I'M OK, YOU'RE NOT OK

If you are in the *I'm OK, You're Not OK* position, then you place yourself in a 'one up' position in relation to others. This can take two principal forms. You may have a need to do things for others, with the implicit, and sometimes explicit, message that they don't have the ability to do these things for themselves. You are also unlikely to check out with them whether they want these things doing anyway. Alternatively, you will blame, berate, oppress or criticize them for all the things they (from your perspective) get wrong. You may make them the cause of all your troubles – 'without you, my life would be so much better'. This is an angry position, and ultimately leads to your wanting to 'get rid of' them. John was in this position in the vignette at the start of this chapter.

I'M NOT OK, YOU'RE NOT OK

The *I'm Not OK, You're Not OK* position is 'hopeless'. If nobody is OK, then everyone is to blame for things that happen. This can happen in the low point in an argument – where you have reached a 'stalemate', 'get nowhere' place.

Attributes and OKness

Attributes and adjectives can be assigned to the different positions (Berne, 1972), For example, manager–worker. Here are just four examples:

a.   I am a Manager and therefore OK; You are a worker and therefore Not OK.
b.   I am a Manager and therefore Not OK; You are a worker and therefore OK.
c.   I am a worker and therefore OK; You are a Manager and therefore Not OK.
d.   I am a worker and therefore Not OK; You are a Manager and therefore OK.

The traditional western view about status is that those who have it either have innate superiority (for instance as members of the aristocracy), or have achieved status because of their hard work. In contrast, according to this view, those without status are in the position they are because they are lazy, or not as worthwhile human beings as their 'betters'. Managers who accept this view would correspond to position (a) above. Conversely, those without status who take on the diametrically opposite view to this would correspond to the position (c).

This highlights the subjective nature of the Not OK positions – ideally if you believed in the innate value of all human beings, you would hold none of these four views on status.

Context

No relationship exists in isolation. All of our interactions, whether with one, or more, people, take place in a variety of contexts – families, friendships, communities, teams, organizations, society at large and, increasingly, the global context. People are dealing with a complex web of relationships in their living situation, at work, in their family and local community. They may view themselves as 'OK' within their family, for instance, where they experience positive relationships. They may experience bullying at work, leading them to move to one of the Not OK positions for at least the period they are working. Their existential Life Position will play a part in this too – if this is one of the Not OK positions, then the bullying will simply reinforce this. In contrast, if they have a strong *I'm OK–You're OK* base, they may well ride through the negative experiences at work.

The OKness Mix

Moment by moment, you are influencing others and being influenced by them in terms of your experience of OKness. You put out invitations for other people to respond to you from one of the four positions, and they are simultaneously doing the same. Different people will have differing levels of energy that go into their invitation. This means that one invitation may be more powerful than another. An example of this would be when a group of people who are all behaving in an OK–OK way with each other are joined by someone who is overbearingly negative. The mood of the group may then shift. The opposite is of course equally possible.

Messages from the Environment

The following diagrams aim to illustrate this phenomenon. The first diagram illustrates the way in which people in our environment are giving you invitations in relation to OKness. They may be treating you as if you are OK or Not OK and you can decide if you wish to go along with this or not. It is, however, important to stress that this process is likely to go on out of your awareness most of the time. If the invitation fits with your own internal self-talk and beliefs then these are likely to reinforce your position, whether this be negative or positive.

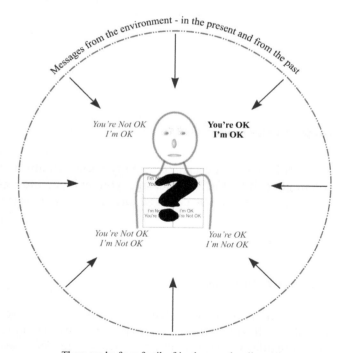

These can be from family, friends or work colleagues

Figure 2.5   Messages from the Environment

Messages to the Environment

The second diagram illustrates the messages which you communicate to others – whether in your awareness or not. Your perspective on the world will affect your relationships and the responses you get back are likely to reflect this – and very likely reinforce your view of yourself and them. As with the messages from the environment, you are giving out invitations to people to respond to you in a particular way.

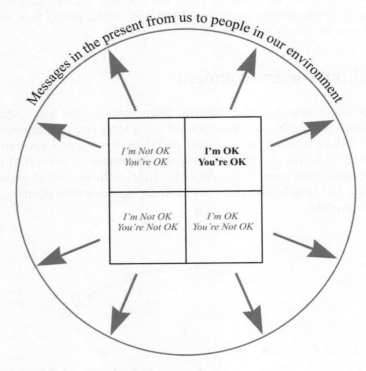

Figure 2.6   Messages to the Environment

The importance of this lies in the fact that many social situations are much more changeable than you might think. With the messages you send out and receive, a situation which seems hopelessly negative, can be changed, often without a great deal of effort.

Resilience

Our inner well-being has two broad aspects:

1.   The overall way in which we see ourselves. This represents, as we have seen, our existential Life Position. In other words, the overall way we see ourselves and others – that we return to regularly – especially under stress. The four basic permutations revolve around whether I see myself as OK or not, and whether I see the other person (I am currently with) as OK or not.

2. The more momentary changes in our perspective dependent on many factors:

*   the extent to which we are thrown off balance when things go wrong
*   whom we are with – and what our intuitive 'antenna' says about them
*   the internal OKness state of the person/people we are with
*   how tired/energized we are
*   our physical health
*   any beliefs that are current for us – maybe related to recent events for instance

An Example of Resilience

Resilience isn't the same as stamina – here is an illustration of what we are talking about:

SCENARIO 1 – LOWER RESILIENCE

You get up, feel good, have a shower, but the water runs cold before you finish. You mutter an expletive, and go down for breakfast. Whilst you are eating your cereal, you knock over your coffee, spilling it all over your clothes. You mutter another (stronger!) expletive. You leave the house, only to see your bus disappearing over the hill – your watch has stopped. You decide you have had enough of today, and go back indoors and retire to bed in a huff.

SCENARIO 2 – HIGHER RESILIENCE

You get up, feel good, have a shower. The water runs cold, so you get out sharpish and resolve to call a plumber to see if you need a bigger hot water cistern. Whilst you are eating your cereal, you knock over your coffee, spilling it all over your clothes. You wonder what led you to do that, and get changed. You check your watch, realize it has stopped, and that you will miss your bus. You phone in to work to let them know you are running late and need to make the urgent work calls from home now before going in.

The different outcome in each scenario is not to do with the triggers – which are the same – but the sense/meaning you make of it, and what you do in response to what happens. In the first scenario, the person appears to be a Victim to what happens to them, and their initial sense of OKness with themselves and the world is fairly easily knocked off course by the three, relatively minor, things that happen. In contrast, in the second scenario, the person 'problem-solves' as each incident occurs. Although this could be seen as stoicism or toughness, the crucial variable in terms of resilience is the internal experience of holding a sense of OKness, rather than just that the person 'deals with' things.

Putting the OKness Model into Practice in Dealing with People

Imagine a situation where you are in conflict with some at work.

Some useful self-monitoring questions are called for here:

1. Is this person significant to me?
2. Am I generally having difficulties in my dealings with them?
3. Do I sense that they are generally having difficulties dealing with me?
4. Do I need to work with this person, regardless of my liking/disliking of them?
5. Can I actually work with them even if I disagree with them on some issues?
6. Is there a recognizable pattern here for me in terms of other times and other relationships?

These questions do not in themselves provide the means to change the patterns of OKness in a situation. They do, however, provide a way of making sense of the way you relate to others, and enable you to realize that you have options. Life Positions are not facts – they are beliefs and beliefs can be changed.

Ultimately, you need to have an internal sense of OKness. If your sense of OKness depends on others continually giving you reassurance, then your sense of self will be fragile and illusory – when people go away, or this continual reassurance is not there, then you are likely to lose this sense.

You cannot will other people to move to an OK–OK position. However, you will increase your chances at some point of succeeding in this aim if you consistently stay in an OK–OK position in your dealings with them. It may come as no surprise that, very often, people who you find difficult experience *you* as difficult. Many years ago, one of the authors worked in an office where the postman arrived each morning, grunted, threw the post on the desk and disappeared. We resolved in the office to make sure that we enthusiastically welcomed and thanked the postman each morning. After just one week, he came in and said animatedly 'Good morning!' After a further few days, he said that this was the only place he went to where people were friendly. So from his perspective it was other people who did not welcome him, rather than he who behaved in this way. We can fantasize that people's actions are intentional and conscious, when, instead, they may be conditioned, and arising from a narrow range of experience of how to be with others in this particular situation.

OKness is about relationship and connection. If there are problems with these two areas in an organization then it is highly likely that effectiveness will be hampered. In the above example of the postman, the staff were proactive in making connection and developed the relationship. This proactive stance enabled the postman to develop a sense of belonging and in response he changed his behaviour with them, even though he may not have immediately altered his beliefs. That might (or might not) follow later. Neither the staff nor the postman were looking for a deep, meaningful relationship in this context – they simply needed to do their job, and if that can be done with hassle-free, clear communication, they can be more productive, and find their contacts with others pleasurable.

The culture of leadership and power within the organization will have an influence on the workforce's beliefs about themselves and others. For instance if managers describe their reports in negative, Not OK ways, this is highly likely to lead to a drop in motivation and hence productivity.

You can decide to enter situations with a resolve to hold an OK–OK position, and this can be an effective strategy, but to be successful you need to be congruent in terms of your philosophy and your behaviour.

Ascendant Organization and OKness

In this section we are going to take a look at the application of OKness to the macro perspective of the organization.

Wickens (1995) writes about the 'Ascendant Organization' – a term he uses for an organization that combines high levels of commitment with control of the processes to 'achieve a synthesis between high effectiveness and high quality of life leading to long–term, sustainable business success'.

In order to obtain commitment, employees need to be valued along with their experience and expertise, and need to have the opportunity to further develop their skills. Wickens' basic Model corresponds with TA's OK Corral. The Ascendant Organization quadrant falls within *I'm OK and You're OK*. This type of organization is the one in which there is most prosperity, power and happiness.

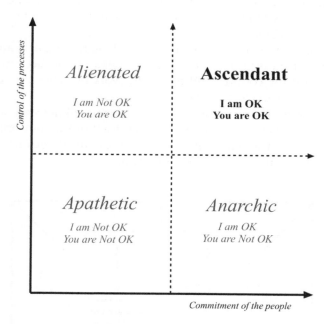

Figure 2.7   The Ascendant Organization with the OK Corral

The anarchic quadrant has high levels of individual commitment but little control. People do what they individually think is right for the organization or themselves without much thought for any corporate objectives. This is within the *I'm OK and You're Not OK* quadrant on the OK Corral.

The alienated organization utilizes top-down imposition of rules and procedures, with no attempt to involve people or get their cooperation, except by edict. Managers may be autocratic. This fits with the *I'm Not OK and You're OK* position.

With the apathetic organization there is neither commitment nor control, no centrally respected authority or any attempt to involve the workforce. People broadly do what they want, without any shared objectives or sense of direction. This is in line with *I'm Not OK and You're Not OK* position on the OK Corral.

Wickens sees the ascendant organization as requiring 'high-quality investment, engineering, financial control and product development. Above all, it requires high-calibre, highly motivated people, and a culture and leadership committed to these goals'. So the organization needs to be seen as a whole from his point of view. This fits in with the Organizational Transactional Analysis perspective.

The Three Dimensional Model of OKness

The original OK Corral implies that there is only one other person in the equation, when in reality there are often more than this. For example, the behaviour of a team member in an organization may suggest that they believe they are OK and that other members of their team are OK, but that individuals from other teams (or other teams as a whole) are Not OK. You find other people whom you like and then gossip and put other people down. You are therefore saying that you believe you and your fellow gossips are OK but those you are gossiping about are not.

Another example would be in an organization where the senior managers are seen as Not OK by the administrative staff and the finance departments because they are seen as 'swanning off' around the country and not really working. Therefore two departments join forces to make the managers Not OK.

Diagrammatically, if we are to take account of this third dimension, we need to extend the four Life Positions to eight. It can be seen that each of the four original positions is related to two three-dimensional positions – where the third person/s are either OK or Not OK – as indicated by the arrows in the diagram.

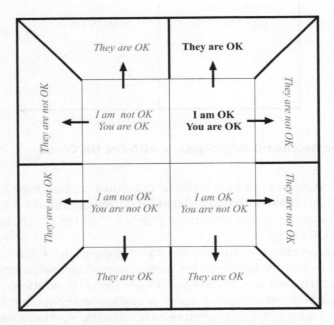

Figure 2.8   The Three-Dimensional Positions

Education into this format starts early. Parents talk to their children about how the world is – an exciting place, how people are – whether they can be trusted and so on. Children start to build up a view of themselves, of the specific people they directly relate to and 'people out there'.

New employees equally get socialized into the culture of their new organization. 'The people in finance are a waste of time' or 'The boss is great as long as you agree with him/her'.

The extension of the two-dimensional *I'm OK, You're OK* to include the third dimension of 'They' offers a way to understand a person's social context and accounts for differences in your sense of your own and others' OKness. The Model can be used to work with an individual or a team to assist them in understanding their transactions with others and to put words to some of their experiences. It can also be used from the perspective of a manager, or colleague to help make sense of an employee's responses in relation to others.

This Model has been successfully used in organizations with teams of individuals struggling to relate to each other in effective ways. The Model enables them to recognize the patterns they perpetuate, and this goes some way towards individuals making changes.

An Example of 3-D OKness

In April 2005 The Rover group of companies had to call in the receivers. Several employees when interviewed for television news blamed the British public for buying foreign cars – 'this is their fault'. Some commentators saw the possibility of the government putting in funding to prevent the closure of the company being misguided or even an immoral use of taxpayers' money – their view was that the directors of the company had taken out large sums of money in bonuses. So the public and their buying habits were Not OK from some workers' point of view, the directors were Not OK from the point of view of those who felt that they had exploited the company's assets and others saw the government as Not OK because they were seen as bolstering the bosses by bailing out the company.

Examples of 3-D OKness in an Organization

The following figure looks at some specific examples in each of the eight three dimensional positions. They do not represent a sequence – just a set of fictional examples that could arise from one situation.

It can be seen from the examples in the three-dimensional chart that it is really easy to fall into one of the negative positions. However, if a manager has a positive approach they are likely to be influential in changing a negative culture. However, if this were a real situation they are likely to need additional support – since maintaining resilience in the face of this level of negativity would be very difficult. Fortunately, in such situations there are usually others we can align with in an OK–OK way who will act as the 'encouragement committee'.

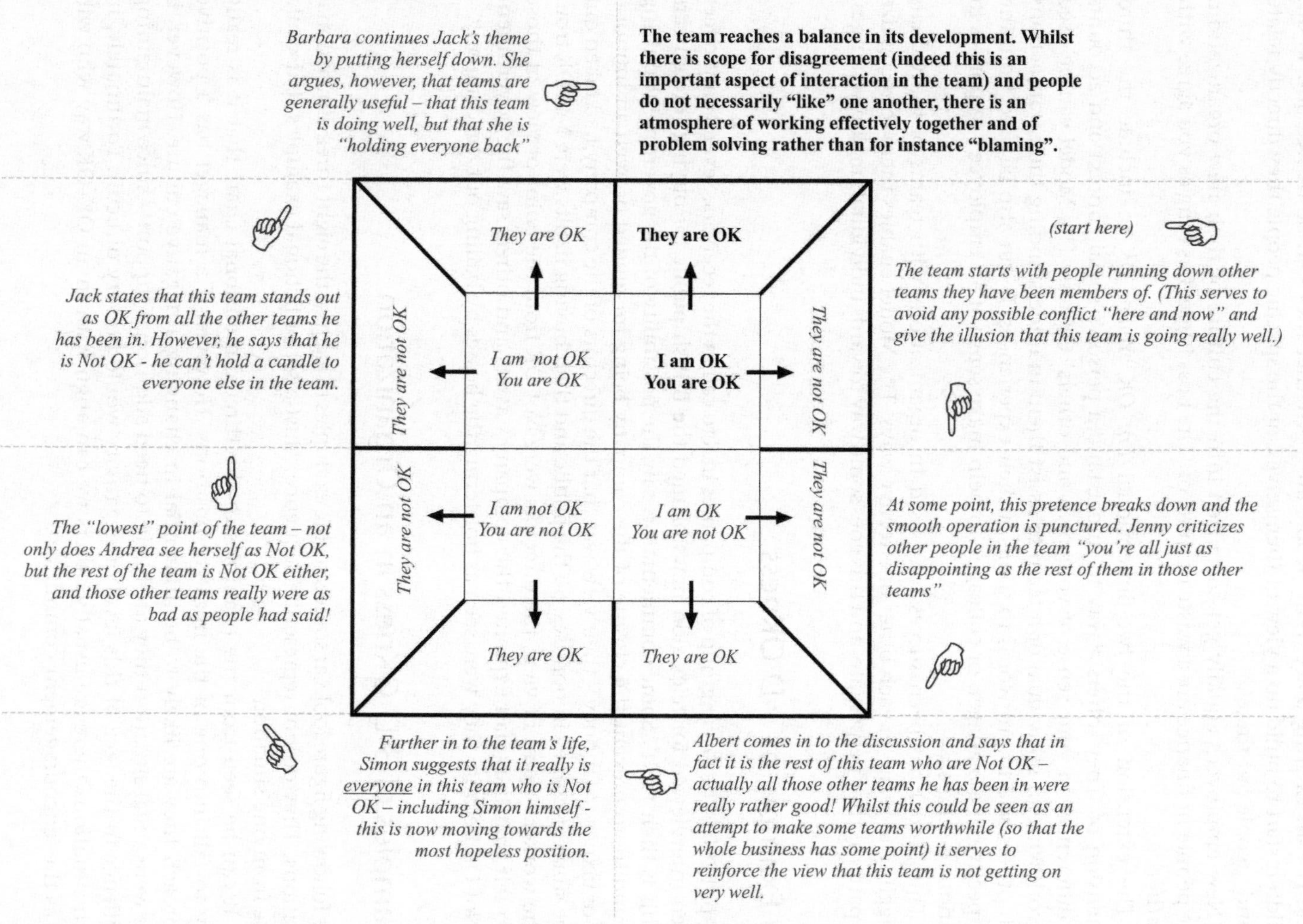

The team reaches a balance in its development. Whilst there is scope for disagreement (indeed this is an important aspect of "interaction in the team) and people do not necessarily "like" one another, there is an atmosphere of working effectively together and of problem solving rather than for instance "blaming".

(start here)

The team starts with people running down other teams they have been members of. (This serves to avoid any possible conflict "here and now" and give the illusion that this team is going really well.)

At some point, this pretence breaks down and the smooth operation is punctured. Jenny criticizes other people in the team "you're all just as disappointing as the rest of them in those other teams"

Albert comes in to the discussion and says that in fact it is the rest of this team who are Not OK – actually all those other teams he has been in were really rather good! Whilst this could be seen as an attempt to make some teams worthwhile (so that the whole business has some point) it serves to reinforce the view that this team is not getting on very well.

Barbara continues Jack's theme by putting herself down. She argues, however, that teams are generally useful – that this team is doing well, but that she is "holding everyone back"

Jack states that this team stands out as OK from all the other teams he has been in. However, he says that he is Not OK – he can't hold a candle to everyone else in the team.

The "lowest" point of the team – not only does Andrea see herself as Not OK, but the rest of the team is Not OK either, and those other teams really were as bad as people had said!

Further in to the team's life, Simon suggests that it really is _everyone_ in this team who is Not OK – including Simon himself - this is now moving towards the most hopeless position.

They are not OK

They are not OK

They are OK

They are OK

**I am OK
You are OK**

They are OK

They are OK

*I am OK
You are not OK*

*I am OK
You are not OK*

*I am not OK
You are OK*

*I am not OK
You are not OK*

They are not OK

They are not OK

Figure 2.9   Examples of Three-Dimensional OKness within a Team

OKness and Teams

OKness can be observed in everyday action in the continuing dynamic interplay between people – which can often change dependent upon the situation.

In teams where there is an absence of structuring and/or supportive leadership, not-OKness develops. Somehow in the vacuum of what people need, there is an out-of-awareness belief that something is wrong and so someone must be Not OK. The meaning that is attached to this is likely to relate to the person's Life Position. For example, if this is *I am Not OK, You are OK*, then they will be more likely to believe that something is wrong with them – this could be about who they are and/or what they do (or do not do). This may not necessarily be explicit in their behaviour.

The social situation can also be seen as a co-creative mix of what people bring to the situation, how others respond to them, and how this pans out. On a day when someone is in an especially good mood, they are less likely to take up other people's invitations to move to a Not OK position.

To develop a sense of OKness, you need to monitor your own internal reactions, which will be a mixture of your responses to deeply based beliefs about yourself and others and the invitations from people around you to move to different Life Positions. You are much more likely to remain effective in your communication with others if you stay in an OK–OK position. When you do this, apart from communicating clearly, you are inviting the other person to join you in the OK position.

Factors Involved in OKness

The following table examines some of the factors that are linked to OKness.

Table 2.1   Factors Involved in OKness

Area	How this is relevant/important
Quality of Relationships	The quality of relationships which people experience in a team or an organization is a crucial variable in the level of OKness at a social level. This includes all permutations of behavioural OKness, both within a team as a whole, between individual members of a team and between the team and other teams within an organization.
Self-Esteem	People with low self esteem give strong invitations to others to move to *Not OK*'ing them. Being held in low esteem by others may of course result in the same outcome but from a different cause. High self-esteem can be developed and maintained by positive colleagues and bosses, as well as ourselves. Ideally we start work motivated and this needs to be maintained.
Cohesion/ Belonging	The extent to which people experience a sense of belonging and cohesion is important, since it provides encouragement of OKness at a behavioural level.
Blame	One way of seeing the three *Not OK* positions is by looking at who is assigned 'blame' for the way things are (Davis – unpublished – see earlier in this chapter). High levels of blame in a team can be seen as a fairly obvious sign that people see themselves or others as *Not OK*.

Table 2.1   Continued

Area	How this is relevant/important
Openness to learning	This measure is more a gauge of how willing people are to consider change as a way of improving life in a team or an organization. Are they willing to let go of old behaviours or is the need to hold on to the old ways of doing things too strong?
Volatility	The greater the level of volatility there is in a team, the greater the chance that change can be effected. Where the OK positions are rigid and unchanging, the more likely it is that there are one or more individuals in the team whose negative, social level OK positions are strongly linked to their negative existential Life Position.
Management	The ability of management to provide a positive structuring and supportive environment within which people may work is a crucial inoculation against behavioural Not OKness. The lack of either structuring and/or support in the style of the manager (or the management structure as a whole) leads to a vacuum in which Not-OKness becomes the explanation for why all is not well.
Hope	Hope is a way of focusing on the future, rather than the present. We all need to maintain a sense of hope to enable us to remain emotionally stable in the present.
Investment	What has each individual got invested in this situation (either positively or negatively)? If their primary energy is elsewhere (home, hobbies, friendships) then they may not be willing to invest energy, time or short-term discomfort to resolve the team situation – indeed, they may not experience themselves as being particularly affected by it.
Resilience	Much has been written about resilience in relation to children and their ability (or otherwise) to ride through difficult experiences. Increasingly, this same term is being used in relation to managers' ability to hold the tension during the process of change (see Conner, 1998).

Summary

We have looked at the many aspects of OKness in the workplace, in both one-to-one relationships and the larger networks within an organization. Whilst there are undoubtedly situations in which problems in relationships seem more intractable, this chapter has proposed that many, if not most, difficult situations between people can be more easily understood than is commonly believed. That understanding can then be used to find a solution to the situation.

EXERCISES

EXERCISE 1

When you get stressed, or when things so wrong, are you more likely to look to yourself or to others as the cause? Relate this to the Life Positions. Having worked that out, decide what you could say to yourself to enable you to shift back to the positive OK–OK position. Who could you receive support from to do this? What could you do in future to maintain the OK–OK position?

EXERCISE 2

- Think about someone from an identified group (or a specific person) whom you regard as OK. What would this person need to do for you to see them as Not OK?
- Think about someone from an identified group (or a specific person) whom you regard as Not OK. What would this person need to do for you to see them as OK?
- Consider what this tells you about:
  - how stable or fragile your views of yourself or others are
  - how likely you are to move people from one position to another
  - how the positions are about perspective and beliefs, not facts
  - your investment (or not) in any relationship and what kinds of factors make a difference
  - how other people may also be doing this with you and your actions

What will you do with this awareness from now on?

EXERCISE 3

This exercise is useful when there is a need to develop understanding between teams or groups of people. It is particularly helpful to enable meetings to progress amicably. Make slips of paper for each of the first three descriptors (described below).

Descriptors

- You have high individual commitment. There's no real leadership and you individually do what you think is right for you and the organization. You believe in the approach of 'dog eat dog'. You do your bit so that you get on.
- You don't have any commitment and there's no one you respect at your level or in authority. Generally you don't think anyone knows what they are doing or why they are doing it. At your worst you believe everything is pointless anyway.
- You are in a top-down rule-bound organization with autocratic managers. You look up to others and when things are going wrong believe you can't get things right. At these times you feel pretty helpless about things.

Final Descriptor

- Your organization involves you in the decision-making process. You are encouraged to go on courses and improve yourself. You get on with others and are happy to listen to their point of view. You are also happy for the final decision to be made by the team leader or manager if there is uncertainty about what to do.

Procedure

- Ensure that each person has a slip with one of the first three descriptors on it, and ask them not to show it to the others.
- Then hold a meeting about a potentially real situation that could occur in your organization, such as making a decision about how to spend a certain budget. It will be difficult for the meeting to come to a resolution.
- Next give each person a slip of paper with the final descriptor on it, again without sharing what is on the piece of paper, and ask them to have a meeting from that position. The meeting should go more smoothly with greater listening on all sides, even if they disagree.
- Next debrief the exercise drawing up the Wickens quadrants (see page 21 above) and ask the group to read out and decide which each of the descriptors related to.
- Discuss how this relates to your organization and/or to each individual. This latter will depend on how much trust there is in the group as to whether discussing this is appropriate.

Feel free to develop other exercises based on this.

3 *The Basis of Communication*

Introduction

Getting communication right in the workplace is essential to the creation of a positive, trusting, organizational culture. This in turn enhances productivity – whether that be manufacturing output, creative ideas or the quality of a service provided. This chapter will explain the origins of misunderstandings, assumptions, irritations and conflicts and, together with Chapter 4, explore ways of developing effective communication. In short, these chapters and the Models within them will help to develop effective communication and enhance relationships.

We will outline two different Models; one concerned with observable behaviour – the *OK Modes Model*, and the other with what goes on inside us – the *Inside Picture*.

OK Modes Model

EXAMPLES

Here are some examples of how a person's behaviour can create misunderstandings in communication and alienate listeners:

1) Deirdre seems to manage to annoy her colleagues. They experience her telling them what to do even though she is not their manager. She always seems to know the answer and know better than everyone else.	*Deirdre might believe that she is only OK as long as she is in control. This causes her to alienate others since they experience her as treating them as though they are Not OK.*
2) John comes across to his colleagues as childish. He has a great sense of humour, but this is sometimes inappropriate. John's colleagues like having him around as he brings energy into the team. However, there are times when they find him difficult. His boss sends him for coaching as a way of trying to enable him to develop.	*John is not able to assess situations and respond appropriately. He seems to believe that humour will get him by. John's behaviour might indicate that he believes he is Not OK. He then covers this with jokey behaviour.*

And in contrast:

3) People value Jack's style as a manager. He is clear in decision-making, the way he structures his team, and he is supportive towards the workforce. He comes across as being reliably in touch with what is going on.	*Jack values those he works with and is happy to treat them as equals (I'm OK and You/They are OK). This invites others to value themselves as well as others (which is also the I'm OK/ You're OK position).*

The Model

For those of you who have come across TA before you may not have heard of the term 'Modes'. This comes from a variety of TA theorists including Porter (1975), Lapworth, Sills and Fish (1993) and Temple (1999, 2004) and our OK Modes Model provides a visual way of representing how we behave and interact with other people. It has 10 different communication 'Modes' – four of which are effective and prompted by the process of Mindfulness, that is, taking account of current reality and acting accordingly, with the other six being ineffective.

Definition of Effective

By effective, we mean:

- that a communication is likely to achieve the intended response or result; information is received, necessary action(s) follow and good relationships are maintained or developed
- that communication will (if necessary and desired) be able to continue – either now or later
- that each party to the communication, whether they agree with each other (or not) or like each other (or not) maintains an *I'm OK, You're OK* position

Definition of Ineffective

By ineffective, we mean that any or all of the following apply:

- the intended communication is not understood
- the person receiving the communication is themselves invited into a 'Not OK' position or invited to make someone else 'Not OK'
- communication may be broken in some way and so does not continue, or it escalates to even more discomfort or misunderstanding for those involved. In extreme cases the rift may be permanent
- what needs to be done is less likely to be done – or may be done incorrectly

Colours

As usual in this book, the Model uses the **bold black text** and *grey italic text* to represent the effective and ineffective areas respectively. Adopting this approach makes it easy to visualize the stop and go (or flow) to each exchange in a conversation and therefore to track and understand what went on. If you have access to colour and are drawing the diagrams, green (for go) would represent effective and red (for stop) ineffective – just as traffic lights.

The Diagram

We will now build the OK Modes diagram bit by bit. We have incorporated miniature OK Corrals into the diagram to reinforce the message that ineffective Modes reflect and invite a Not OK response and that the four effective Modes reflect and invite an *I'm OK, You're OK* response.

EFFECTIVE COMMUNICATION

When you are in the one of the effective Modes you are responsive to the present situation. Generally when something is said from an **effective Mode** the response from the other person is likely to be from an **effective Mode**, and vice versa. Of course, in reality, there are not simply four effective ways of behaving, and these descriptors are intended as impressionistic rather than definitive. It is also the case that some behaviours will fall on a continuum between two or more of the Modes.

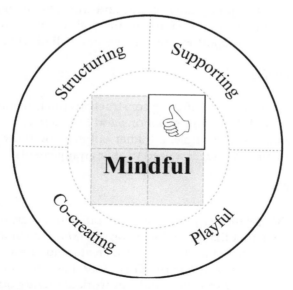

Figure 3.1   The OK Modes of Behaviour

Effective Modes

THE MINDFUL PROCESS

Human beings do not just respond or react – they also initiate. How you behave in any particular moment will depend upon whether you respond in a reflex or automatic way, rooted in the past, or are in the present moment, dealing with current reality.

The central area of the diagram is called **Mindful** as a reminder that you need to bear in mind the totality of the situation and possible consequences of any actions and interventions. This is not a behaviour as you cannot actually see someone being Mindful but you will see their subsequent actions which reflect their **Mindful** process. The **Mindful** process is circular to represent being in 'the flow', taking into account the current reality and being effective in the moment.

When in this central circle you have incorporated and developed the positive behaviours from the past and brought them appropriately into the present as resources to draw on. In the diagram above, we have therefore placed the other effective Modes within Mindful process to reinforce this. When here you can discuss and debate with others, be interested in opinions and have thoughts and feelings that are related to the present. Should circumstances change you can decide whether to move to a different **effective Mode**. You may not always be overtly aware of doing this because, when in this Mode, you are relaxed and creative. However, there are times when you need to stand back and observe a situation before deciding what to do next which is why **Mindful** is in the centre. All of the **effective Modes** communicate **I'm OK, You're OK, and They're OK**.

SUPPORTIVE MODE

When in this Mode you are appropriately caring and affirming in your behaviour and do not take away the other person's power, or assume their inability to do something. You will be consistent and your support will be reliable, and will fit what is actually needed.

STRUCTURING MODE

This is the boundary-setting Mode, offering constructive criticism and being caring whilst firm. You respond to, and deal with, situations and take action when a limit has been reached and overstepped. For example, a trainer outlines the schedule for the day and ensures this is kept to, unless there is a need to alter arrangements.

CO-CREATIVE MODE

Co-creativity in this Model means being willing to join with others to develop and create something different, whether that be in discussion or in practical or logistical terms. From this Mode you are able to recognize that you can create something together with others that is greater than the sum of the parts. This Mode has developed through learning the rules that help you live with others and can work alongside others for the good of all. Both leaders and team members need to be co-creative and cooperative, which is a very different behaviour to that of being compliant. When relating from this Mode you behave in ways which keep you and others OK. You are able to consider the pros and cons of each suggestion and work with others. Indeed, productivity would lessen and little or no work would be possible unless people were willing to cooperate. This includes such basic administrative details such as when and where you will meet and who will do what so that you can develop mutuality and co-creativity.

PLAYFUL MODE

This is the creative, fun loving, curious and energetic Mode and is closely related to the Co-creative Mode. One of the strengths of this Mode is that you can confront others playfully as a way of dealing with a difficult situation. This can diffuse a potential problem and get the message across. You can be appropriately humorous and also encourage others to be playful.

When in the **Mindful Process** it is possible to choose which – if any – of the effective Modes to use – depending on the situation. If someone is invited to go into an *ineffective Mode* they have a choice – though it may not always be a conscious one. They can accept the invitation, and move to a subservient or domineering position in the conversation, or resist this invitation by staying in an OK–OK stance and responding from one of the effective Modes – thus remaining in the Mindful Process. This is referred to in TA as *crossing the transaction* – in that it will be an unexpected response for the other person. We cover *transactions* in the next chapter, and in the following examples we will start to use transactional diagrams to provide a visual way of plotting a conversation.

From in the Mindful process you will be treating yourself and others as OK and are more likely to achieve a positive response. You can also have healthy fun from here and enjoy co-creating with others. This follows Berne's idea that when we are operating in a Mindful, 'integrated' way, we *are* charming and courageous and are appropriately utilizing our past experiences in the present moment. This is differentiated from someone who is operating in an ineffective, 'unintegrated', Mode and who may '*revert* to being charming, and may feel that he *should* be courageous' (Berne, 1961).

Ineffective Modes

We will now add the ineffective Modes to the previous diagram.

If you slip into one of the *ineffective Modes* you have left the present and are operating as you did as a child or as a significant person from your childhood behaved with you. In the diagram these are shown as boxes to symbolize the process of defaulting to the past behaviour, and in so doing, being rigid and inflexible.

The *ineffective zones* all reflect outdated and unintegrated experiences from your past. They will seem to 'pop up' out of the blue in the same way that your leg shoots out when a doctor taps your knee to testy our reflexes. You don't seem to be in control of these responses – which would more accurately be described as reactions. They are the 'overdone' counterparts of the positive ones within the Mindful Process circle and are likely to be 'hooked' by a trigger, which could be:

- another person's ineffective communication
- when someone presses your 'button' – a sensitive issue or area for you

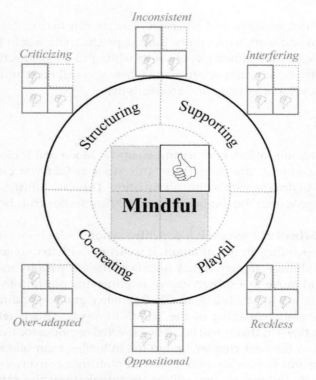

Figure 3.2   The Complete OK Modes Diagram

CRITICIZING MODE

When in this Mode you can be authoritarian and act as though you believe that others cannot do things as well as you. In this Mode you will either persecute, prohibit, or patronize. Leading from this Mode is unlikely to develop a loyal supportive team or culture as the workforce will be tense and ill at ease. This Mode communicates *I'm OK and You're Not OK*.

INCONSISTENT MODE

Leaders in this Mode tend to be inconsistent in style – changing their behaviour in unpredictable and apparently random ways. For example, you may sometimes take control when others are capable of doing things for themselves, and then, at other times, sit back and leave the workforce to take control. This behaviour is confusing for those concerned as they do not know which of these options you as the leader will take. This Mode also communicates *I'm OK and You're Not OK* because you either act as if you can do things better than others or you appear to be ignoring their needs.

INTERFERING MODE

When in this Mode, your behaviour is of 'Rescuing' others (see Chapter 9 on Games – the Drama Triangle), that is, doing things for others which, in reality, they are capable of doing for themselves. You could also be overindulgent or fussing. Here you will behaviourally be expressing *I'm OK and You're Not OK*.

OVER-ADAPTED MODE

When in this Mode your behaviour is one of over-adapting to others that is, trying to please others without asking them what they want and being passive and compliant. If you are a leader operating from this Mode you are likely to become stressed as you cannot please all the people all of the time. When in this Mode you express *I'm Not OK and You're OK* or *I'm Not OK and You're Not OK*.

OPPOSITIONAL MODE

The behaviour in this Mode will be resisting and opposing without any objective or consistent basis for doing so. Employees who do this earn a reputation for being obstructive, saying 'No' when others are saying 'Yes' and vice versa. When in this Mode you are unlikely to be willing to hear others and consider their perspective, and you will express *I'm OK and You're Not OK* or *I'm Not OK and You're Not OK*.

RECKLESS MODE

When in this Mode you express *You're Not OK (or You're Irrelevant)*. At work you will tend to behave in ways which indicate unwillingness to take responsibility for your actions. Your energy appears unfocused, you fail to keep to agreed time boundaries – by for instance frequently being late. This Mode is different from oppositional Mode in that the actions will not be a response to another person, but more you *doing your own thing*, regardless of the people around or the situation.

The Inside Picture

The second part of this chapter is concerned with what goes on *inside* us. Sometimes when you observe someone's behaviour, you won't be able to make sense of it. Thus some further explanation to add to the Behavioural Model might serve to further your understanding.

THE STRUCTURAL EGO STATE MODEL

This Model is used to describe how people develop and what happens inside their heads. This is a great Model for gaining better understanding of ourselves and others.

The word structural is used because this is a Model which describes the structure of our personality. An ego state refers to a coherent pattern of attitudes, thinking, feeling and behaving in an individual. At the simplest level we refer to Parent, Adult and Child as the building blocks of our make up. In relation to the previous OK Modes Model we can think of this like a Russian Matrushka doll. The OK Modes Model is the outside doll and the Structural Ego State Model would be that which we cannot see, one of the inside dolls.

The Structural Ego State Diagram

We draw the Parent, Integrating Adult and Child Ego States as three stacked circles.

Since there are more complex ways of representing ego states in a diagram, this version of the diagram is called a first-order diagram.

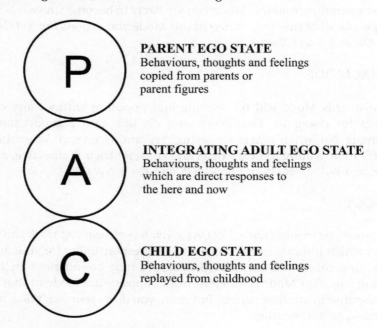

PARENT EGO STATE
Behaviours, thoughts and feelings
copied from parents or
parent figures

INTEGRATING ADULT EGO STATE
Behaviours, thoughts and feelings
which are direct responses to
the here and now

CHILD EGO STATE
Behaviours, thoughts and feelings
replayed from childhood

Figure 3.3   Parent, Adult and Child

PARENT

The Parent Ego State is a collection of attitudes, thoughts, behaviours and feelings copied from parents and other significant people in a person's life. Since no one goes through life meeting only 'perfect' people, the content of this ego state will be a mix of positive or negative elements. This copying process can be experienced in action when someone says something one of their parents may have said to them. They are likely to do this almost without thinking about it and, the person may well feel uncomfortable when they realize what they have said. Older children often do this with their brothers or sisters, talking to them just like mum or dad might have done. If their parent overhears this dialogue they may well feel a bit embarrassed as they recognize themselves!

There are positive aspects of this Parent Ego State as it provides us with:

- a ready made blueprint for how to manage yourself and your relationships
- a set of values and beliefs about the world so that you don't have to think every single situation out from scratch
- ways of being nurturing and supportive to others as well as ourselves

The downside of these benefits is that they are second-hand. This is because they are aspects of the image of the person you have taken into your mind. It is often the case that this side of you is less flexible, and, because no one is perfect, almost certainly some of these views and ways will not actually serve you well. Because you are likely to have lived for a long time with your parents or carers you tend to incorporate their views, actions and beliefs without realizing it.

The Parent Ego State can also be punitive, criticizing or smothering toward self and others. For example, if a person were to be very self-critical they may well be so because their parents taught them that their shortcomings were unacceptable and that they deserve criticism. So another downside of the Parent Ego State is that that real life parent no longer has to be around to do that criticizing – we do it for ourselves!

Whether someone's Parent Ego State is generally positive or negative will largely depend on how the actual parents, relatives and important other figures – like teachers – treated them. They are likely to replay automatically their experience of those people, and are likely to hold the same values about what is acceptable and not acceptable without ever having questioned them.

When growing up, the development of a Parent Ego State can make our lives easier as we don't need to constantly think about everyday choices. In example (1) above under the OK Modes Model Deirdre would seem to be either in the Parent Ego State as she keeps telling others what to do or in the Child Ego State, acting as bossy and precocious. However, unless we ask Deirdre we cannot be sure about whether she has learned this behaviour from watching her parents, or if she was bossy as a child and developed this behaviour as a response to some other situation. If she did behave as her parents (or another significant person) had done then she would be in a Parent Ego State rather than a Child Ego State.

CHILD

The Child Ego State is a set of behaviours, thoughts, and feelings which are replayed from our own childhood (rather than copied from someone else as is the case with the Parent Ego State). In example (2) above, John's behaviour is sometimes inappropriate and at these times, to the outside observer, it would seem that he is in a Child Ego State. John might also move into his Child Ego State when his boss, Jane, calls him in to ask him about a report he is writing. John immediately thinks that Jane wants to see him in order to tell him off about something. He feels anxious and, when he goes into see Jane, he lacks assertiveness and confidence. When Jane asks him for some factual information about the report he realizes that he has been worried over nothing. He gives her the information and returns to his desk. He describes the situation to his coach and realizes that this is a recurring issue for him. He becomes aware that this is how he felt at school and that the feeling is an inappropriate response in the present. Even if his boss was going to tell him off it is not helpful to act as if he were a child, which is how he tends to react.

INTEGRATING ADULT

The Child and Parent Ego States are from a past time. In contrast, the Integrating Adult Ego State is the part of us that is in the present moment.

When a person is in the Integrating Adult Ego State they can be both creative and responsive. Their behaviour, thoughts and feelings relate to the present and are not just copied from parents or parent-figures, nor are they regurgitated aspects of childhood. The Adult Ego State integrates the positive aspects of parents and significant others, as well as taking the best experiences from the past child to use them appropriately today. This is undertaken with thought, rather than purely emotional reaction, which is what happens when we are in the Parent or Child Ego State. In the example above, Jack would appear to be in Integrating Adult Ego State as he responds appropriately, is structuring and supportive and thinks clearly. All of these traits enable Jack's team to respect him. However, it is important to say that when in Integrating Adult Ego State we also have feelings. Years ago it was taught that the adult was like a computer, emotionless. If this were the case being present and being in the Adult Ego State would be rather one-dimensional! However, thankfully TA has moved on and we now recognize that when in Integrating Adult Ego State we think, feel and behave appropriately for the situation. For example, if we are sad because something has happened it is important to appropriately express our feelings without it being seen as 'coming from the Child Ego State'.

Ego State Assessment

Ego states are internal but are manifested in our behaviour. To be truly certain which Ego State someone is in we need to assess the situation in four different ways. Without doing this we can only use guesswork.

BEHAVIOURAL ASSESSMENT

Firstly, we can get an indication of the ego state someone is in from how they are behaving. Parent behaviours include nurturing and empathy and the posture of a person in this ego state may be leaning forward (as if towards a child) or standing in a rigid manner. The vocabulary the person uses may contain value judgements, for example, 'I think you are really selfish' or 'I don't think that's a sensible idea', or 'Let me make you a cup of tea, you look tired'. If we combine their language with their tone of voice then this might reinforce our assessment. We can also look at the tempo of their speech and their expressions. If someone were coming from a Parent Ego State their tone may be staccato, abrupt and controlling, they might have or a stern expression or a wagging finger along with a clenched jaw. These are all possible indications of the Parent Ego State. However, in our childhoods we will all have learnt slightly different behaviours and body language from our parents and significant others, so we need to continue with the assessment.

If the person's words are clear and coherent then they might be in the Integrating Adult Ego State. This assessment would be reinforced if they were standing tall, without being rigid with a sense of flexibility and preparedness a readiness to take a different position if required. They are also likely to show both a sense of assuredness and acceptance of others.

Continuing with our behavioural assessment of the ego states, the Child Ego State behaviour would show up in language and behaviour that is as playful, sulky, rebellious, creative, enthusiastic, excited or inappropriately vulnerable – for example, if you are scared of something that most other people would take in their stride. If you are in the Child Ego State your body language will also mirror that of a child. For example, if you are trying to please someone else you might have your head on one side and be nodding in agreement. Your voice would also be higher in your throat, or squeaky. You might also be quiet and withdrawn or noisy and showy.

SOCIAL ASSESSMENT

This assessment concerns the kinds of transactions a person is having with other people. For example, if it appears that someone is responding from Parent Ego State it is likely that the previous communication came from someone in a Child Ego State. If we were observing a conversation this interaction will be a way of assessing which ego state each of the people may be coming from. On the other hand a transaction from Integrating Adult Ego State will invite an Integrating Adult Ego State response. the Parent Ego State can also invite responses from the same ego state; as in the case of two individuals who are jointly critical of a third person, a group or some other target: 'It's disgraceful how Members of Parliament can claim so much money against the public purse' … 'Yes, I think it is a great pity to see MPs who do not respect the office they hold in the way they used to in the past.' If we look at the words used in this example we can see that 'disgraceful' and the tone of voice and posture may also indicate a Parent Ego State.

Again, if we only use social diagnosis we can only surmise the ego state of the other person. Use of both the social and behavioural assessments offers greater clarity but two other assessments are required to be certain.

HISTORICAL ASSESSMENT

The person's past also provides important information. If, as a child, you had feelings similar to those you are experiencing now, it is likely that you are in Child Ego State. If your mother or father behaved or talked in the same way that you are behaving or talking now then you are probably in Parent Ego State. For example, perhaps you were angry at someone and on reflection feel that you responded in the way your mother did when angry.

Alternatively, if the boss calls you into his office and you immediately think that you are about to be told off for something, on reflection you realize that this is how you felt, aged 12, when your head teacher called you to her office. In this case you would be in a Child Ego State.

Things can get a little more complicated. For example if you feel that your actions are incongruent with how you usually are and your behaviour is more childlike. You know that you did not behave like that when you were a child so don't know where this behaviour comes from. Further enquiry leads you to understand that it is the way one of our parents behaved in a similar situation. In this case it would be a Parent Ego State but from the Child in the Parent. This diagram would look like this.

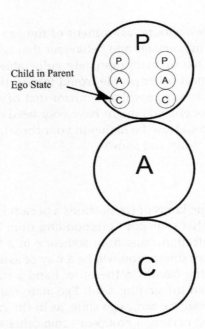

Child in Parent
Ego State

Figure 3.4   Child in the Parent

PHENOMENOLOGICAL ASSESSMENT

Phenomenological wins the prize for the longest word in TA! It relates to times when we re-experience the past instead of just remembering it. This assessment uses the feelings and sensations we are experiencing to understand whether we are here and now, or in the past. For example, we are walking into the reception area of an organization. As we walk toward the doors we pass through a landscaped area where we smell lavender and are immediately transported back to being a child in our grandmother's house – she always polished her furniture with lavender polish. In this instance the smell triggered us to re-experience this rather than just remember it. For those few seconds we would be in Child Ego State.

So a detailed assessment of ego states can reveal a further layer of information and understanding. In organizations, however, this level of detail and probing would not normally be appropriate – or part of the contract.

Relationship between Ego States and OK Modes

Ego states are a way of making sense of what goes on inside us. To be really sure which ego state another person is in we need to do the four types of assessment outlined above. It is not always appropriate or indeed practical, to use historical and phenomenological assessments. In organizations we tend to rely on behavioural and social assessment as it is hardly appropriate to go up to someone who had just snapped at a colleague and ask them, 'Is this how one of your parents used to talk to you?' If we did this we are likely to get short shrift!

Whilst this basic Structural Ego State Model has been criticized as being over-simplistic, it is useful when considering your internal dialogue, and your actions associated with it. It is therefore a useful concept for your own development. It is helpful to reflect on your own ego state/s and in which situations you may move into either Parent or Child Ego State so that you become sufficiently aware and learn to remain in the integrating adult. So understanding the Structural Ego State Model is relevant for your own use or with others when your role permits such detailed enquiry.

All transactions that originate from the Parent or Child Ego States are carried across from the past and are what we call 'transference'. This concept is useful when considering why you might be reacting to certain people in particular ways, for example, to those in authority, or to women who come across as powerful or perhaps to a certain type of personality. It may be that you are 'putting someone else's face' onto the person and therefore you treat them in a way that is not connected to the present. We talk about this later in relation to leadership and followership.

The OK Modes and Ego State Models are linked. If you have integrated effective role Models and are able to use your creativity and be fun then you probably have an effective Integrating Adult Ego State. This will then show up in your behaviour and, in the OK Modes Model, you would be in the Mindful process.

Most other books on Transactional Analysis use the Structural Ego State Model for representing transactions between people. We do not do this as the only way to be sure which ego state someone is in is to undertake the four types of assessment. Therefore the most appropriate Model to use to represent conversations is the OK Modes Model.

By becoming aware of your behaviour and from which Mode you are relating to others, you can change and improve the way in which you communicate with others. When you do this you are likely to receive a different response form the other person.

EXERCISES

EXERCISE 1

Watch Your Language!

This exercise is to familiarize you with the vocabulary of different Modes of behaviour so that when you come across these words and phrases in every day life you can recognize them in yourself and others and decide on the appropriate response.

- Spend a few minutes considering all the messages, words and phrases that may come from the different Modes. For example: Where would 'What time do you call this?' come from? Or 'That's not fair!'?
- Take a look at what you have come up with and consider if you use any or these words or sayings on a regular basis and if so, what beliefs are behind them?
- Are these expressions helpful for good communication? If not what will you do to change these beliefs and behaviours?

EXERCISE 2

The Ineffective Zones

Watch one of the 'reality' programmes on television and identify all the Modes of behaviour.

- Are they examples of effective or ineffective communication?
- Do situations escalate that could have been avoided?
- What options do the characters have that they did not use?
- Could they have said the same thing in a different way?
- Could they have responded differently? As preparation for the next chapter, list some examples of how.

EXERCISE 3

Role Models

If you have made a decision to change and wish to find ways to support this, it is helpful to find positive role Models. These role Models don't even need to be in your life today. You could focus on a great boss you had years ago. Then, when you are in a difficult situation, you can remind yourself what they might have done in a similar situation and behave in a similar way. This will include any positive messages they might give. Eventually, the new, copied behaviour will feel more and more natural as you integrate or incorporate it.

4 *Getting to be an Effective Communicator*

This chapter is the second of two linked chapters – the previous one being on the OK Modes and Ego State models.

Introduction

Even great leaders and strategists can experience difficulties in putting across their message. In organizations, energy needs to be spent on production, not on conflict and disharmony. Organizations need people to come into work at ease, ready to cooperate to get the job done. One of the strengths of Transactional Analysis is that it has ways to develop clear communication and these can be taught and understood by most people, across cultures and across the hierarchy in organizations.

One aspect of TA is its attention to analysing sets of transactions between people. Indeed, not surprisingly, it was this aspect that got TA its name! By analysing transactions, you can develop effective relationships and understand what to do when things go wrong. In addition you can develop your understanding of what works. By being aware of the options available to you when communicating you become emotionally literate, which enables you to defuse situations where there is a potential for conflict.

A single transaction is a communication from one person to one or more other people. This can include speech, but may also include a variety of non-verbal signals. Since the purpose of communication is primarily two-way, you can expect that transactions normally go in pairs – stimulus and response.

The idea of exploring transactions is that you can track a conversation – or a segment of it – and make sense of what took place. Of course you don't need to do this if everything went well. However, it is good to understand the processes that helped it to go well so that you learn to do this consistently. For example, it might be helpful to understand:

- What went well and why?
- At what point did you manage to bring someone round to a common ground?
- At what point did the argument get lost?

What follows are some different concepts that will help to develop an awareness of why communication may go wrong.

Co-Creativity

One of the aims of Transactional Analysis is to be in a positive relationship with yourself and others. To achieve and maintain this, you need to be in the Mindful Process (see Chapter 3) in dealings with other people. If you do this, you will remain flexible and more able to deal with current realities, rather than simply reacting in an automated and maybe rigid fashion. This will be the case regardless of the other Modes people may be in when they relate to you. We are using the term co-creative here (see Summers and Tudor, 2000) as this is an essential part of true dialogue, hence using it as part of our OK Modes Model.

When you are co-creative you are allowing the relationship to develop where you can come together to create something over and above what you may have created on your own. In this way you are more than just responsive. Being purely reactive means that you simply respond to others, whereas in the co-creative space you are, and invite other people to be, assertive, confident and respectful.

To develop a shared understanding with others you can use the OK Modes Model to help explain what goes on during communication. When considering *your own responses* and the way you relate with others you can use the Structural Ego State Model.

Transactions

Let us take a look at some examples of transactions using this model. We will now use two OK Modes diagrams side by side to represent each person involved in the transaction.

PARALLEL TRANSACTIONS

A *parallel* transaction is an exchange (or *stimulus* followed by a *response*) where the Mode to which the first person addresses their communication is also the Mode from which the second person responds. This therefore results in a predictable response, and communication is likely to continue in a similar vein.

Barry – Stimulus: What do you think about the need to maintain the training programme during economic downturn? **Philomena** – Response: Research shows that where training programmes are maintained they are more likely to increase when the upturn happens. How about I get some more information and we have another discussion at the end of the month. That way we don't need to take any action until we have the info.	*This is what we call a parallel transaction and because it is a dialogue it could go on indefinitely. Both people are being respectful to each other. It is the co-creative space where more could happen if it were necessary and appropriate.*

Diagrammatically, the conversation between Barry and Philomena would look like this:

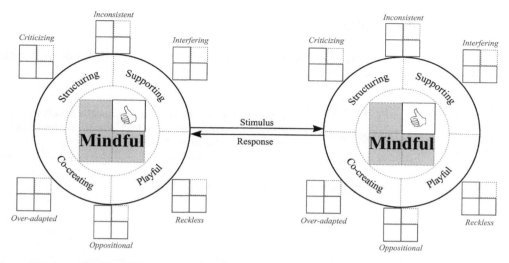

Figure 4.1   Parallel Mindful to Mindful

On the other hand a parallel (or 'complementary') transaction can also lead to more uncomfortable dialogue such as:

Brody – Stimulus: What sort of time do you call this to get in to work? **Tammy** – Response: *(in a whining voice)* I can't help it, the cat was sick on the carpet and the bus was late. I am doing the best I can!	*In this situation there is no co-creativity only an invitation to conflict and resistance. Brody's communication comes from Criticizing Mode and Tammy responds from the Over-Adapted Mode. This process, if it continues indefinitely, is likely to go nowhere and this gets in the way of developing (or maintaining) a positive relationship.*

This would be represented as:

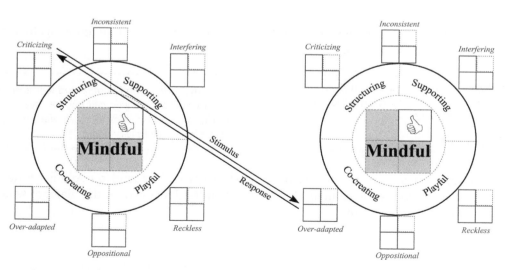

Figure 4.2   Parallel Criticizing to Over-Adapted

CROSSED TRANSACTIONS

A second type of transaction is a crossed transaction. These can be helpful or unhelpful. Let's take an unhelpful example first.

Felicity – Stimulus: What time is it? **Angus** – Response: Time you got yourself a watch!	*In this situation the stimulus came from the Mindful Process but the response came from the Criticizing Mode. Again, the effect is to push Felicity away.*

The diagram for crossed transactions would look like this:

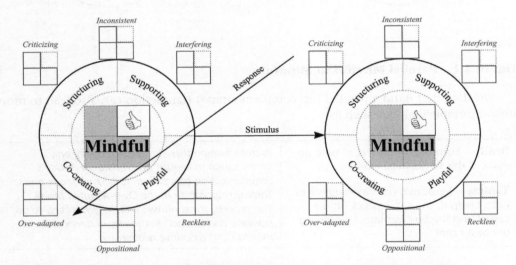

Figure 4.3   Crossed Transaction: Mindful/Criticizing to Oppositional Mode

Alternatively, the person who asked the time might cross the transaction again as an attempt to obtain an answer.

Felicity – I realize you might think I need a watch but in the meantime would you tell me the time? **Angus** – OK – it's 3.00pm.	*Felicity invites Angus to be Mindful, and whilst he may not have actually fully joined her, he does give her the answer and is less likely to move to Criticizing Mode with Felicity again.*

The diagram for the second set of transactions would depend on Angus's tone of voice. But if we assume he came back from the Mindful Process then the diagram would be a parallel communication.

ULTERIOR TRANSACTIONS OR IMPLIED MESSAGES

When you have beliefs and thoughts that are not congruent with the words you are using then you send out a mixed message. For example, internally you may be thinking 'Oh damn, it is her again. How can I cut short this conversation?' In a situation such as this the other person is likely to pick up something from your demeanour, attitude or tone of voice.

Consider the following unspoken statements and how they might affect those with whom you are in dialogue:

- I'm really in a rush – I don't have time for this conversation
- I'm wondering if all the things I've heard about you are true
- I nearly had an accident on the way into work this morning and I can't get it out of my mind
- I've just had a row with the boss and I'm going over and over in my mind the things I'd like to have said
- I'm bored with work and bored with this conversation
- I'm desperate to go to the toilet and I'm too embarrassed to tell you
- I need to get my own way on this so that I get that promotion
- I haven't forgotten the last conversation you and I had on this topic – you're not going to get away with those tactics again

If you were to be thinking any of the above thoughts it is likely that they will be expressed in some way or other, even if not intentionally. The other person then picks up the hidden, psychological or ulterior message and responds to that. Therefore psychological messages have a tendency to create conflict. You often hear people saying something like 'I know that's not what you said, but it's what you meant!'

For example, 'That's a really nice top. Didn't you wear it to a previous conference some years ago?' or 'It's great that the CEO wants you to go to Brussels with her. You go to the same gym club don't you?' Both of these comments appear to be stating fact but have an additional underlying, negative message. For instance, 'I see you are still wearing the same old clothes', or 'no wonder you get to go on the jolly to Brussels when you're mates with the CEO'. It is important that you know how to deal with such transactions.

Sometimes you are not sure what the message is that you are picking up but you just feel uncomfortable. You could blame yourself and say it must be that they don't like you and then try to avoid having contact with them. It might be that they were preoccupied with a problem they had and this was why they were distant with you.

Let's take an example of a communication process that has the potential to escalate and to make at least one person feel bad and see how to avoid that.

In this instance you are doing a presentation and write up something you wish to teach on the flip chart. You teach from this and then, after some discussion, one of the participants says: 'You've spelt 'behaviour' differently three times'. There appears to be an ulterior transaction here – one that implies something without actually saying it. In other words, 'you can't spell the word behaviour'. You, as the receiver of this comment, then have a choice. You can feel stupid and shamed by the comment and become defensive, in which case the process will get very messy. Alternatively, you could keep yourself and the other person OK, saying, in an even voice, that you had not noticed, and then check if this is a problem for the participant. In this way, if there was an attempt to show you up, this does not happen and you seek to understand the other person's concern – for there may have been some reason for the comment that you do not understand.

So where you appear to be invited into a fight or to feel bad, you have choices about how you respond. You need to keep yourself and others OK and still deal with the situation in a way that is also boundary setting. Remember, in this respect at least, suffering is optional!

Of course, the psychological message might be positive which would happen when you experience the other person as showing good will toward you as a matter of course.

Ulterior transactions are those where what is said carries a second, hidden and contradictory message. When this happens distrust will develop and conflict is likely to ensue or, at best, the person or people on the receiving end of such communication are likely to withdraw and/or not commit to a course of action.

Below is another example of an ulterior transaction:

Tom – Stimulus: Just when will you be able to get that report in to me (said with a hint of sarcasm and implying 'You have been too long with that report it should have been in by now').	*If these types of transactions continue it is likely that Tom and Tilly's communication will deteriorate as neither is actually expressing their frustrations with each other. As they are not saying it straight their communications come across in a sniping or 'crooked' way.*
Tilly – Response: By the end of the week (said a bit curtly meaning 'Get off my back. You are always giving me grief').	

To illustrate ulterior messages diagrammatically we still use the OK Modes Model because without further enquiry we do not actually know which ego state someone is in. The opening stimulus purports to come from the Mindful Process – though of course if we were Mindful we would say something straight rather than with an ulterior message. The ulterior message will come from an old way of being and will therefore not be a straight communication.

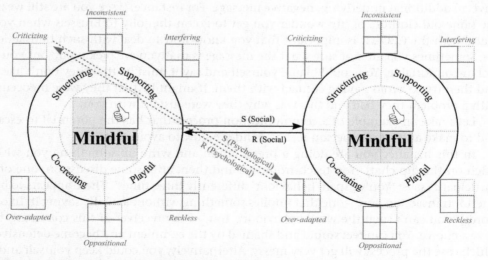

Figure 4.4   Ulterior Transaction: Behavioural Version

Table 4.1 Detailed Example

	Transaction	Mode of behaviour	Life position	Transactions from OK Modes Model (Jo) (Joan)
Jo	Joan, come into my office, now!	Criticizing Mode	*I am OK and You're Not OK*	
Joan	Thinks 'What have I done wrong now?', and not saying anything, just follows Jo into the office without considering the work she is currently doing. (Once in the office) What is the problem? (In a small meek voice, trying to be conciliatory.)	*Over-Adapted Mode.* This will later lead her to believe that life is tough and that she is useless. / *Over-Adapted Mode*	*I'm Not OK and You're OK*	
Jo	At last, you're here. Now, I want you to find out how many new sales we have had this month and I need to have the information on my desk by 4.00pm.	*Criticizing Mode*	*Still acting as if she believes that Joan is Not OK*	
Joan	OK, I have a lot on but I guess I can work late to finish off the other things you wanted by today (said in a sharp terse tone). On return to her desk she finds that she has lost all her work.	Joan is being passive, and is still in *Overadapted Mode.* There appears to be a greater percentage of resistance than compliance. She is saying she will work late but there is an ulterior message here, namely that she resents having to do this. Had she not returned to her desk the tension might well have moved into an argument with her boss asking what her tone of voice meant and this would have escalated the process.	*She sounds as if she is in the position of I'm Not OK and You're Not OK either*	

Consider the above.

Instead, this is how the communication could have gone:

Table 4.2 Detailed Example: Alternative 1

		Transaction	Mode of behaviour	Life position	Transactions from OK Modes Model
Jo		Joan, come into my office, immediately!	*Criticizing Mode*	*I'm OK and You're Not OK*	
Joan		I will be with you in two minutes. I just have to save my work on the computer.	**Mindful Process, opting for Structuring Mode,** crossing the transaction.	*I'm OK and You're OK*	
Jo		At last, you're here. Now, I want you to find out how many new sales we have had this month and I need to have the information on my desk by 4.00pm.	*Criticizing Mode*	*Still in I'm OK and You're Not OK position*	
Joan		Right now I have a great deal of work on, all of which was a priority for today. If I get this information for you now, which other pieces of work would you like me to delay?	**Mindful Process, opting for Structuring Mode,** acknowledging this new priority and wanting to cooperate – **Co-creative Mode.**	*Still I'm OK and You're OK*	

Alternatively Jo, as the manager, could have changed her approach as follows:

Table 4.3　Detailed Example: Alternative 2

	Transaction	Mode of behaviour	Life Position	Transactions from OK Modes Model
Jo	Joan, would you mind coming into my office a moment? I need to discuss some statistics with you.	Jo is behaving from **Mindful Process – mixture of structuring and Co-creative Modes.**	*I'm OK and You're OK*	
Joan	Fine Jo, give me a minute whilst I save what I'm doing on the computer (she saves her work and goes to see Jo).	**Mindful Process – mixture of structuring and Co-creative Modes.**	*Jo's invitation to Joan to stay OK is effective and Joan also chooses to keep herself and Jo OK*	
Jo	I urgently need the statistics for this months sales. Could you get this to me by 4.00pm?	Jo is giving information from **Mindful Process – Co-creative Mode** and is enquiring rather than demanding the stats. This offers Joan the option to co-creatively problem-solve.		
Joan	I can do this, Jo, but I will need to stop doing the other things on my priority list. It sounds like this is the most important task for you right now so if it is OK with you I will drop the items you asked me to do this morning and get on with this.	Joan acknowledges the current reality – for instance that her time and the new task are important and therefore she needs to negotiate dropping other tasks in favour of this one.	*She remains OK/OK*	
Jo	Yes, that's fine. I realize I have just thrown this one at you and of course something else has to give. I trust you to manage your time.	Jo keeps her demands reasonable.	*By expressing her trust in Joan she keeps the relationship OK/OK*	

It is likely that the external behaviour will not be congruent with the internal experience of the people concerned. Rather like the Russian Matrushka dolls, the doll that is on the outside is the only one we can see. However, the internal doll influences our external behaviour. Ideally the internal and the external behaviour are congruent, but when they are not you are likely to experience an ulterior message and get into difficulty with the communication.

Rules of Communication

In TA, here are some basic rules of communications (Berne, 1961):

When communication lines are parallel (or 'complementary') the communication can go on indefinitely – this can be from Mindful to Mindful, or from one of the ineffective Modes to another ineffective Mode.

When messages at two different levels are conveyed at once, the response will be to the psychological or ulterior message rather than the overt, social message. When Joan said she would stay late to complete the work, she was not being straight about how she felt and had Jo picked this up, the situation could have escalated. With these types of situations you tend to say things like 'What did you mean by that?' then receive a response such as 'What do you mean, I said I would do it' moving on to 'Yes, but it's not what you meant', and so on. When this happens an argument can ensue but very often there is no resolution because no one is really saying what they need to say.

Crossed transactions can end up in a break in the conversation in some way – this can be done in a healthy way when you are invited to move into an ineffective Mode and instead you cross the transaction and come from the Mindful Process (Joan crosses some of Jo's transactions).

The break in conversation can be for a few seconds. Crossed transactions are not necessarily bad, and complementary transactions are not necessarily good. It is important to cross a transaction when the other person is inviting you into a behaviour that is not appropriate. For example, when a team leader approaches their boss saying they don't know what decision to make, when in fact the boss knows they are capable of making this decision. The boss is being invited into an ineffective Mode to do the task for the person. It is better for the boss to cross the transaction and invite them to think about the problem and the options and consequences of each. In this way, if the crossed transaction intentionally comes from the effective Mindful Process, the other person is invited to move into their own Mindful Process as well. That will have been the aim.

However, Felicity in her first request for the time (page 46) did not get the response she had hoped for, and in that instance this was not helpful or effective.

Communication may go wrong not because something was said from an ineffective Mode, but because someone *heard* it as coming from that Mode. For example, someone may have heard a comment you said and responded from the Oppositional Mode, using defensive behaviour, which would be an indication that they believed your statement to be coming from Criticizing Mode. If someone adopts an ineffective Mode in response to something you said, you still need to ensure you stay in the Mindful Process and (if appropriate) check out what they heard you say and clarify the situation.

Developing awareness of your own communication processes is important. When you philosophically believe that everyone has a right to be in the world, you value the people you are communicating with *and your behaviour reflects this*, effective communication will follow.

Self-Talk

Effective communication starts with your own effective internal dialogue. You need to ensure that this internal dialogue, as well as the dialogue you have with others, is supportive towards finding a solution to a problem or dealing with a situation.

An example where the person is talking to themselves in an unhelpful way:

At work Max is asked to give a presentation on the work he is doing. Having prepared it thoroughly Max undertakes the presentation. He is congratulated on an interesting and informative presentation, senior management now feel up-to-date, and one or two people show an interest in the project which they previously did not have. He is asked questions, some of which he cannot answer, as he does not yet have the information. Internally, Max beats himself up for not knowing the answer to all the questions, and for forgetting to tell them something. He ignores the obvious interest from the group, and instead focuses on the minutia even though, given the current stage of the project, he could not have answered all the questions anyway. He becomes withdrawn and loses connection with the group.	*In this example, Max's internal dialogue damages his communication processes with others. Max needs to develop positive self-talk which will develop his confidence and his communication with others will improve. He believes he is Not OK.*

As a child, when your parents (and significant other people) were talking you did not question their attitudes and actions. Instead you are likely to have incorporated these behaviours or attitudes into your own and, as an adult, you sometimes respond to situations in the same way they did, without questioning whether this is now still the best option. You are also likely to talk to yourself in the way you were spoken to by them. In the above example we can see that it is likely that Max is talking to himself from his Criticizing Mode in the OK Modes Model. This may well be how a significant person, perhaps a teacher or parent, behaved towards him, and it affects his communication with others.

Children make decisions about self, others and life based on very limited life experience. Fortunately, as adults, we have the potential to make new, self-aware decisions based on a wider range of experiences. These may have shown us that negative self-talk is damaging and that we need to find new ways to talk to ourselves.

How much better it would be if Max had congratulated himself on a great presentation. If there had been faults he could have reviewed them later and used them to learn from in order to develop his presentation skills, rather than just criticize himself. The original criticism in his childhood may have had a positive intent, such as to protect him from others' ridicule. Perhaps he kept on alert so that he did not get criticized. Whatever the reason, this way of living is no longer helpful to Max. It prevents him from excelling, since he loses confidence and self-worth, and it hampers his relationships. He therefore needs to develop more appropriate positive self-talk.

Here are further examples about our internal conversation.

Table 4.4 Case Study: Lynn

Case study	Mode of behaviour	Life positions
Lynn is a manager. She was appointed six months ago. The previous post holder, Jamie, was dynamic and creative. He left behind a legacy of new initiatives which the workforce value as they have made life easier. Lynn comes in to post and learns about the previous manager and her self-confidence begins to ebb. When others say to her 'You have a hard act to follow' Lynn starts to say to herself 'I sure have, and I am not going to be able to. I am not as creative and dynamic as Jamie was.'	When informed that she has a 'hard act to follow' Lynn moves into Over-Adapted Mode.	Lynn's beliefs about herself and the previous incumbent are detrimental to her and to her ability to perform. She believes that she is Not OK in some way and that others are better than her. This keeps her in the one-down position and prevents her from taking her power and her self-esteem lowers. Melinda and John are making themselves OK and Lynn Not OK. They liken themselves to the previous manager, Jamie, and the ulterior is that she will never be like them. In this instance no one is OK. Morale is low and there are no solutions and no options for change.
Whenever Lynn makes a mistake she allows this to reinforce her belief that she is not good enough and others are better than she is.		
During her induction Lynn meets with managers. During these meetings Melinda and John reinforce the stories that she has heard and say that Jamie was great, funny and intelligent. The three of them were good mates and often went out and about – they were in fact three of a kind, able to lead and who are valued up at HQ.		
Lynn starts to believe all of the stories and seeks out people she can relate to. She finds other managers who do not feel good about themselves and who moan about the organization. They go for a drink after work and there they sit and say how bad things are and that it is okay for people like Melinda and John, who are not very nice but they know how to manipulate others to get where they want to be.	This is a difficult decision for her as she wants to belong. However, the cost is too high as no one ever talks about solutions and the options they have to improve things.	Lynn's position is: I'm Not OK and You're Not OK, They are OK

Table 4.4 Continued

Case study	Mode of behaviour	Life positions
After a few weeks of going to the pub and talking about how bad things are Lynn decides that she always ends up feeling worse after going for a drink and decides not to go any more.	Lynn's ability to stand back and be objective assists her to take a new look at the situation, develop her Mindful Process and take action to assist her with the new post.	
Having stopped going to the pub Lynn eventually starts to think about why she was appointed and how much faith they must have had in her. She begins to look at initiatives she had taken in her previous job and how well she was thought of there. She writes everything down so that she can see how successful she was and gets out her c.v. and looks at everything she has done to get to this point. She realizes that she has got herself into this negative frame of mind. She decides that she will see her boss and ask for positive recognition and also see if her boss is willing to pay for a coach for her while she feels her feet in the new job.	With her new attitude about herself she responds differently to the comments about Jamie, the previous manager, or to implied messages that are negative about herself. She crosses these transactions, stays in Mindful Process because, internally, she is saying positive things to herself about her abilities and skills. In this way her transactions follow a Mindful Process rather than colluding with the implied messages about her ability.	Lynn is moving to I'm OK
In this way Lynn starts to achieve her goals and, over time, people stop talking about the previous manager and she begins to get positive recognition for her initiatives and achievements.		Lynn took her power back and shifts to the position of I'm OK, You're OK, and They're OK.

Out of the different positions it can be seen that Lynn's 'favourite' or default position is *I'm Not OK and You're OK*, shifting to *I'm Not OK and You're Not OK*. The case study highlights the fact that OKness is often three-dimensional, for example, Lynn's drink with colleagues who did not feel good about themselves. When they got together they could make everyone else Not OK, including John and Melinda and the organization. As soon as Lynn caught up with what she was doing she was able to shift to *I'm OK, You are OK and They are OK*. In this way she took her control back (see Chapter 2 for more on the three-dimensional Model).

In order to establish effective dialogue with others you need to establish effective dialogue with yourself. It is important to praise yourself for a job well done and to nurture yourself when tired – in fact at any time. It is also important to offer yourself encouragement rather then criticism when things are difficult. When you do this you are more likely to consider options and be able to think about the consequences. In addition you can be creative and spontaneous when your internal dialogue is supportive rather than repressive. Also you are unlikely to enable others to be creative if you are unable to do this for yourself.

EXAMPLES

1) Derek's manager, Robert, shouts from his office, demanding that Derek come and see him immediately. Derek looks worried and sheepishly rushes into the office.	*Derek is used to this style of communication with his manager. He 'knows' that when Robert calls him he has to come straight away. For his part Robert expects those who report to him to jump at his command. Robert would appear to have developed a Criticizing Mode to Derek's Over-Adapted Mode. This type of relationship can go on forever. However, it is possible that one day Derek will shift from Over-Adapted to the oppositional Mode and conflict will ensue. Alternatively, Derek may become so stressed that he goes off sick having taken a grievance out against Robert for bullying. For his part Robert may be stressed but because he uses his Criticizing Mode from which to transact there is little awareness of his stress by other people, and even if there were he is unlikely to receive very much sympathy.*
2) Jane takes a promotion in another company. A couple of weeks later she meets up with Sam, a former colleague. Sam tells Jane that she is really pleased to see her again. Jane senses, however, a different, more ambiguous message underneath this welcome.	*Jane needs to have a positive view of herself to prevent any suspicious thinking about her colleague's ulterior transaction. Jane could spend hours trying to work out what it was that her colleague, Sam, was not saying when in fact it could be that she was envious of Jane's new position and fed up that she is still back at the old place of work. Jane will never know unless she checks this out with her. Therefore she has to decide whether she will do this or whether she will just ignore her intuition and get on with having lunch with Sam. Whichever option she chooses will depend on the level and importance of this relationship to her. It is, of course, also an (unhelpful) option to develop fantasies about what the ulterior message could be about and feel bad.*

3) Alison asks her colleague for some advice on how to handle a client call. Her colleague snaps back at her, saying she has enough of her own work to do without running advice sessions for everyone.	*There are times when someone will give us an unexpected response such as this. In these situations you need to ensure that you do not try to match the other person's Criticizing Mode with your own even more ferocious Criticizing Mode, or even with your defensive Oppositional Mode. There are options for Alison. She needs to cross the transaction and come from the Mindful Process, perhaps using some techniques from assertiveness such as 'I can understand that you must be frustrated if you experience yourself as running advice sessions. Would you prefer it if I asked someone else for advice in future?' In this way Alison would cross the transaction and reflect back to her colleague what she had said so that she experienced being heard. This aligns with her colleague's frustration, shows empathy, and aims to set an agreement for the future. In this way Alison keeps herself and her colleague OK and maintains relationship. How different it would be if Alison took the option of moving into her own Criticizing Mode to respond. If this had happened it is likely the communication would break down.*

The OK Modes Model helps to explain what goes on during communication. A small series of transactions represent and reflect a relationship in miniature. So the general pattern of the relationship is frequently to be seen in the smallest pairs of interactions between the people involved.

Troubleshooting

Naturally, when things are going well, analysing transactions in this way seems a redundant activity. However, if a communication has gone awry, or if you generally have difficulties with relationships, then time spent on analysing what went wrong will be worth it and will repay the time spent on it.

When Communication goes Awry

Sometimes it seems that connecting with each other is one of the most difficult things in the world, when it should be as easy as breathing. The difficulties come when you, for example:

- have the need to control
- aim to prove you are better than others
- put yourself down
- feel put down and then try to do the same to the other person
- get defensive

Within communication there are so many nuances – the words you choose, the tone of your voice, the way you stand or your facial expressions. There also different types of communication – ones where you are talked to like a child, talk to others as if they were a child, talk about others as if they were less than you or imply something without actually saying it. There is also, of course, effective communication where you care about the other person, know that you can have an impact on others, really want to relate and learn about what the other person thinks and are prepared to adjust your thinking accordingly. Of course it is sometimes appropriate to put in a boundary and be firm, but this can be done in a way that is not punitive or 'out to get' someone.

Examples of Communication Difficulties

Mavis was not very socially skilled. She used to approach others with the opening question about what projects they were doing and how busy they were or were not. All these questions were put in a patronizing and aggressive tone. Her fellow team members felt irritated with her and tried to avoid her. If anyone attempted to challenge Mavis' behaviour they got short shrift or even shunned for days at a time. The team started to gossip and moan about Mavis and the more they did that the more arrogant her behaviour became. She began to relate more and more to the team leader and less and less to them. The team leader saw Mavis as a good worker and tended to favour her when new pieces of work came in. This only served to alienate her further from the rest of the team.	*Here it is clear that effective communication has broken down. Mavis has no idea what the issue is as she lacks awareness. No one has been able to raise this issue with Mavis without being shot down in flames or ignored. The team leader shows no apparent awareness of the problem.*

Effective supervision and team development could sort this out, for example, when people have limited awareness they project onto others what they may be thinking or feeling. Mavis may not even be aware that the other person is feeling anything. The team's assumption may be that Mavis does not have any feelings.

Even when someone's behaviour is experienced as invasive or patronizing this does not mean that they don't have any feelings. However, it may be that they have moved away from feelings as a defensive position and it becomes difficult to make a relationship with them in the work place. In instances such as these it is important for the manager to address this issue through the appraisal system and ongoing supervision.

Sometimes people like Mavis are able to shift and become aware of their jarring interactions with others, whilst others are unable or unwilling to take the challenge and make the changes necessary. When this occurs leaders need to consider the most appropriate response to ensure cooperative team work and to ensure the organizational goals and values are maintained. Occasionally this lack of social skills develops into bullying behaviour and this is something we deal with in Chapter 14.

Most people become interested in communication when it starts to go wrong. Most of the time we have fairly good rapport with others and we can tell that we have that rapport. However, there are times when there is some sort of miscommunication, conflict or confusion and then we begin to take an interest in how we could do it differently. This is particularly so when the difficulty keeps happening with the same person or with a range of others. It is then too simple to say 'It must be them'. All of the suggestions here can apply to ourselves as well as others. We are often part of the problem, and we also need to be part of the solution.

Summary

This chapter outlined ways to ensure that your communication is effective. Whilst you may be invited into an ineffective Mode, you need to make the decision to stay here and now. To do this you need to keep in touch with the sense of self, what you think about what you feel and what you feel about what you think. In this way you will be able to stay present and Mindful and decide what you want to do. You need to be interested in others and in the co-creative process of dialogue because through this you will develop effective communication.

EXERCISES

EXERCISE 1

Take a recent real life conversation and plot the pairs of transactions on the diagrams below. The best portion of the conversation to plot is from just before the problem occurred to just after it happened. It may be that your conception of when the problem occurred changes as you do this exercise.

Think first about what was the first thing that either they or you said. On reflection which Mode of behaviour do you think this stimulus came from? Then draw a line from that Mode to the Mode you believe that it was directed to. Next consider the response, which Mode did that come from and where was it directed to? Continue to do this for each transaction, plotting them on the diagrams below. Depending on the number of transactions you may need to draw more diagrams.

1

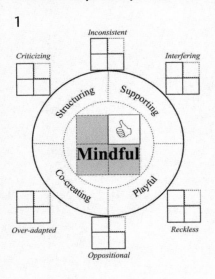
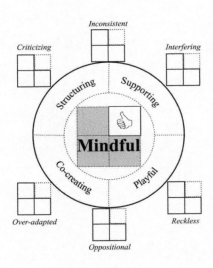

2

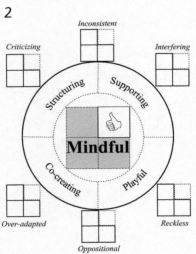
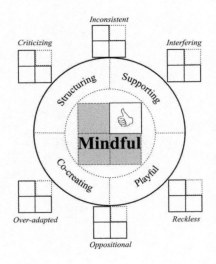

3

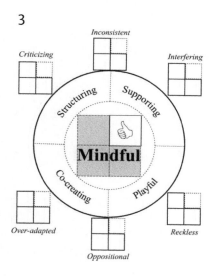

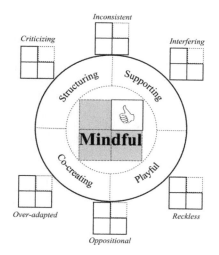

4

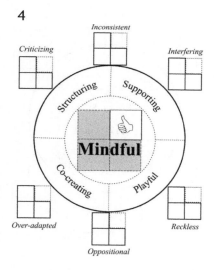

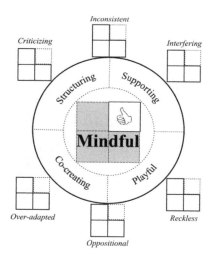

Now, using the knowledge you have gained form this chapter, plot an imaginary alternative – where you respond differently – and what you predict would be the different outcome.

1

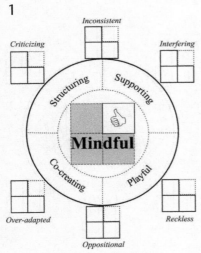

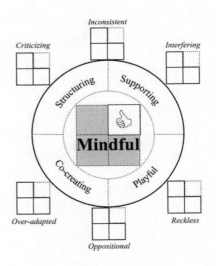

2

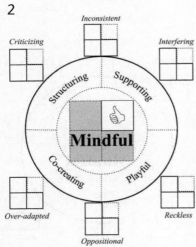

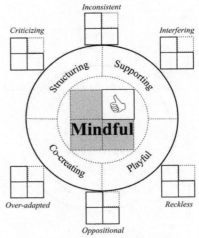

3

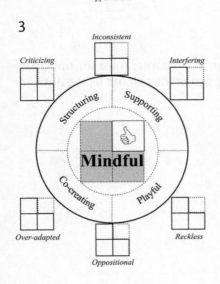

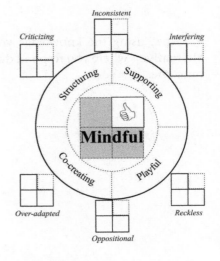

4

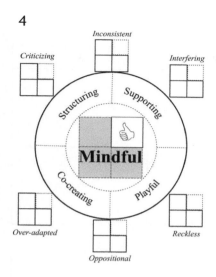

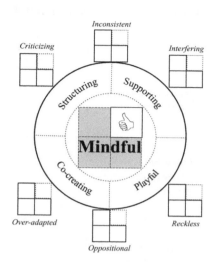

EXERCISE 2

Think about the times when you make life harder for yourself.

- What do you say inside your head?
- Is that helpful?
- What would you like to do differently?
- Who could you draw on that would be a positive role model in this process?

Take a look at the chapter on OKness (Chapter 2) to see the link between how we communicate with ourselves and how we communicate with others. When you talk to yourself in negative ways and believe that you are not as good as others, then you are saying *I'm Not OK and You're OK.* On the other hand you might get irritated and angry with other people's frailties and shortcomings and talk negatively to them from Criticizing Mode in which case you are saying that you are better then others (*I'm OK and You're Not OK*). By changing your beliefs you can change your communication processes and therefore improve your relationships.

EXERCISE 3

Consider the following and then complete the chart below:

1. Take three beliefs or self-criticisms that hold you back
2. How does each belief or criticism affect you?
3. Write what the opposite beliefs or positive self-talk would be
4. Consider what it would be like to comfortably hold these new beliefs
5. How will you change your behaviour?

Fill in the three columns with the belief or criticism that holds you back and then follow down completing each column before going on to the next.

Table 4.5   Beliefs and Self-Talk

	1	2	3
Negative belief or criticism:			
How this affects me and/ or others:			
Opposite belief or criticism:			
New self-talk:			
How I will be if I gave myself this message:			
I will change my behaviour by:			

5 *Recognition*

Introduction

When an organization acknowledges its staff, they are more likely to feel positive about coming into work and energy will be productively focused. This chapter explores the effect of positive recognition on the establishment of a healthy organizational culture.

Positive recognition is the means by which people express their sense of belonging, attachment and appreciation of self and others. This is not just about giving praise to people it is also about actions. For example, bothering to greet someone, stopping to talk or say 'Good morning' when they come into work, are all forms of recognition. Recognition can also be expressed through our behaviour in other ways, for example, by trusting someone to undertake a task, or asking them for their opinion. In Transactional Analysis acts of recognition are traditionally called *strokes*.

Berne coined the name 'strokes' from the infant's need for touch. Spitz (1946) had observed that babies reared in orphanages largely failed to have their needs met and, more specifically, lacked touching and stroking by their carers. He argued that children need stimulus to be provided in order to promote and enable neural development. In contrast, children who spent large amounts of time in hospital seemed to fare better, since although they were unwell, their care necessitated much physical contact – even though this was for medical reasons.

This need for recognition does not stop in adulthood. Most people value being acknowledged when they have completed a task for someone, or when they go into work in the morning. If this is not forthcoming then something that may have started as a lack of awareness on someone's part can escalate into outright hostility, affecting the whole department or team. Further, the higher up the management ladder someone goes the fewer people there are to offer strokes and people can become stroke-deprived. This deprivation can lead to psychological and emotional difficulties.

Why is recognition so important? It is one way in which you show that someone is accepted and perhaps even more than this – that they belong. So recognition is one way of showing that the other person is significant and that, at the very least, you acknowledge their presence and/or their efforts. You therefore ignore the need for recognition at your peril.

Myths and Antidotes

People develop different ways of giving and receiving recognition or strokes dependent upon how strokes were exchanged in their families. Some of these will be healthy and some unhealthy. For example, there is a belief that children will become arrogant if given too many strokes or if a child asks for recognition they must be very needy. These childhood beliefs tend to stay with us in adulthood and there is a tendency to maintain the same patterns about giving and receiving strokes.

Steiner (1971) came up with five myths about stroking:

- don't give strokes when you have them to give
- don't ask for strokes when you need them
- don't accept strokes if you want them
- don't reject strokes when you don't want them
- don't give yourself strokes

The fourth myth above concerns the rejection of strokes that are given in a manipulative way. The classic one being from the teenager in the family who says 'You look really great today, mum' and from past experience you know that this is likely to be followed by a request for a lift into town! When rejecting a stroke the intention is not to make someone else Not OK, but just not to allow manipulation. In the mother and teenager example the mother could be in the Mindful Process and responding from the Playful Mode, with a smile on her face respond with 'OK, what do you want?'

Rather than follow the stroking myths you need instead to acknowledge that:

- giving strokes is an important part of relationships and growth
- it is OK to ask for strokes when you need or want them
- accepting strokes will increase confidence and positive feelings
- rejecting strokes can be a healthy thing to do when done in OK–OK ways
- giving yourself strokes is important and will promote good feelings

Some of these may seem simple to do but many may, subconsciously, believe the myths. When reading the acknowledging list above you might say to yourself, 'I'll just become big-headed if I do that', or 'If I have to give myself strokes, they won't be worth much, they only count if given by someone else'. When you give yourself negative strokes for who you are and for things not done well, this lowers self-esteem. Instead, when you give yourself positive strokes this will develop to feelings of positive self-worth, creativity and your levels of energy will increase.

You can give yourself strokes through positive stored memories, dreams, movement and nature as well as positive self-talk. When you use your negative stored memories as a way to give yourself recognition you will become depleted. For example, when you do something at work for which you were criticized you might then revisit all the other times when you got it wrong and use these to reinforce your view that you are useless. When stressed how much better it is to go for a walk in the park, recall the times when you have dealt with things well and use this to feel good about ourselves. You can feel the breeze on your skin, feel the warmth of the sun and begin to feel relaxed and at ease in this moment, despite any difficulties there might be in the workplace. You can then obtain a sense of perspective and return to work able to deal with the difficulties being encountering.

Obtaining Balance

When you give out a lot of recognition and get very little back you become depleted. When there is a balance you are more able to maintain your energy and positive outlook. You can give yourself positive recognition through massages, walks, luxurious baths, holidays, seeing friends, positive self-talk. That way, when there are few people around to give you strokes, or you are receiving negative strokes from others, you still have a healthy balance.

The Value of Recognition

When someone gives a considered stroke which is well timed and relevant it is likely to engender a positive feeling and increase feelings of self-worth. The person receiving the stroke is likely to feel closer to the giver of the stroke as they experience being seen and valued.

People have a tendency to give strokes at the level of the relationship they have. For example, if a new manager walks up to you on the first day in an organization and tells you that you are fantastic, you are not likely to take them seriously. Strokes therefore relate to the nature of the relationships you have.

We all value different strokes in different ways; you might be the sort of person who likes being asked what sort of weekend you had, or how the family is, whilst someone else might find this intrusive. Others might accept strokes for being clever but not for being creative. Unfortunately, people have a tendency to value strokes more highly if they come from a person in a senior position than someone who is a colleague. Strokes can also be devalued if they come from someone who is not respected or they give rather too many strokes as this indicates they may not be genuine. Conversely, by limiting the nature or type of strokes you accept you are discounting the giver of the stroke and the stroke itself. The more open you are to a variety of different types of positive strokes the better you will feel about yourself and what you do.

RECOGNITION FOR WHO WE ARE AND FOR WHAT WE DO

In broad terms, strokes can be exchanged in two areas – for the person you are and the things you do:

- **Being and Doing Strokes** (also known respectively as unconditional and conditional strokes).

Being strokes are *unconditional* for the logical reason that you haven't had to do anything to earn the stroke, since it is for *who you are as a person*. An example in a work context would be:

'I really enjoy you in this team.'

So all that needs to happen for the strokes to continue is to carry on being yourself.

In contrast, doing strokes are *conditional* for the logical reason that they are a response to *something you have done* (or achieved). An example in a work context would be:

> *'That was a great report you put together there – it's increased our chances of getting that contract. Thank you.'*

Here you would need to produce another report or do something else to earn another 'doing' stroke (though of course we can receive more than one stroke for something we have done!).

People have preferences for these different kinds of strokes – usually as a result of their experiences in early life. For instance, some people may be uncomfortable with *being* strokes – preferring to get recognition for what they do. Others are less interested in *doing* strokes and want to be recognized for their personal qualities. Ideally, we benefit from a mixture of the two in terms of both giving and receiving.

POSITIVE AND NEGATIVE RECOGNITION

We have used the word *positive* several times so far in this chapter. We define a positive stroke as one which invites an *I'm OK, You're OK* response (see Chapter 2). In contrast, a negative stroke invites either the giver or the receiver of the stroke (or both) to feel Not OK. So to illustrate this in the context of appraisal, feedback about areas in which the employee needs to make changes does not in itself constitute negative recognition. The crucial factor will be the way in which the feedback is given. Sometimes, especially if it is done mechanistically, the 'sandwich' approach to giving feedback (say something nice, then hit them with the feedback, then say another nice thing) is so transparent that the recipient feels manipulated and therefore decides either that they are Not OK, or that the person giving feedback is Not OK. If the individual feels that a genuine effort is being made to help them develop and improves their performance, this is less likely to happen.

People sometimes respond negatively to quite mild feedback, and one way of seeing this is to consider that it has its origins in the way in which parents give feedback to their children. When children do something wrong, a frequent statement form parents is 'you bad boy/girl' rather than 'what you have just done is wrong'. Many people thus grow up with the sense that getting something wrong is equivalent to being Not OK.

RECOGNITION AND MOTIVATION

There is a link with strokes and motivation. When there is an absence of positive strokes, and sometimes just an absence of strokes in general, this can lead to apathy and demotivation. We all need to be recognized and have our work valued, as well as value it ourselves. When neither of these occur you are likely lose interest in what you are doing which will affect productivity. If this situation goes on for a while then your self-confidence is likely to be affected. However, as this book highlights, recognition is not sufficient on its own as a way to improve morale.

Stroking Examples

1) Joan's manager, Cedric, is efficient and popular with management. However, Joan finds him difficult as he frequently criticizes her work. Cedric tends to take the praise for work Joan has completed. When she tackles him about this, he says that she gets paid, and shouldn't need praise.	*Cedric's criticism of Joan will affect her commitment to the job as well as to her boss. It is clear that Joan is assertive as she has raised this issue with Cedric but was only met with defensiveness and further criticism. It is likely that she will look for a transfer or a new job where she feels she will be valued.*
2) The area sales team have low morale. Their organization is target driven for which there is no recognition. Despite this the team enjoy their work and are good at it – and meet tight deadlines.	*The expectations are all about results and yet, when these are achieved there is no recognition. Their extra effort has not resulted in more pay, any thanks, or strokes. The final outcome is likely to be a loss of good will with an accompanying slowdown in productivity.*
3) Sharon is a newly promoted manager with quite an abrasive style, although she is not argumentative or aggressive. She describes herself as a 'tasks' person not a 'people' person. Despite being abrasive she is experienced as fair. Sharon recognizes that she needs to develop a different style and in the meantime has appointed a deputy manager who is much more of a people person.	*Relationships can suffer if people have difficulty with giving or receiving positive strokes. Sharon is accepted as good at her job despite not being so good with people. In this instance a good deputy initiates processes that encourage positive strokes. Had this not been the case then the outcome may well have been low morale, as in the previous case study.*

Strokes and Relationships

We all have different ways of dealing with life and for some people the strain can be eased by teasing one another. This teasing or banter can be a way of releasing stress and can be a sign that someone belongs – 'If we didn't like you or feel safe with you, we wouldn't tease you in this way'. For example, the brother of one of the authors (Mountain) used to tease her and today, when friends tease her, this offers a positive link to the relationship she enjoyed with her brother and brings her closer to those friends. This type of good-natured teasing is particularly evident in the armed forces as it can create a bond between individuals and is one way they cope with traumatic situations.

One thing which needs to be ensured in a culture of banter is that everyone experiences it as a positive sign of belonging. If you are in a minority in a team, or a newcomer, you may not share this understanding. For example, if you have not experienced positive teasing in the way that Mountain did, then the banter in the workplace may be experienced as bullying and shaming, which of course, it may well be.

If you start the banter you need to be sure that there is no underlying negative intent. For example, you might say to something like 'Here comes Paul, we know who'll they'll be letting go in the next round of redundancies! Ha, Ha, Ha.' This is called a 'scorpion stroke' and challenging it can be difficult as the retort might be 'It was just a joke, we all joke around here, don't be so soft.' If you initiate the teasing you need to ensure that the aim is to be inclusive and from an OK–OK position.

The development of a positive stroking culture promotes a trusting environment. Trusting environments promote individual responsibility, rather than blame. When this occurs the organizational culture will be dynamic and creative.

Biological Hungers

There are three main biologically driven needs that are the motivating force for human beings. Berne's term for these was 'Hungers'. He called them:

- stimulus or sensation
- structure
- recognition (belonging – authors' amendment)

STIMULUS HUNGER

We all need stimulation. We get this through the art we put on our walls, the activities and studying we undertake, and the conversations we have. Insufficient stimulation and we become apathetic, too much stimulation and we become burnt out. We all have different thresholds regarding the amount of stimulation we enjoy and can handle, and learning what this is will be helpful. When you are overwhelmed by too much stimulus you have usually failed to notice the signs that things are becoming too much and have not taken the appropriate action.

STRUCTURE HUNGER

We all need to find ways to structure our time. We do this in a variety of ways:

- withdrawal
- rituals
- pastiming
- activities
- games
- play
- intimacy

(See Chapter 15 for a fuller account of Time Structuring.) By paying attention to the way in which you structure time you are able to better meet your overall stroke needs and maintain your motivation throughout your working lives.

RECOGNITION HUNGER OR BELONGING HUNGER?

Berne maintained that gaining recognition is one of our primary motivators from the time of our birth. However, recognition could be seen as a specific form of stimulus. A 'stroke' consists of a *stimulus* coming from a *specific person* and which is *specifically directed at us*. If we contrast that with stimuli generally, such as sounds around us, the warmth of the sun, or the sensation of a breeze on our skin, we can see that those stimuli are 'out there' in the environment – for anyone to access – they are not specifically directed at any one person.

We therefore consider 'belonging' to be the second hunger. If we see someone and exchange greetings with them this is a stimulus and we obtain value for being recognized. However, everyone needs to feel a sense of belonging and it is this aspect that enables us to feel safe enough to offer our thoughts and opinions since we feel valued. This links with the Concepts for Thriving (see Chapter 16). When we feel we *belong* we are also more likely to contribute and our loyalty will increase. The development of belonging in the workplace is an aspect often insufficiently considered but invaluable in order to achieve effective participation during day-to-day working as well as during change.

We can see how important belonging is when agency staff are used as they rarely have the same commitment to the organization. They do not know its culture, structure and systems and are more likely to undertake their basic workload with less motivation. Agency staff's attachment can be influenced by acknowledgement and inclusion and they are then more likely to return with increased enthusiasm for a permanent post, or return on frequent assignments.

These situations reinforce the idea that recognition is not the hunger, the hunger is belonging, and that positive recognition is the means by which we express this with other people. This would serve to explain the apparent contradiction that people who meditate experience high levels of fulfilment and connection when there is no visible stroke exchange – they are experiencing a sense of belonging and connection to themselves and the universe.

Put another way, recognition to and from other people, and to ourselves, is one of the primary means by which we satisfy our hunger to belong to:

- another person in a relationship
- feel part of the whole when involved with a team or group
- an organization
- a culture
- the global community
- humanity
- nature and the universe

A grid which is a variation of the OK Corral (Ernst, 1971) may help to illustrate this (please see the following page).

The sense of belonging could be negatively affected by many factors including:

- the lack of choice of one's colleagues at work
- high levels of turnover
- lack of a sense of common ownership
- threat of redundancy
- the level of commitment a person has to their work
- the level of fulfilment a person experiences from their work
- people's script decisions (see Chapter 10)
- The way in which strokes are given – for instance, with ulterior messages such as 'I am doing this because I have been taught to on my management course, not because I think you deserve it'

- our stroke 'filters' – the way we screen out certain kinds of strokes – for instance, positive strokes about who we are

Table 5.1   The Recognition Grid

I experience myself as out of connection with myself and as not wanting/having any belonging with you. *(I'm Not OK, You're OK)*	I experience a sense of connection with myself and of belonging with you. **(I'm OK, You're OK)**
I am disconnected from myself and from you and I see you as being just as disconnected. Belonging feels a long way away. *(I'm Not OK, You're Not OK)*	I experience myself as better than you and I am putting you out of connection with me. *(I'm OK, You're Not OK)*

However, these can be offset in a work context by the extent to which people feel there is genuine concern for them as individuals. The stroking culture (Hay, 2009) can be seen as the backcloth which aids or impedes workers' sense of belonging in the organization. The organizational stroking culture consists of exploring the issues of success, failure and how the good enough person is stroked in that culture, and there is an exercise at the end of this chapter to assist you to do this.

Stroking Audit

By taking an 'audit' of the quality of relationships in the workplace you can consider the outcomes and decide if, and what you need to change. Sometimes there is a lack of positive stroking across the whole workforce, from colleague to colleague, or up and down the hierarchy.

Sickness levels give an indication of the workforce's relationship with the organization. High rates of sickness indicate, amongst other things, that there are insufficient positive strokes within a team, department, division, or across the whole organization. As far back as 1951, Homans stated that when rewards are withheld this leads to apathy. Conversely, when you are over-stroked the value of the strokes you receive is reduced. Therefore it is necessary to obtain a balance between these two aspects.

Some Questions to Consider

1. Is there any way in which the quality of relationships is getting in the way of effective working or productivity?
2. Is turnover uncharacteristically high?
3. Are sickness levels unacceptably high?

4. Is morale low – and for reasons that are not particularly connected with external realities?
5. If you were to walk into any workspace area, what would be your sense of the predominant mood?
6. Is the well-being of people a priority for you?
7. What are your core beliefs about people? Is this reflected within the organization?

Having asked these questions you are in a better position to consider if the development of a positive stroking culture would at least go some way to improving the situation. However, changes in the way that people exchange strokes and recognition need to happen with care and be genuine. Instituting changes needs to be done at a slow enough pace for people to develop a sense of trust.

Some Questions to Answer Include

1. What is the purpose of this change in culture? Does this change include benefits to the workforce as well as predicted ones for the organization?
2. Does the change directly relate to a problem in morale, communication or productivity?

When considering the stroking culture it is not about how many strokes are exchanged but what investment there is in the workforce and their interactions. If new office premises were obtained and not painted, insured, maintained, or kept locked at night, this would be considered highly irresponsible. Yet, over time, there is a huge comparable investment in the workforce and positive recognition needs to be a part of this.

Be Aware About What You Stroke

Sometimes we give attention to unhealthy behaviour which can actually reinforce the very thing we want to change. This happens because the criticism comes from the Criticizing Mode of the OK Modes Model. The person on the receiving end is therefore likely to develop resentment and move into their Over-Adapted or Oppositional Mode in response (See Chapters 3 and 4). If they go into Oppositional Mode then the outcome is likely to be more outwardly aggressive, or passive-aggressive behaviour, all with negative outcomes. Given that 'what we stroke is what we get' putting the focus on what someone is doing well will be more productive. This is not to say we ignore the more negative aspects but they need to be in a context of acknowledging the positive.

An example of this is when someone, let's call him Pete, is argumentative and defensive when asked a question. Feedback at the appraisal highlights this issue and Pete decides that he will change his behaviour. However, his boss and colleagues tend to focus on how often Pete does it the old way, as opposed to noticing when he does it differently. When this happens Pete feels demotivated and returns to his old defensive ways. What we focus attention on grows greater in our lives and if everyone showed Pete support when he did things differently he is more likely to be motivated and manage the change.

Types of Strokes

Positive strokes are intended to be pleasurable and carry an *I'm OK, You are OK* message and foster self-esteem. Negative strokes carry an *I'm Not OK* or a *You're Not OK* message (or both) which can result in damaging self-esteem. Whilst strokes can be positive and negative they can also be conditional and unconditional. If we were to say to someone 'You are a great orator' there are no 'conditions', from our perspective the person is a great orator. However, if we were to say 'You would be a great orator if you spoke more slowly', being a great orator is conditional on the speed of the other person's speech. Conditional strokes are very useful when offering developmental feedback, particularly when there is an agreement or 'contract' for this. Naturally, the conditional stroke needs to given in an *I'm OK and You're OK* way, and in a context of a positive stroking culture.

The unconditional negative stroke would sound something like 'You are irresponsible' or 'I don't like you'. These are unhelpful ways of talking with people and we would be coming from an ineffective Mode within the OK Modes model and also inviting the other person to come from an ineffective Mode. This will do nothing to promote productivity, let alone harmony, and will only serve to reinforce any feelings of low-self worth.

Conditional strokes are helpful when learning a skill as they point the way forward. They need to be specific and given immediately after the action, as well as just before the person is undertaking that action again. Let us take the example of training others to facilitate workshops. James has taken his turn to facilitate and there is a contract for developmental feedback. We might say 'I liked the way you made contact with the group and responded well to questions. You clearly know your material and can put this across. You sometimes speak very quickly – moving on before I had taken in what you'd said. I suggest that you speak more slowly so that your audience can glean your knowledge'.

Boosting the stroke by being specific is likely to have greater effect; for example, we could simply say 'You did a great job' or 'You really put a lot of energy into everything you do and I really appreciate the way you saw that project through, despite the difficulties'.

Summary

There are different ways to give strokes to others and to yourself. For some it may be another's actions that are valued, rather than what they say, whilst for others it is the other way around. Some people become uncomfortable when given any positive recognition and therefore when wanting to give a stroke to this person you need to do so sensitively without going on too much. Others believe they do not need any recognition at all and whilst they may discount the strokes they do receive it is still important to offer them when you have them to give. What they do with your stroke is up to them.

You need to take into consideration the person, their culture, and the organizational culture and therefore the appropriateness of the stroke, otherwise you may inadvertently insult someone. If you are new to a country or culture it is important to find out about it, and listen and watch, before being too liberal with strokes and what or whom you stroke.

When giving feedback and recognition you need to decide if the intention is to:

- value the other person
- make developmental comment about their work or behaviour
- put them down, which is more about you and your need to believe you are better than others

To be effective you need to consider:

- the context of the relationship in relation to the nature and degree of intensity of strokes exchanged
- the current pattern of strokes the person is familiar and comfortable with
- strokes not simply from a manipulative, 'let's squeeze more work out of them' way but from a way to improve relationships and self-esteem which will in turn improve productivity
- ideas around what motivates people – because this will have an impact on the kind of strokes you may choose to exchange
- what makes a 'target' stroke for an individual – in other words what makes it special and therefore more powerful for them to receive

The giving and receiving of strokes is a dynamic process which promotes or inhibits relationships. The atmosphere, trust and cooperation within the workplace can be enhanced by the genuine giving and receiving of positive as well as conditional strokes. Obtaining the balance between the nature and type of strokes for each individual is an important part of management and leadership.

EXERCISES

EXERCISE 1

Strokes and You

This exercise is designed to promote awareness. Once you have answered the questions consider what options you have and how you will make any changes required to ensure a positive stroking balance in your life.

- How do you manage your relationships with people?
- Is there a fairly equal exchange of recognition and appreciation?
- If you are a manager, how did your web of relationships change when you became a manager – do you receive fewer, and give out more strokes?
- If this is the case what can, and will you do to achieve the balance between giving and receiving?
- If you give too few strokes to others what will you do to redress this?

EXERCISE 2

Scenarios Exercise

Below we have written some short scenarios followed by some suggested questions for discussion. These can be used by consultants and trainers as well as heads of department and those responsible for encouraging the development of a positive culture.

Scenario 1

Your boss had asked everyone to 'pull out all the stops' for the current project. You put lots of effort in, worked extra (unpaid) hours, and exceeded all expectations with results in terms of a major contribution to the project. Your boss makes no response to this. You tell your boss that you'd like some praise for all your effort. He tells you the satisfaction of doing the work should be enough praise in itself.

Some possible questions/points for discussion:

- How might you persuade your boss differently?
- Is there any truth in what you boss says?
- Will you 'pull out all the stops' next time?
- Assuming you are committed to your job – and enjoy and value other members of your team – how might this incident impact on you and them – and what could you do about it as a team?

Scenario 2

You are the manager for a team of eight people. You have learnt the basics of TA and understand the importance of giving your team recognition for their efforts. However, one person in the team never seems to be satisfied – they always want more encouragement and praise. You are pleased with their work, which deserves praise, but this seems to be a personal issue that is getting in the way of the team's smooth working.

Some possible questions/points for discussion:

- Would you broach the idea of this person getting help (therapy/counselling/coaching) for this problem?
- Even if this is a personal issue – generate some strategies for what you could do to aim for some change with this person.

Scenario 3

You have a work colleague whom you really value working with – you enjoy them as a person and like having them around. They work really well too. When you have tried to tell them how much you value them as a colleague, they become embarrassed, and 'ward off' your compliments. This concerns you, and you want to understand how this could be.

Some possible questions/points for discussion:

- Review/Generate ways of giving strokes.
- What could you do as an alternative to giving *being* strokes?

Scenario 4

You went on an introductory course in TA a couple of months ago, and the concept that struck you the most on the course was stroking and recognition. This is probably because it resonated so much in terms of how you could improve your awful work situation. No one at work gives anyone any recognition – not the manager, nor any of the team between themselves. Everyone just 'puts their head down' and 'gets on with it' – even though morale is at rock bottom. When you raised recognition at a team meeting a couple of weeks ago, everyone ridiculed it as 'pop psychology'.

Some Possible Questions/Points for Discussion

- Generate other ways of putting your argument across.
- What are your options personally?

EXERCISE 3

How I Exchange Strokes with People I Know

Consider all the relationships you currently have – think of a spectrum from close relationships to vague acquaintances. Pick a relationship at each of the extreme ends and one somewhere in the middle. Finally, choose someone you work with. Choose someone who is typical of the kinds of relationships you have with people at work. We invite you to take care of yourself in how much you decide to write down in this questionnaire – bearing in the mind who else might get to see it. There is no right or wrong here – just your answers for you. However, the intention of the questionnaire is to help you recognize more about the way in which you exchange strokes in your life at present and to decide if there is anything you will change about this process.

Give five examples of what you consider to be typical stroke exchanges in the four relationships from Table 5.3.

Table 5.2   Stroke Exchange: Examples

Person			
1st example			
2nd example			
3rd example			
4th example			
5th example			

Table 5.3   Stroke Exchange

Name of person	(close) ←	← (middle) →	→ (acquaintance)	(Work colleague)
On a scale of 1–10, how important to you are the strokes you exchange with this person?				
How *often* do you have contact with them?				
How *long* on average do you have contact with them each time?				
On a scale of 1–10 how intense would you say this relationship is for you?				
Is the exchange of strokes equal between you (in terms of giving and receiving)?				
If between 5 and 6 is the average, score the balance between positive strokes (higher the number) and negative ones (lower the number) that you normally exchange in this relationship.				
How many other relationships have you that are similar in intensity to this relationship?				
How much of your need for exchanging strokes is met by *this* person – as a percentage? Since these four relationships are just a sample, your total here may well not come to 100 per cent.				

Review your answers. Are your relationships how you would like them to be? Is there anything you would like to change? What will you do to ensure your relationships and stroking patters are in line with how you want to be?

EXERCISE 4

The Organizational Stroking Culture (Hay, 1993)

Does your organizational culture leave something to be desired in relation to giving and receiving positive strokes? If so, then the following questions, taken from Hay's work, may be of assistance.

Very often when someone is successful they are given extra benefits, bonuses or strokes. When someone is failing they may receive coaching, mentoring, and additional attention in a variety of ways, even negative attention. However, there are people who are doing a good enough job, who may be doing their best even but who are not interested (or able) to be a high flier. These people may not receive any, or many, strokes. They may then experience themselves as having few options as to how to obtain strokes. In these circumstances some people may go off sick as a way to receive recognition, or even fail in a task (or in general). For some people receiving negative recognition is better than receiving no recognition at all.

Consider the following questions:

- What is success in your organization and how is it given recognition?
- What is failure in your organization and how is it given recognition?
- How is the 'good enough' person given recognition?

Consider your answers and then decide what actions you can take to change the stroking culture of your organization, department or team.

6 *Agreeing the Way Forward*

Introduction

The workplace depends on people agreeing with each other about pretty well everything that they do – both singly and collectively. Often when things go wrong in organizations, it comes down to the quality of these agreements – or the lack of them. These agreements may not be explicit, or conversely, they may be written in stone in procedure and policy documents. Some will be made in the moment, other times people may simply follow the way things were done last week. Sometimes people simply go about their work with no reference to anyone else.

In this chapter we will be considering the art of reaching agreements, including:

- different types of agreement – or *contract*
- the process of reaching an agreement – referred to as *contracting*
- tips on ensuring clarity, professional effectiveness and goal-led outcomes

When all these aspects are in place, there is a far higher likelihood that goals will be met and that people will be clear about roles and tasks.

Defining a Contract

We can define a contract as:

an openly made agreement to commit to a specific action or outcome, which involves all the people who will contribute to making it happen.

In an ideal situation, each person is motivated to take on the tasks they have agreed to. In Transactional Analysis we use this concept as the bedrock of our work. Effective contracting leads to effective working. We consider a contract to be as small as checking out with someone that this is a good time to call, to establishing agreements between large numbers of stakeholders on a major project.

Effective contracts are made when each individual is clear about:

- what they are doing
- why they are doing it
- who else is involved
- what their role and responsibilities are, and
- when the tasks need to be completed

All too often people make assumptions about who is doing what, with resultant misunderstandings and things not getting done.

EXAMPLES

Let's take the following examples:

1) John manages a team of sales people. They met a month ago to establish a new strategy, which everyone agreed to. None of the agreed actions have been implemented since then, and John is confused and angry as to what is going on.	*It would appear that people are not actually 'signed up' to the new strategy.* *Questions John needs to ask include:* *Was a time frame agreed for implementing the agreed actions?* *Were disadvantages to individuals talked about and/or dealt with?* *John needs to consider his communication with the team:* *Which Mode did he relate from?* *Which Mode does he think the team members related from?* *Perhaps he discounted something in terms of their workload and their motivation and commitment. It is likely that through reflection he can become aware of something now, that he was not aware of then, in terms of establishing the contract.*
2) Fred was recently unsuccessful as the internal candidate for a promotion. The CEO suggests that Fred will be the best person to carry out much of the induction programme for the successful applicant when he starts next month. Fred is approached and agrees to do this, though internally he thinks 'I wasn't good enough to get appointed and now they want me to help the person who pipped me to the post!'	*Using the OK Modes Model, it would appear that neither CEO nor Fred were Mindful in this situation. Which Mode do you think Fred is in when he agrees to the contract but in fact resents doing the induction? What would motivate Fred to help with this induction other than simply doing as he is told, and what other options does he have? It looks as if Fred moves into the Oppositional Mode with his boss. It would be appropriate if his supervisors gave him some feedback about his interview and let him know why they thought he would be good to induct the new incumbent. If Fred is to undertake this contract he needs to do so from within the Mindful Process or decline the task.*
3) Jack and Jenny agree to hold a meeting of all those involved in the implementation project. They decide that it will be a great idea to get Jackie, the Personal Assistant (PA), to come to the meeting to take and then circulate the minutes. That way they will all be free to take full part in the discussion. Jackie is not at the meeting but in her absence everyone agrees she will produce the minutes. Jackie is annoyed when she hears that she has been volunteered and feels overwhelmed with the amount of work she already has.	*There is little here to make this a contract in the way we consider it in TA. As a person lower down the hierarchy the PA is clearly not being treated as equal in the decision– making process because Jack and Jenny are senior to her. In an open healthy culture where the workforce is encouraged to be autonomous, people would not be 'volunteered' but consulted.* *How much easier it would have been to establish in advance that Jackie would be able to attend the meeting, than to make assumptions and then risk her not being there on the day. Even having made the error not to invite her, the group could have consulted with Jackie to see if she had the capacity to take this job on.*

Power and the Contracting Process

Effective contracts are made between people who share power equally. This does not necessarily mean hierarchic power. It could be that the organizational culture promotes autonomy and individual roles and boundaries are acknowledged. For example, the role of PAs or administrators should not mean that they are subservient to others. In fact the administrative departments have an important part to play in voicing their perspectives on situations as they often know how certain systems and processes can be improved. If an organization wishes to promote a culture of autonomy and respect, those who are party to the contract will be encouraged to express their opinions without fear of reprisals. Fear of reprisals is likely to result in the workforce moving into either their Over-Adapted or Oppositional Mode and this would lead to difficulties in terms of effective communication, relationships and productivity.

The vaguer the agreements, the less likely the goals will be achieved. The less account we take of people's hopes and fears, workloads and skills, the more likely there will be sabotage or inaction in fulfilling the contract.

Contracting is the means by which we reach agreements with others about the goals we will collectively seek and the means by which we will achieve them. At its simplest, this will involve just two people. However, in a work context, it will be very rare for only two people to be involved. The more parties that are involved, the greater the complexity and the more important it is that the contract is clearly drawn up with everyone involved.

Getting to "Yes"

When we first make contact with someone we wish to collaborate with, we need to establish if we can really be of assistance. If the aim is to collaborate then you would need to find out if your skills complement one another. In terms of purchaser and providers, let's take an example of a networking event. Very often people spend time relating to someone they think will be a potential buyer of their services only to find that they are not in the market for training, coaching, buying their product or that they, as the provider, don't have the right skills to meet the needs of this particular organisation.

This can be avoided. First of all you need to make relationship with the person and then find out what their needs are by checking what issues they are currently facing in their organisation. (This fits with the Winner's Pyramid on page 137). By asking this you can find out if what you have to offer fits with their needs. Once you have established that you do have the skills and/or products that will be of assistance you can then check if it is worth meeting to discuss how you might be able to help and set a date. All stakeholders and decision makers need to be at that meeting as this prevents any delay in the contracting process and offers the opportunity to relate more widely in the organisation. You can also check if there is anything that might get in the way of that meeting and, if there is, set a date that would not be cancelled.

Once the meeting has been set up then we can put the following contracting processes into action.

Meetings and Contracting

One area where contracting can be applied is with meetings and the way they are conducted. How many times have you been to a meeting and come away with the following thoughts?

- I don't know why I went – the meeting didn't relate to me
- No one listened to what I had to say
- No one listened to each other
- I came away with more work to do than I can manage
- I am not sure who is going to do that task, or by when
- I thought Jack was going to do that job and he thought Jenny was, and so here we are three months on and it has not been done. What a waste of time!
- I think that the way we do things at our meetings is so competitive

These situations can be circumvented by developing clear agreements with those with whom we are relating. The chair's job is to ensure that agreements are reached about who is going to undertake a particular task and by when. Everyone at the meeting needs to be clear about how they will know when they have achieved the goal. Additionally it is vital for people to understand why they are doing it and how this will be beneficial. If the task is project-based then the group is responsible for deciding when they will meet to undertake the project, how often, and so on.

Types of Contract

At the basic level there are three types of contract:

Administrative Contract: this deals with all the practical arrangements such as time, place, duration, fees, agreements between departments and agencies, confidentiality and its limits. It includes aspects of policy and legal administration, as well as monitoring and evaluation.

Professional Contract: this deals with the content of the project or goal, and more specifically with the competence of the various people to carry out the tasks they are undertaking. It is also about responsibility, purpose, benefits and limitations. When people involved in a project are not clear what they want, then a preparatory contract to explore this will need to come first.

Psychological Contract: this concerns the *unwritten and unspoken* set of expectations and obligations that are held between all employees of the organization. In these terms 'obligations' are stronger than 'expectations' and if broken have deeper, more emotional, reactions. Broken expectations can lead to disappointment, whilst broken obligations lead to anger and resentment. This psychological contract is more about the way things are done than what is done. Because it is unspoken, it has a powerful influence on behaviour in organizations.

The *psychological contract* is equivalent to the psychological level of communication (see Chapter 4), that is, where the outcomes of the transactions are determined at the psychological, rather than social, level. The psychological contract can be experienced as 'the way things are done around here'.

Let us take an organization that appoints a new director, who undertakes a restructuring of the organization. People who lack experience are moved up into leadership positions and in this way the new director exerts greater power, since these people owe their rise in status to the new director. One day a deputy attends a management meeting in their team leader's place and starts to challenge several decisions. The meeting ends up by agreeing with this deputy manager that the direction they were going in was not necessarily the best option. Following this meeting, the director puts a stop to anyone deputizing. The implicit (ulterior) message conveyed here is that the director is not going to have people at the meeting who disagree with the current line of development. A psychological contract therefore starts to develop around the sense that it is not safe or acceptable to challenge decisions and, more particularly, the director. Eventually, the organizational culture is likely to be fed by stories around such incidents as these. They are likely to become even more exaggerated as they continue through the organization, making it less and less likely that others will challenge.

The psychological contract includes the system of rewards in an organization. The workforce will have beliefs about how they should be treated, involving rights, expectations and obligations and the ways in which these are dealt with by the organization. Makin et al. (1996) point out that the psychological contract is a powerful determinant of organizational behaviour and that this can change as circumstances change within the organization. The psychological contract, even though not explicit, is still an agreement – in that people tacitly 'agree' not to challenge, or clarify the situation in point. Therefore to ignore this type of contract is to deny a powerful psychological force.

The Purposes of Contract Making

Busy people may well say that they do not have the time for the kind of detail we are suggesting. However, if detailed contracts are not made and misunderstandings and assumptions occur then this can take even longer. Contracting ensures:

- that all parties are actively involved in the process and energy is directed toward a clear vision and goal thus minimizing game playing (see Chapter 9); this enables the potential energy to become freed up to take purposeful action
- there is a clear commitment to change
- that all parties know clearly when their work is complete
- against the imposition of goals on others
- open processes, discouraging the pursuit of hidden agendas

Contracts Need to Specify

- Who is going to be involved

This is important, however obvious it might seem. Often a crucial party to the contract is not brought into the discussion and subsequent processes and tasks will be hampered and perhaps not completed.

- What they are going to do

  Again this is seemingly so obvious. However, lack of precision about this is frequently where agreements fall down. The more people who are involved, the more important it is to be clear who will do which aspects.

- How long it is going to take

  Assumptions here can lead to misunderstandings – 'I assumed you'd realize that I was talking about a deadline of the end of the month – surely that didn't need saying'. Therefore stating and writing down agreements about timings is essential. Should an external event take place preventing completion by this time then re-contracting is required to address the shift and notify others that there is a difficulty.

- What the goal is

  Almost always when contracts do not succeed, it is because of lack of clarity about the goal or goals. Goals and outcomes need to be specific, measurable, manageable and motivational.

  There are times when there may be conflict about goals. For example, an individual, team or department may have their own agenda and their own goals which dissipates the energy that should have been directed toward the organizational goals. This can happen when someone wants to move to another organization and loses interest in the organization's goals.

  We can draw this dissipation of energy in the following way:

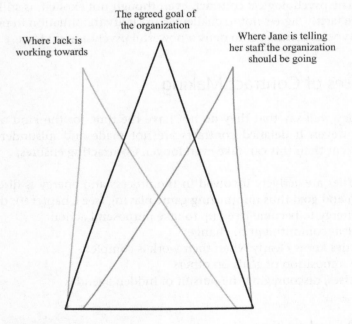

Figure 6.1   Energy Model

Source: Unknown.

- How you will know you have completed the process or task

  You can evaluate whether the task has been completed when the outcome is specific. If the outcomes are less tangible or measurable, for example, 'improve our sales', or 'work more effectively together', those involved in the contract will not know when they have achieved the outcome. The question needs to be 'How will we measure this?'

- How the goal will be beneficial to those concerned

  If you are party to the contract you need to know what the benefits will be for you and for the organization. This will promote motivation. We are unlikely to be highly motivated to help achieve outcomes that have a negative consequences for us.

- How the completion of the contract will be marked

  Whether this is framed in terms of celebration, recognition for people's contributions or simply acknowledgement of the end of a process, it is an important aspect of completion. People become demotivated when there is no recognition that projects have been completed before going straight on to the next one.

Assumptions and Expectations

Clear contracting helps to prevent assumptions. By working through answers and responses with everyone involved, any underlying assumptions and expectations can be brought to the surface and addressed. An example of this process follows. A coach is contracting with their client:

EXAMPLE

Coach	So what is the outcome you are looking for by the end of the session?	*The coach needs to agree what the client is aiming to achieve in this session and so asks a question to develop clarity. The contract for this session needs to be in the context of the overall contract of their work together.*
Client	I am not sure really. I don't really understand how to contract with others in my organization. We talk the theory but I tend to understand by feeling it. My contracts don't seem to hit the mark and things tend to get messy.	*The client is given time to consider the question and work out what the issue is.*
Coach	So you haven't really got a practical understanding of how to contract. You understand the theory but not the process of how to do it, is that right?	*In order not to rush the client the coach uses reflection. This also ensures she understands the client.*
Client	Yes, I tend to learn by being involved.	*The coach is already on track with the client about his learning style – learning by doing and is using the process to do just that.*
Coach	So would do you know if a contract were sound and effective?	*The coach asks another question that 'involves' the client.*
Client	I feel a sense of relief; my tension goes away in my stomach.	*The client offers a somatic response and learns something about themselves.*

Coach	So when you understand how to contract you will experience a sense of relief. What do you think you and I are doing now?	*The coach uses the here and now Co-creative Mode to develop understanding.*
Client	Contracting. Oh, I'm beginning to understand.	*The client understands that the very process they are engaged in reflects what he needs to undertake when contracting.*
Coach	So what am I doing that aids your understanding?	*Again the coach uses the here and now process to develop the client's learning.*
Client	Well, you keep asking me how I will know, and you are aiming to understand me. When I am contracting I forget that part of the process. I have just realized that I tend to just look at the administrative part, and what the tasks are. You keep with me to help me to unpick what I want and how I will know. I realize that I need to slow down so that I can get the detail when I am contracting, rather than rushing on.	*The client recognizes that he needs to be detailed in his process and not take things for granted or make assumptions. He realizes that he needs to track with his colleagues and ensure they are all really understanding and communicating with each other.*

Even if you are part way through a project and realize that you are unclear or lack direction you can always get everyone involved around the table and check out what outcomes are sought, who is responsible for what or how these outcomes will be measured. Once you have an overall contract it is then easier to ensure that the short-term goals fit within the broader outcomes offering focus and direction.

Complex Contracts

Where there are more than two parties to the contract it is helpful to make a diagram of the process. If we start with three parties to the contract, using a triangle, each party can be placed at its points (see Figure 6.1 on page 86). Drawing this out enables the complexity to be recognized and ways can then be found to ensure communication flows freely between everyone. Clarifying expectations on the part of all parties will aid the process and progress of the contracts. Each party will have a view of the relationship between the other two – sometimes based on conjecture, sometimes on fact. We will use an example to illustrate this.

A marketing director is brought into a company by the board to work with the CEO. At the start, there are three parties to the contract, the *Board* – who are commissioning this work – and are the 'big power' (English, 1975) – the *CEO* and the *Marketing Director*. The marketing director may view the board and the CEO as people who know each other and who are closer together because they work together – and of course initially there will be a reality to this. This distance between him and them becomes problematic if he (or whoever it might be on the farther flung corner of the triangle) continues to feel less valued, party to less relevant information or less part of the process of making decisions. In Transactional Analysis we call this the *psychological distance* (Micholt, 1992). One way of symbolizing this 'view' is to place an eye in each corner of the triangle – the arrow coming from each eye points to the dotted line opposite, which symbolizes the *perceived* relationship (Figure 6.2).

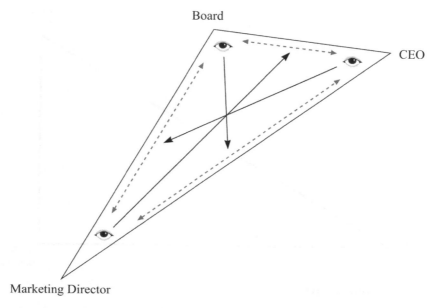

Figure 6.2   Three-Cornered Contract with Eyes

This psychological distance can relate to any of the parties of the contract. For instance, if the new marketing director is known to some of the board, the CEO may see her as 'a good friend' to them and therefore closer with them, which may affect how safe he feels in relating to her. Alternatively, if the work goes well, the board might become concerned that the marketing director is getting on a little too well with the CEO and, in their turn they may become guarded (see later in this chapter for more on Psychological Distance). Of course, in an environment of trust these dynamics are much less likely to occur.

The progressive diagrams below show the range of different parties and relationships involved in the process of working with this company. Although the work could be seen as 'one to one', in reality various other stakeholders will be affected by the work, need to be involved with it, or contribute to it.

Ensuring that all parties agree their expectations is a difficult but important task. Doing this prevents frustrations and misunderstandings, and better ensures the success of the intervention. It will not always be the case that every party needs to communicate directly with every other party, but each line of each triangle should always be considered.

EXAMPLES

If you were the marketing director working with the chief executive you might well need to give consideration to the middle managers of the company and their relationship with the CEO (Figure 6.3).

The present and future customers of the company, and the CEO's vision about them, are another important aspect of the contract. The board and the CEO need to reconcile their views and vision about the company's customers (Figure 6.4).

So we are progressively adding in each of the triangular relationships. In some instances detailed discussions will not be practicable with a particular party to the contract – and

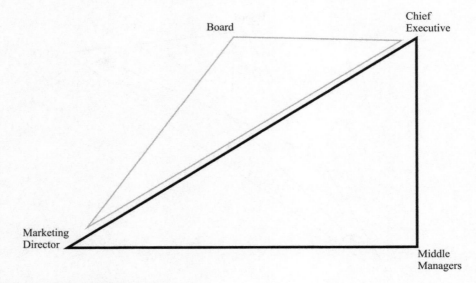

Figure 6.3   Second Diagram

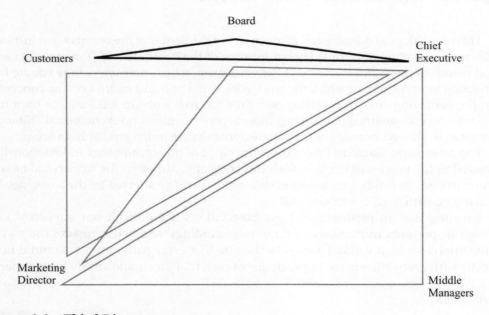

Figure 6.4   Third Diagram

customers would be a case in point. However, in that instance it would be a question of agreeing an approach to those customers.

The board and the CEO also need to agree a contract with the middle managers of the company so yet another dimension can be drawn in here (Figure 6.5).

Perhaps there is also a brief for the marketing director to work with the middle managers and the customers in which case the diagram would look like this (Figure 6.6).

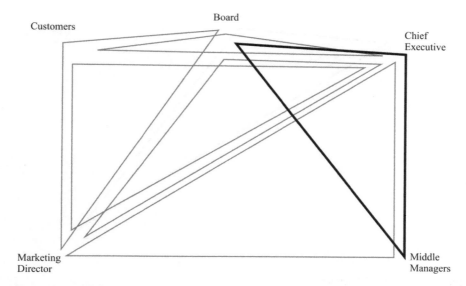

Figure 6.5   Fourth Diagram

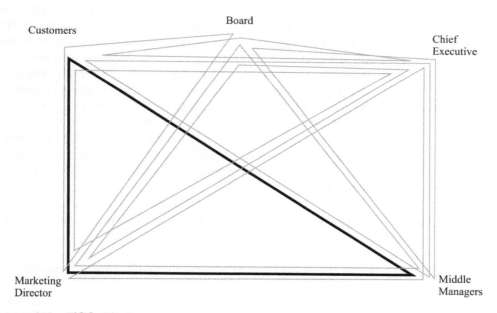

Figure 6.6   Fifth Diagram

Finally the board, the middle managers and the customers have a contract (Figure 6.7).

By drawing these diagrams the complexity of the contracting process is highlighted, and if a diagram is made at the start of the project then this complexity can be addressed, including any gaps in membership. Not all the permutations can be actively discussed with each party (for instance, customers) but each permutation does need to be considered.

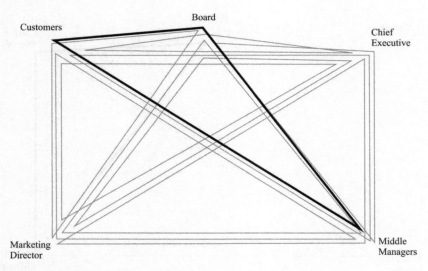

Figure 6.7   Sixth Diagram

As a specific example, let us consider a global organization with its software development department in Detroit and its warehousing in the UK. The UK teams need Detroit to develop software that will help them keep tabs on the stock. This request needs to go through their head office in Germany and be checked with both the financial director and the president. Detroit develops the software and sends it to the UK. On arrival the workforce in the UK are frustrated with the product because it does not really meet their needs. When the situation is investigated the problem is in the communication processes. They did not check out their understanding with each other; no one came from Detroit to the UK to obtain a clear picture; and there was no communication in between the request for the task and its delivery. Unbeknown to the workforce in the UK, the president in Germany had also told the financial director to make savings and so he had made his own amendments to the UK's request. How different this could have been if:

a.   There had been at least a video conference with all parties concerned – Germany, Detroit and the UK.
b.   All expectations and limitations were on the table.
c.   Each party checked that the other had understood the remit – and this would mean more than just saying 'yes'.
d.   Someone had come from Detroit to the UK to obtain a clear picture of the commission.
e.   Communication had been maintained throughout the project to ensure that things were still on track.

Here's another example:

Jane, CEO	I have been getting complaints about the increased work loads. I think one way we can deal with this is for all regional managers to delegate the task of project management to their team leaders. However, we do need to consult on this to ensure that this would work at local level. As I am not in the regions I need to be informed about how this would impinge on current practice. I have asked Jim, my PA, to take notes so that after the meeting, we are all clear about who has agreed what.	*Jane outlines the issue and suggests an option for dealing with it. She also demonstrates her lack of awareness of the situation in the regions and wants to be informed so that the appropriate strategy can be implemented.*
Jack, Deputy	What would be the limits to this new role for the team leaders? Will they have the authority to make all decisions in relation to a particular local project?	*Jack is getting into the detail of the changes.*
Jane, CEO	Good point. We do need to decide what the limits to the decision-making would be. However, if we don't give them an increased level of authority, we will be limiting their effectiveness.	*Because all parties are in Mindful Process, keeping each other OK/OK, the discussion can build.*
Tim, Finance	We also need to consider the implications for this increased level of responsibility. The unions are likely to seek a salary increase and this will have implications for next year's budget.	*Everyone's role and responsibility is accounted and here Tim is able to raise the financial implications.*
Jane	OK, will you sort out a finance package for this, getting in anyone else you need to support you with thinking this through? I would like this information by 31 March. Are you able to deliver this in that time?	*Jane is clear about the deadline and contracts to see if this is possible.*
Tim	Yes, that's fine. I will set up a working group to look at the budget and report back to you.	
Jane	OK, we also need to talk with the regional managers about the implications, and attempt to ascertain if there is the good will for this. Will you organize this, Jack? Perhaps a questionnaire over the Internet would be a way to ascertain their thoughts, though we had better put in a bit about our rationale for this – for instance that I have heard that they are concerned about the work levels increasing and therefore I am looking at a way in which we can increase the delegation, so that this puts it in a context. We could also raise this at the next regional managers meeting. Jim, will you ensure this is put on the agenda? Let's set a date for the next meeting. Jim will you get the this meeting's notes out, with agreed actions, by midday tomorrow?	*It is clear that Jane wants to consult all those who will feel the consequences of any decision. This is likely to promote good will and invite honest and open discussion. She is clear about whom she is asking to do what and checks this individually with each person, rather than just assuming they will do it. Writing down the decisions also confirms and clarifies the outcomes.*

The above is an example of good contracting. Everyone at the meeting takes responsibility for their roles and actions. The tenor is one of OK–OK and there is clarity about outcomes, deadlines, and responsibilities.

Berne defined treatment contracts as *hard* or *soft*. In a hard contract the goals are clearly defined in behavioural terms; for example 'I will find myself a new job in this geographical region in computer technology within a year, with an increase of £2,000 in salary'. Soft contracts are more subjective: 'We want to become the best company making widgets'. The way in which they will be the 'best' is not stated and therefore this cannot be termed a 'hard' contract. Soft contracts can be useful at the early stage of a relationship before there is clarity about the tasks, relationships or outcomes. However, these need to be firmed up as soon as possible.

Not everyone can play an equal and equivalent part in decisions and some decisions are, and should be, made from the top and are 'givens'. However, consultations regarding new developments should take place with the workforce with regular updates including developments, new thinking, possible changes, the limits to these changes, the possible implications, time frames and any protective measures that will be taken to maintain jobs. In this way anxiety can be minimized and where there are impending employment changes people can start to prepare themselves.

Psychological Distance

Micholt (1992) highlights the need to be aware of the varying levels of closeness and distance between the different contractual parties. Her work is seminal in the organizational field of TA as it ensures clarity of role and relationship. This enables the development of awareness that is required before, during, and after the setting up of a contract. She diagrammatically outlines the different relationships between the parties to the contract and highlights the necessity for the 'psychological distance' between them to be equal. In other words, if one of the parties experiences themselves as being out on a limb, this will have an impact on the contract.

For example, if an MD were a close friend of a consultant and were to bring that consultant into their organization to work with staff, then a number of possibilities could arise:

- If people know of the friendship they may well be wary of opening up to the consultant, and/or mistrust the motivation for choosing this particular consultant
- If people do not know of the friendship, they may observe tell-tale signs of closeness in the dealings of the MD and the consultant and infer the friendship or, alternatively, sense that something is not being spoken about openly
- The MD may well take more account of the consultant's views than those of the workforce, regardless of what other evidence may be present

Here the MD and the consultant are psychologically closer, and this leaves the workforce feeling at a distance from what is going on, or what is being decided. Awareness of psychological distance as an ever-present issue leads to greater amount of time being spent in the Mindful Process (see Chapters 3 and 4). Ideally all sides of this contract will be equal. If they are not experienced as equal, or account is not taken of the realities of differences in relationship, something is likely to go amiss in the process and problems can ensue.

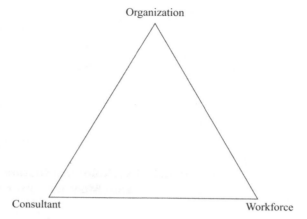

Figure 6.8   Psychological Distance

Let's suppose that the MD of the organization has been told of a legal duty to have the workforce undergo some form of training. The MD is not convinced of the value of this training making clear to all employees that this is not high priority. The trainer coming into the organization is likely to experience the psychological distance between himself, the MD, and the participants, as they are not fully cooperating in the training. As this lack of involvement by participants has the MD's psychological sanction the trainer has an even harder time completing the contract. In this case the psychological distance would look like this:

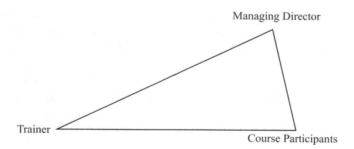

Figure 6.9   Psychological Distance: Trainer out on a Limb

Another variation on this would be where the course goes exceptionally well, leaving the MD having a sense that the trainer has got on too well with the participants. It may be that he is concerned that perhaps too much information was shared about company business in the process, or perhaps participants are more assertive than they were prior to the course and he is uncomfortable with this. The diagram might look like this for the MD. (Figure 6.10).

Where leaders and managers have dual roles and relationships things can get confusing. This is most clearly shown when a consultant coaches the team leader, as well as undertaking team development with that person's team. It would be very difficult for the team leader to be totally at ease with the coach turned trainer and for the team to be totally at ease with the trainer either. Each party might believe that the coach/trainer would inappropriately use some information about them. If we take the perception of the team the relationship

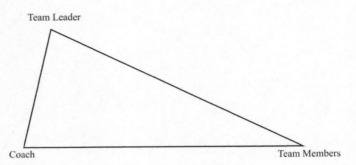

**Figure 6.11 Psychological Distance:
Team Members out on a Limb**

**Figure 6.10
Psychological Distance:
MD out on a Limb**

between the coach and the team leader the psychological distance would be drawn like this (Figure 6.11).

It does not make any difference what the level of expertise is of any of those involved, including the coach/trainer. The situation itself does not enable the development of emotional safety on the part of the team and therefore team development will be compromised.

This situation can occur in other situations too. For example:

Sara, the Department Manager, is close friends with two members, Ann and Resi, of a small team of six people she manages. Sara regularly comes into work and jokes about the nights out on the town she, Resi and Ann have had, and the others feel left out.

The group dynamics at play here are likely to develop into resentment on the part of the other team members and productivity will lessen as energy is spent on emotions rather than tasks.

This situation would be seen by the other team members like this:

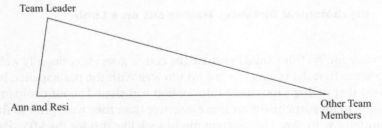

Figure 6.12 Psychological Distance: Specific Example

Ensuring that roles and relationships are clear, without duality, prevents friction between team members and enables everyone to feel valued. It also reduces the likelihood of game playing (see Chapter 9) and promotes the development of equality and trust within the organization.

Making Effective Contracts

In TA we consider that contracts need to be established from the micro to the macro levels. On the micro or individual level one of the first considerations in the contracting process is timing. Let us take an example of a one to one contracting process to highlight the importance of this. You have just received an internal email from someone that you experience as curt, criticizing and controlling. Instead of firing off a response in the same vein you decide to go and see them. The first thing you need to do is check with them that now is a good time to see them. If you fail to check this out you can get them on the hop and they may respond from a defensive position, and the difficulties are likely to escalate. Prior to any meeting you need to consider what outcome you want rather than just going to see them to be angry. (There is more about this in Chapter 17 on countering conflict). You also need to state how long you think you need for the meeting so that you do not arrive and find they only have 10 minutes.

At the meeting with your colleague you need to remain in the Mindful Process and contract for outcomes. Using emotional literacy (Steiner, 1984) you need to state why you have asked for the meeting, and express the outcome you seek. The subsequent statements might look like this:

The opening transaction	I would like to discuss your email with you, are you willing to talk about that with me?
Their response	Hopefully this will be 'Yes' *(We need to establish a clear contract to ensure there are no misunderstandings. Without a contract we are also likely to reflect the controlling style of the other person. If they say 'No' then we need to consider our other options.)*
Your transaction	When I received your email I felt ... and wondered what your thinking is about the tone of it. Were you aware how I might experience your email?
Their response	...
By remaining in the Mindful Process you have a range of options dependent on their response	In future what I would like is ... Are you willing to do this?
	I am sure you did not mean to offend me, however, I do find your manner ... and would appreciate it if, when you are irritated with me you would come and talk with me about it or to ask me about it, in the way I have just done with you. Are you willing to do this?

The 'Are you willing to do this?' is a mini-contract and invites the other person to join you rather than assume they will. This micro contract is as important in a different way as that for the setting up of a project group within a company – all parties involved need to decide who will be responsible for what and by when.

Naturally the goals and outcomes need to be achievable. It is no good saying that you will undertake a task when in reality you are already overwhelmed with work.

When considering the contract you need to ask 'How will I know and how will others know when we have achieved the goal?' making the contract measurable.

CONTRACT LET-OUTS

The following are all phrases to watch out for – they are ways in which we, outside our awareness, build in get-out options before work has even started:

- I'll 'work on' the problem ('and I may find it's not soluble')
- I'll 'try' to do it ('but I probably won't succeed')
- 'I want to', or 'will' do, something about it ('but I don't know when')
- 'I can' ('but I might not')
- 'I think I will' ('but I'm not sure')

Making effective contracts involves positive phrasing. When you say things like 'I want to stop doing ___', the Oppositional Mode in you is likely to rebel as we rarely appreciate 'stop' contracts. This also means that you are going away from something rather than going toward a vision or goal, which is much more motivational.

When you set contracts you are future focused and moving toward something. This energy dynamic is positive because, when you are looking back, your energy is dissipated and less motivational, except perhaps through fear. When you set contracts in the present you are able to set a vision for the future and take the action required to move toward that goal, however small that goal may seem to be.

Complexity and Problem Definition

When contracting you need to consider what the issues are and who is defining them, as each part of the structure is likely to have a different perspective. For example, top management may see the issue as too much decentralization as it is difficult to coordinate, whilst middle managers' perspective may be that there is too little decentralization. Therefore working out where the focus will be, and ensuring that the contract is outcome focused is part of the complexity of working in organizations.

This complexity is very apparent when undertaking coaching and mentoring. The traditional intra-organizational mentoring schemes, where the more experienced employees acted as mentors and role-models for newer recruits, highlighted a range of different aspects of contracting. The more traditional mentoring role involved the psychological contract or obligation on the mentor. The mentor would be expected to induct the new recruit in the ways of the organization. This was, and sometimes still is, a hampering process for the organization, as the mentors may not be challenging of organizational processes and systems. In contrast, the use of external coaches who are free from any affiliations to the organization can assist the coaching client in their professional development, from which the organization will inevitably benefit. They are also more likely to think 'outside the box', enabling greater flexibility and creativity. The possible disadvantage of using external coach/mentors is their less detailed knowledge of the business.

Each person who is party to the contract needs to experience themselves as confident, and capable with the right to question and challenge should the need arise. When contractual members experience equality in the process this tends to lead to greater creativity. In short what is required is that each person develops a secure sense of self.

Time Pressures and Contracting

There is almost always pressure, and the idea of taking what seems to be undue time on the process of contracting may feel wasteful. However, two questions are worth considering:

- How crucial is this outcome – what will be the cost if it is not achieved?
- How crucial are different people's various contributions to it – how will that compromise the overall project if they do not fulfil their part of the contract? (There are links here with project management and critical path analysis.)

Who will Facilitate the Contracting Process?

Organizational contracts need to be clearly stated and be measurable, manageable and motivational. The difficulty is that one person's motivation may be another's demotivation. Therefore clarity about who is the commissioning agent, who negotiates the day to day contracting process, and who is the client are all parts of the complexity when working with groups and organizations. As the number of parties to the contract increases it becomes increasingly important to keep track of the complexity of the relationships.

What Skills are Needed for Contracting?

You need to develop an eye for detail and awareness of the context, be able to relate and negotiate with others and have the willingness to listen. Through the process of listening you can find out what all parties to the contract are seeking, assuming and perhaps even projecting. Listening means that you can reflect back what you have heard so that those involved develop clarity with the way forward specified – with dates, times, roles and responsibilities agreed.

The most subtle and sensitive skill is in the consideration of the psychological level of the contract and in the avoidance of 'game playing' (see Chapter 9). By noticing and challenging any ways in which aspects of the contract are being ignored, you are able to make effective contracts that promote the positive and channelled use of energy that may otherwise be used for game playing.

Summary

The largest and smallest decisions and activities you undertake with people can benefit from effective contracting. It is relevant to every sphere of life – home, work, leisure. The way we are using the concept of contracting here is more as a frame of reference. It guides what we do and our interactions with others and is therefore the bedrock of Transactional Analysis approaches. Whilst we have written one chapter on contracting, others have written whole books but we hope that this chapter goes some way to promoting the use of the concept within a variety of situations in order to channel the energy toward positive outcomes.

EXERCISES

EXERCISE 1 – CONTRACTING FOR OUTCOMES

Take a current, or past project. Using the pro forma below, consider which aspects of the contract may have been overlooked or insufficiently dealt with.

Table 6.1   Contracting for Outcomes Pro Forma

The Goal/Outcome	
Is the goal/outcome *agreed* or *proposed* at this stage? (This is always a dilemma – how widely to share alternative possible proposals before there is a realistic prospect that a specific line will be followed through.)	
If proposed, how will the transition from 'proposed' to 'agreed' be achieved?	
What is going to be beneficial about this goal and to whom (that is, in different ways)? (If the outcomes of this goal are not primarily beneficial, then acknowledging this as a source of people's resistance will be very important.)	
Who is affected by the outcome/goal Are there going to be negative/challenging outcomes for some of these people? (As above, acknowledging this as a source of people's resistance will be very important. Peripheral players can still impact outcomes.)	
If so, how will this be managed?	
Who needs to play a part in agreeing the details? (There is almost always a hierarchy of decisions – from the strategic to the very localized, practical. However, managing the process of involvement is still important.)	
And then who? (Double-check for those left out of the first list!)	
What are the secret fears, hopes, connected with this goal and its implementation? (This is the 'psychological level' of the contract. It will be in this area that the greatest potential for failure lies if these areas are not addressed/acknowledged.)	

Table 6.1   Continued

The Goal/Outcome	
What is the timescale for this goal?	
How will people know when the goal is achieved?	
How will the achievement of the goal be celebrated?	

EXERCISE 2 – MULTI-PARTY CONTRACTING

Consider a project or goal which in reality involves several people. Draw up a diagram to show the multi-party contracts which need to be considered. Decide which are essential to ensure the completion of the goal and which are desirable, and which ones are impracticable in real terms. Consider the detail of the contracts that are required for the parties to this goal and what you need to do to ensure that everyone is 'on board'.

EXERCISE 3 – THE PSYCHOLOGICAL CONTRACT

Consider a project that you are currently involved with – what are the psychological level aspects of the contract for you and for others involved?

- What are your secret hopes for this project?
- What are other people's secret hopes – as far as you can intuit them?
- What are your secret fears for this project?
- What are other people's secret fears – as far as you can intuit them?
- What do you expect to come out of this project that is not the primary aim?
- What do you think others expect to come out of this project that is not the primary aim?
- Are there any actions you need to take now that you have this awareness?

7 *Extending Your Styles Repertoire*

Introduction

Very often people talk about 'personality clashes' and use this almost as an excuse for difficulties. However, if we consider that we all have different styles and ways of being in the world we might then find effective ways to communicate with each other. This chapter will outline the concept of Working Styles as a way to increase understanding, develop tolerance and expand your ability to relate with others.

In TA there are five different Working Styles: Please Others, Be Strong, Hurry Up, Be Perfect and Try Hard. When growing up we received and made decisions about ourselves and how to be in life. This is clearly linked to our sense of OKness – for instance, I will be OK as long as I am strong or perfect. These early decisions will influence our personality and these influences also have a positive side.

It is sufficient here to take a look at the different traits of each Working Style to get a sense of the two we major in. When we are in the worst of this behaviour we call it a *Driver* because we are driven by it and are using it as a defence. When we are working well we can use the positive traits of it as a 'Working Style'.

In response to your life experiences you develop *Driver behaviour* as a defence when growing up. You will have decided how to be in the world and this will have been influenced by your family. These styles developed in response to lots of 'Don't' messages. For example, don't be you, don't be close, don't be successful, don't be healthy, don't be important, don't be the gender you are, don't feel (in TA these 'Don'ts' are called 'injunctions'). As a way of dealing with these 'Don't' messages you develop Driver behaviour as an attempt to keep yourself OK (to counter the negative message).

In a marketing company a team has been brought together that includes Alan who has been included because of his expert knowledge. The team consists of dynamic creative people, but no one person coordinates processes. Everyone believes their job is more important than other people's and all come to the table not knowing how to get the best out of each other for the benefit of the client. The person who received the briefing and achieved the contract is clear about what needs to be done and knows that the skills are there. Alan's task is clear but some of the team expect him to do more and more, going beyond his skill area. Alan wants to please others and is worried he will not be accepted if he asserts himself and therefore he takes on more than he can manage. This makes him short tempered and unreliable in terms of deadlines.	*Alan believes: 'I will be OK as long as I please others'. Please others is the Driver here. He is therefore 'driven' by the need to defend against some of the 'Don't' messages he received about not being important. If someone were to become angry with him because he has not completed a task he will become stressed and start to find life more and more difficult.*

The Five Drivers

PLEASE OTHERS

If, like Alan, you were someone who decided that you need to Please Others in order to be OK, you will put yourself down in relation to others. You would tend to be compliant and express this through your body language, by putting your head to one side, look up toward others but keeping your head down and so on. You would speak higher up in your throat, thus raising the pitch. As a person with a Please Others Driver you would tend to believe that your views are not as important as others' and therefore expressing an opinion is difficult for you. When criticized you take this to heart and become stressed even if the criticism is unwarranted. You can be experienced as weak because you rarely take a stand on anything. You can, therefore, be experienced as frustrating because of this, whilst others may exploit us by getting us to do things you would rather not do.

You need to know that you, and your opinions, are important and that you can please yourself. Tasks where you have to make decisions for yourself will be good for you, though if this is imposed without your agreement and decision to change, this will cause you too much stress.

BE STRONG

On the other hand if you are someone who has developed a Be Strong Driver you will often appear aloof, and will have difficulty in expressing feelings. You have a tendency to talk in the third person as a way of avoiding staying in touch with yourself and your feelings. Your facial expressions tend to be motionless, and you see asking for help as a weakness even when you are overloaded. Others tend to project a range of things onto you – for instance that you are capable of dealing with anything, that you don't need to be loved, that you are not vulnerable and so on. As a person with a Be Strong Driver you need permission to feel and to ask for help when you need it as this will counteract your Don't Feel and Don't Be Vulnerable messages. In fact, very often you do feel but do not think that it is OK to express these feelings or, that if you did express your feelings, you believe would be overwhelmed by them. A trusting relationship with colleagues who will challenge you will help to promote change, as long as you have contracted to be challenged and are able to acknowledge that all your feelings are fine and manageable.

HURRY UP

If you have a Hurry Up Driver you have a tendency to finish others sentences for them because you are frustrated at how slow they can be. You act in agitated ways, tapping your foot, fingers or pacing around. You tend to make mistakes as you are in a rush and overlook the obvious because of this. Your haste is a way of avoiding yourself, let alone others. If you slowed down you might actually get in touch with your feelings, your body and with others. Because you forget things people can become irritated with you. You can also be admired by some as they experience you as important because you are so busy all the time, whilst others get frustrated with you because you are in such a rush. If you have this Driver you need permission to take your time. Activities such as yoga, pilates and tai chi can be good for you as you have to be slow and in touch with yourself and your body, though this can be difficult for you as you may become frustrated with the slow process.

BE PERFECT

If you are a person with Be Perfect as a defence you will tend to wear smart clothes, have a tidy desk and be precise in your speech and posture. When talking, you tend to list points by number, such as 'I see it this way (1) that this issue is important (2) it is urgent'. You also over-detail so that your sentences are lengthy due to the number of parentheses you put in. Other people tend to be wary of you as you may have high expectations of others as well as yourself, which others are unable to live up to. Some people with this Driver only have expectations of themselves to be perfect, whilst others want everyone to be perfect. Those of you who expect yourself to be perfect are hard on yourself if you make mistakes and easier on other people if they do. Others see you as reliable, committed and sometimes frustrating as you can keep giving work back as you find more and more errors and omissions. Someone with Hurry Up will clash with you as you tend to take a long time to complete things. If you have this Driver you need permission to make mistakes, to enjoy, and know you are OK for who you are not just for what you do.

TRY HARD

Those of you who have developed the Try Hard Driver will tend to look as if you are struggling to understand things. You tend not to complete tasks as you get interested in something else before the completion of the first task. Your language will be about trying, but not succeeding and you will come across as passive, and hence other people can become frustrated with you as you ask for assistance and then respond with things like 'Yes but we have tried that before and it didn't work'. You can also be grandiose saying things like 'This always happens to me' and the world can look hopeless and therefore when others seek to support you they get nowhere with you. When this happens others may walk away frustrated with you or move down into the hopeless position along with you. If you have this Driver you need permission to make things easy, to complete tasks and to say 'No' and to express your feelings directly. Others are likely to get frustrated with you as you don't finish things and the person with the Be Strong Driver may envy or be disdainful of your high energy behaviour.

From Driver to Working Styles

We might say that when you are 'in a Driver' you are being the way you were as a child and therefore not free. There will be less thinking available as you are acting out an automatic response. Being in the present means that you are Mindful, taking account of the appropriateness of your actions, and the actions of others.

When you receive, and give yourself permission to change, and start to make these changes then your old Driver behaviour can be transmuted into more of a 'style' and used instead, as a resource. In addition you are not always in the extremes of your Driver behaviour as you are not always stressed, and so can use the Driver traits as a strength. When this occurs you use the phrase coined by Hay (1992), *Working Style*.

When in the Working Style of Be Strong, you will have the benefit of staying calm in a crisis and will be good in the leadership position as you remain able to think. You feel energized by problem-solving and are good at giving feedback to others in an OK–OK ways. Alternatively if you have developed the Please Others way of being in the world you will be great at building bridges between people, using your intuition and being considerate of others. When using the resources of the style Hurry Up you will get work done on, or ahead of time, you can enjoy having a lot to do and getting a lot done. If you have a Be Perfect Working Style the resources you have to offer will be your reliability and meeting deadlines, editing others work, being well organized and having plans for most eventualities. And lastly, if you have the Try Hard style you will be great motivators as you enjoy lots of different activities. You will make great project leaders as you enjoy new tasks and will consider a range of different possibilities.

It is important to be aware of the potential to go into your Driver behaviour. You need to consider the triggers for these outdated stressful beliefs and behaviours so that you can notice what the first signs of this might be and change it. For example, once you learn to notice your breathy, fast speech, or that you are cutting across people when they are talking, you can tell yourself to slow down, breathe and ground yourself so that you return to being Mindful.

Alternatively, it may be that you have said 'Yes' to undertaking a task and then realize that your stomach is churned up and that you feel tense. You need to pay attention to these physiological signs and decide on the action you need to take. For example, it may be that you need to re-contract with those concerned and inform them that in fact you are overloaded and cannot do the work after all.

Sometimes after making a new decision, you can start to regret it and feel pulled to return to old ways. In order to avoid this you need to ensure that you develop positive self talk.

If we return to the earlier example of Alan we can see that if he had made a new decision to consider others and take care of, and think for himself, then life would be much easier. To do this he would need to establish which 'Don't' messages he received and counter these with permissions. For example, 'I can think for myself', 'I am important', 'I need to listen to myself and decide what is right for me', 'My opinions are important'.

Alan needs to have an internal dialogue about being important and only taking on what he can realistically do. He needs to be clear about the contracting process to ensure that the aims and objectives are clear. This is part of the leader's task but all team members need to have an eye to clarity about aims and objectives and ensure that the contract is clear.

It is also possible that by changing your behaviour and receiving positive feedback from the environment, you can change your thinking. This may work better with some Working Styles and less well with others. For example, if you have a Please Others Working Style and start to change your behaviour you may be less popular with some people because you will not be doing all the things they want you to do. Being less popular will be difficult unless you are prepared for this and have changed your beliefs and have support with the changes.

Another Example

In order to work well together teams need to form quickly and develop trust. The leader is a key player in enabling this to happen. In the situation where Alan is being pressured to do more by his team, trust is unlikely to develop and he is vulnerable to getting stressed. When this happens, his work, and therefore the project, will suffer. How Alan deals with this situation will be influenced by his internal dialogue. But let us have a look at what he could say to deal with this situation.

Jennifer	Alan, you contact the CEO of the company to check out this question and then get back to us.
Alan	It is a good idea – someone needs to contact the CEO. However, if you want me to do it you will need to wait until next week as I am unable to take on any more at the moment. However, I know that next week will be too late for us to receive the answer.
Jennifer	Oh, go on, Alan. You are so good at these things and always bail us out.
Alan	Thank you for the compliment, Jennifer, but it needs to be someone else doing it this time.

Even if Jennifer had come back again to Alan and asked him to ring the CEO, Alan would need to stick to his original statement that someone else does it. Making changes can be difficult at first because people are likely to try to pull you back to the old way of being. It is rather like someone doing the waltz, everyone knows the steps and then suddenly you start to do the tango and those around you want you to return to the waltz as they know those steps.

As outlined before under the descriptor for the Please Others Driver, Alan himself would need to give himself permission to be important and ensure that he meets his own needs as well. This is exactly what Alan did in the second example above. He maintained the assertive position, using what in assertiveness work is sometimes called the 'broken record' technique – for instance, repeating the same information so that he did not become diverted from the original decision.

It is worth repeating that you go into the worst of your Working Style, reverting to Driver behaviour, when you are under stress. We explore issues of stress later on in the book (see Chapter 15).

Applying Working Styles in the Organization

What follows is a set of examples of people with the different Drivers and Working Styles to show what they might look like in the work place.

TRY HARD

Tom is a great project director. He is creative with lots of different interests. At work he loves initiating new projects and is happy to leave it to others to complete them. He frequently delegates work, which is great for his staff as they feel trusted. On the other hand they become irritated when they experience Tom delegating work that they believe he should be doing. When talking with him his attention can wander, or he goes off at tangents about new things he wants to talk about. His colleagues therefore think that he is not interested in what they have to say or in what they are doing.	*Tom is a person with a Try Hard Driver. So that he gets the best from his staff and the organization gets the best from him, he will need to consider which tasks he should delegate and which he needs to do himself. He will need to give and receive recognition for completing tasks. Project management is actually a great job for him. He needs to learn some people-skills in terms of listening and keeping to the point. If he does not understand someone he needs to ask them to repeat themselves rather than try hard to understand.*

BE STRONG

Next we meet Anne who is a nurse. She has a Be Strong Driver.

People like Anne but recognize that she is unlikely to say how she feels even if things in her life are hard. Her post at work is being withdrawn and if she is to stay in the organization she will have to take a demotion. As there are cuts across the NHS it is likely to be difficult for her to obtain another similar position to the one that she is losing. However, when informing her colleagues about this Anne does not display any emotion. Her colleagues therefore find it difficult to support her and experience being pushed away. Some people tend to think of Anne as Wonder Woman, able to think in a crisis, taking everything in her stride and not showing emotions.	*Anne's manager needs to tell her that she does not have all the answers and that she is there to support her by assisting her to think through her options. This might include enabling her to go on any courses that may help with the development of her skills. The manager would also need to support Anne to manage her work whilst she is also dealing with her stress about her imminent redundancy. Anne needs to tell herself that all her feelings are fine and that she can feel and think together. She needs to know that she can show vulnerability and stay OK with herself and others, and that it is important to reach out and ask for help.*

HURRY UP AND BE STRONG

Like everyone, Freda's personality has its positive and negative aspects:

Freda is a person who is able to deal with a crisis, staying calm when others are panicking. Sometimes she has to make presentations to board members at work. At these times she gets a bit nervous and tends to speak fast (Hurry Up Driver). She tends to use words and phrases that are all about speed, for example, 'Let's go', or 'Let's get on with it', or 'Let's not hang around'. Freda has a tendency to become agitated if she thinks that people are messing around and not getting on with the job or the meeting. At these times she is likely to tap her foot, drum the table with her fingers, or repetitively look at her watch. By being fast Freda is able to avoid her feelings and so her Be Strong Driver is reinforced. Her behaviour irritates her colleagues as they experience her as making them Not OK.	*Freda's manager would need to reinforce that she should take her time. She would like the work done well rather than handed in on time with items missing. When she finishes people's sentences for them Freda needs to be told, from the Structuring Mode, that she needs to let people finish. If she continues to cut across others then her colleagues can tell her how they feel when she does this, and that they would like her to let them end their sentences before she comes in. Freda needs to tell herself that she can take her time. She also needs to let herself know that she is discounting other people when she cuts across them and that she needs to wait for others to finish. Additionally it would be helpful for her to slow down enough to find out what she is feeling about something as well as developing empathy for others.*

BE PERFECT

A new divisional director is appointed to the company and staff find his need for perfection rather over-bearing.

Larry is a great boss to work for. He has drive and ambition and wants his division to do well and improve on previous sales. He has his sights set on expansion. The downside to Larry's style is that he wants everyone's desk to be neat, with no plants or family pictures. He also insists that there is limited conversation to ensure that everyone is concentrating. Whilst the workforce is pleased to be working for someone who is enthusiastic they do find him rigid and tension grows in the office.	*Larry's Be Perfect Driver is likely to be in evidence because he is new and his stress levels are greater. His supervisors will need to encourage him to relax or some members of the workforce are likely to rebel and morale will decrease, as will productivity. If the managers who report to the director are sufficiently confident they too may be willing to share their observations with Larry about the outcomes of his rigidity on the workforce.*

Styles that Clash

Often clashes between people in teams are due to different Driver behaviour. For example, someone who has a Hurry Up Driver is likely to be quite agitated by someone who has a Be Perfect Driver, and vice versa. The more these Drivers are in evidence the more each person will have difficulty. The person with the Be Perfect Driver will want to keep checking things through whilst the person with a Hurry Up Driver will just want to get on with the next task. The way to accommodate these different aspects might be to ask the person with the Hurry Up Driver to complete the task and then hand it on for the person with a Be Perfect Working Style to check it. Alternatively, if each person were aware of the potential for them to move into their Driver behaviour, this very fact may mean they avoid doing so.

If you are aware of your own propensities for certain behaviours then you can find ways to curb these if they are likely to cause difficulties with other people. For example, if you have a Hurry Up Driver and tend to get irritated when another person takes a long time to say something, you can learn to talk to yourself about it being OK for them to take their time and that I need to take my time too. You can even tell yourself to 'stop it' when tempted to interject (done from Structuring Mode, of course!). In this process you are keeping yourself and others OK.

It is worth considering how different employees might work to their strengths. For instance, if a project manager is required then the person with the Try Hard Working Style would be really good here, whilst someone with a Be Strong Working Style would be really good in crisis management. On the other hand it might really frustrate other team members if someone with Try Hard Working Style is expected to undertake long-term jobs and then, through boredom, they continually make mistakes. Naturally, in the long run everyone needs to develop and grow so that the areas that are currently weaknesses become strengths as they give themselves permission to complete, succeed, feel, be important, have opinions, and take their time.

Summary

In summary, Working Styles are the positive resource part of the Driver behaviour that you developed as a way to defend against the 'don't' messages you received, or decided upon, as a child. Your personality will have been influenced by these decisions with the outcome that you believe that you are only OK as long as you are … strong, pleasing others, and so on. Once you realize that this belief is actually a decision you made in childhood you can remake this decision based on the realization that you are OK anyway.

The only fact is 'I am here, You are here and They are here.' In this way we can all get along, even if we don't like each other. When you do this you can then use the positive traits of the styles as a resource. You can then make the most of your Working Style and are more likely to find the job you enjoy, work to your strengths, and also find ways to accommodate others who have developed different styles to you.

EXERCISES

EXERCISE 1

- Consider the people you get on well with, which Drivers or Working Styles do you think they show?
- Consider the people you get on less well with, which Driver or Working Styles do you think they show?
- Which Driver or Working Style do you think you have?
- Do you see any correlation between those you get on with and their Working Style, those you do not get on so well with, and your own Driver or Working Style?
- What could you do or say to yourself that might assist you to get on with the people who you feel more frustrated by?
- How will you ensure you carry out these actions?

EXERCISE 2

- Consider the different Working Styles and how there might be clashes with people who have different ones. Which people are more likely to get on and which people are more likely to clash?
- What could be done so that instead of Driver behaviour, team members show their resourceful Working Styles, and therefore look to the benefits and strengths of each person?

EXERCISE 3

Consider how each of the different Drivers relate to the OKness model. Which style is more likely to be experienced by others as coming from each of the Not OK quadrants (*I'm OK/You're Not OK; I'm Not OK/You're OK; I'm Not OK/Your Not OK*)?

8 *Ignoring Realities: Awareness and Discounting*

Introduction

'They all agreed to the project – why has it not happened?'

'I told them but no one listened to me.'

'I'm sure I don't know what you mean.'

'I had no idea our finances were in such bad shape.'

When you are at your most effective, you take account of the various aspects of yourself, other people and what is happening in the world around you. When you fail to do this, difficulties are likely to ensue. This chapter examines the various ways in which this happens, and presents a model to aid your understanding of how you can change this.

Discounting is the process by which we unwittingly fail to notice something, recognize its significance, or take necessary action in relation to it. We might also be grandiose about something – 'This always happens to me' or 'This will take for ever – that's work for an army'. Discounting is in relation to ourselves, necessary actions, other people or our surroundings. Examples of this might be:

- Not recognizing something which can be seen, heard, smelt, touched, sensed or experienced – in other words, ignoring a sensory stimulus ('Argument? I can't hear any shouting')
- Failing to recognize options to deal with the situation ('Nothing can be done')
- Failing to recognize our own, and other people's responsibility to play a part in dealing with the situation ('I've done my bit – everyone else will have to sort themselves out')

Noticing the Stimulus

In a general way, our perceptions would soon overwhelm us if we did not 'screen out' some of the information we are constantly receiving – sounds, sights, smells. Imagine sitting in a meeting. Through the windows in the meeting room you can see people walking by, and occasionally hear snippets of conversations. Part of our healthy moment-by-moment activity involves monitoring all this information and deciding (usually unconsciously) what to filter out and what to take notice of.

This system generally works well for us and is flexible enough to take account of something peripheral that, due to changed circumstances, now becomes important. For example, conversation in the meeting turns to the importance of urgently contacting a particular person, who happens to walk past the room at that point. Although we relegate all the other people walking by to the periphery, this person walking by now has importance attached to it.

When we discount, we are relegating relevant information into the background and for whatever reason, failing to recognize its significance.

The Types of Discounting

INFORMATION, OPTIONS AND RESPONSIBILITY

These are illustrated by three examples:

1) Amanda looks visibly stressed to all of her colleagues. She is also becoming harder to work with – she has frequent outbursts, has become erratic in the accuracy of her work, and has had more time off work over the last few months. When people talk to her about this, she insists that she is not stressed. Amanda is a good worker. She has a great deal of experience in the company, and maybe that is part of the problem in relation to her stress – she doesn't say no to extra work, and people rely on her for advice, to get them out of a fix.	*Amanda is discounting the observable signs of her stress – which are noticeable by her colleagues.*
2) Jane is an area manager in a company going through major change. The staff she manages are reeling at the changes that have been imposed on them. Jane insists that there are no alternatives, and that things must go ahead exactly as planned. Jane is very skilled, but deep down, lacks confidence in her authority as a manager. When people challenge her, or even ask questions or make suggestions, she feels the need to assert her position and therefore becomes rigid.	*Jane effectively is insisting that there is only one way to do things – that there are no other options.*
3) Jack is sales manager in a busy company, which is struggling to keep its market edge. There has been a clear downturn in sales from his section over the past six months. When he is tackled about it, he agrees that there has been a downturn, and that it is significant, but insists it is not his responsibility. Jack sees it as really important to appear on top of things with his colleagues. He prides himself on managing his work without support.	*Jack is discounting the existence of his responsibility in relation to the downturn in sales (even though he acknowledges that there has been a downturn).*

Amanda is ignoring the information that her own body is giving her about the impact of the stress she is under. She is also not listening to her colleagues, who are reinforcing this message. Although the information is available, she is taking no notice of it. This can sometimes be 'in awareness' – in other words the person knowingly does this. However, more usually, with discounting, this process goes on 'out of awareness' – the person does not realize that they are doing it.

Jane is forging ahead, with a firm line that there are no options for undergoing the change differently. The trap here is in equating the fact that changes need to happen with there being only one way in which they can be implemented.

Jack does not seem to recognize where his responsibilities fit in to the larger picture. Because the problem is going on a larger scale, he somehow takes himself out of the picture.

The Areas of Discounting

There are three broad areas in which you can discount – yourself, others and the reality of the situation.

SELF

You can discount yourself in a number of ways; for instance:

- Your skills, knowledge or ability – for example, a skilled manager saying something like 'I'm just another member of staff here'
- The level of responsibility you have in relation to your role – for example, a manager responding to rebellion in the ranks by shrugging shoulders and saying 'Oh well, if that's the way they want it ...'
- Your feelings – for instance, not acknowledging the distress you feel about losing a member of staff or in breaking the news to a member of staff that they are being made redundant
- Your thoughts/intuitions – for instance, ignoring strong hunches about situations and then wishing later that 'I'd listened to myself'
- The impact you have on others – for example, not acknowledging the impact you have in terms of the way you use your power

OTHERS

You can discount others in similar ways; for instance:

- Their skills, knowledge or ability – 'I'm not interested in what you think. Just do as you're told'
- The level of responsibility they have in relation to you in the organization – for instance, either upwards or downwards or on a level with you
- Their feelings
- Their thoughts/intuitions – an example here would be discounting that someone might have ideas or thoughts on a topic
- The impact you have on them
- The impact they have on you

THE REALITY OF THE SITUATION

Examples of discounting the reality of the situation might be:

- Ignoring immediate relevant information – for instance, unusual smells, smoke, the sound of an alarm, high temperature
- Ignoring the findings of science and others bodies of knowledge which express general truths about people and the world (though to always accept these without question might also be to discount your own ability to think!)
- Ignoring world realities – including political, trade, financial

There are likely to be patterns to the kinds of situations where you discount and recognizing these patterns is one way in which you can develop more awareness. You are likely to discount more under stress, or when you experience yourself as being challenged. You may discount certain groups of people as a result of your life experiences or what you have been taught. Whilst it may well be very apparent to all of her colleagues that Amanda is suffering from her responses to stress, she herself is not aware that she is minimizing this.

Table 8.1 Levels of Discounting

Level	Description	Examples (S timulus / O ption / R esponsibility)
Existence	Here, you ignore the existence of the stimulus, options or your responsibility. This is the most serious level of discounting.	(S) 'What smell of smoke?' (O) 'There's nothing we can do here. It's insoluble.' (R) 'I have no responsibilities for this.'
Significance	Here, you notice the stimulus, option, or your responsibility, but fail to acknowledge the significance, severity or seriousness of it.	(S) 'We often get funny smells here.' (O) 'None of those options would work – they're not worth talking about.' (R) 'Although I do have responsibilities, they are not important here.'
Specific relevance	Here, you notice the stimulus, option, or your responsibility, realize its significance, but fail to account the possibility of its specific relevance.	(S) 'Nothing like this ever changes.' (O) 'The options won't make any difference.' (R) 'Although someone is responsible for this, it isn't me.'
Personal Ability	Here, you notice the stimulus, option, or your responsibility, realize its significance and the possibility of its specific relevance, but discount your own ability to do anything.	(S) 'Other people could manage this, but I don't have the skills.' (O) 'I could never implement those options.' (R) 'It's true that I have responsibilities, but I wouldn't know what to do about this.'

One of the key characteristics of discounting is that it is done out of awareness. When you consciously choose to ignore something, this would not be discounting in the way we are talking about it here. However, in deciding on the basis of just one factor, you may be discounting some other aspect. For instance, you may decide that you are too busy to attend a meeting called at short notice. You may feel that this short notice discounts how busy you are, and therefore your response is not to go. After all, if the meeting was really important, it would have been scheduled with more notice. However, you could, in deciding this, be discounting:

- The reasons the meeting has been called at short notice, which effectively demanded that there be an urgent response
- The consequences of not attending – for instance, not being part of a decision to be made
- The impact on other people of making this choice – they would not have the benefit of your experience, or not be able to make a final decision without you, and therefore the process is held up
- The effect on your reputation as someone who can be relied on to respond in an emergency

You might well have considered all of these consequences, and still made the decision not to attend in order not to discount some other event/aspect. In this case you are assessing priorities rather than discounting.

Change and the Discounting Process

Most organizations are in a state of change a lot of the time. Discounting is a common response to the stress caused by change.

EXISTENCE OF CHANGE GOING ON IN THE ORGANIZATION

From a manager's point of view	From a worker's point of view
'These changes are so minor, they are not really change at all.'	'Things are the same as they always were – Let's just carry on.'
Comment: When managers minimize in this way, the workforce is expected to keep their work activity going through the changes, and little or no space is given for the emotional and practical reactions of people to a number of possible facts: • their job may have changed radically • colleagues may have been made redundant in the process • their own position may have been under threat, even though they survived the process • those colleagues they were familiar working with may have moved on • this manager is not acknowledging the impact of changes on himself, let alone those he manages.	Comment: One reaction on the part of employees is to minimize the reality of changes that are taking place – as a (not very effective) coping mechanism. In this instance the worker is also colluding with the manager. The result of this is that they continue working in the ways that they have always worked, and thereby fail to adapt to the new situation.

SIGNIFICANCE OF CHANGE GOING ON IN THE ORGANIZATION

From a manager's point of view	From a worker's point of view
'These changes are necessary and won't really have an impact on people.'	'What they are planning won't really make a difference to my work.'
Comment: The change is seen as the important factor and the impact is minimized.	Comment: The workforce convince themselves that the changes won't really make a difference.

SPECIFIC RELEVANCE OF CHANGE GOING ON IN THE ORGANIZATION

From a manager's point of view	From a worker's point of view
'Change here is the same as change everywhere – it's how it is.'	'This is the way all companies work – no one can do anything about it.'
Comment: The manager's belief here is that no one can make any difference to the situation – and that people just have to get on with it, whether or not the changes will help.	Comment: The workforce believe they are helpless and become demotivated.

PERSONAL ABILITIES TO DEAL WITH CHANGE GOING ON IN THE ORGANIZATION

From a manager's point of view	From a worker's point of view
'I don't have the skills or time to implement this in any other way.'	'I struggle with change – I don't have the ability to deal with it.'
The manager is discounting their ability to give real consideration to how they could deal with implementing the changes in a different way.	The worker also discounts their ability to be flexible and look at the benefits of the changes and how they can do their part.

More Detailed Examples

The following are two final, more detailed, examples of discounting. They look at the examples given at the beginning of this chapter and place the different levels of discounting and the stimulus, problem and option types of discounting onto a grid, which is referred to as the Discount Matrix (Mellor and Sigmund, 1975).

Table 8.2   Discounting: Example – Sales Manager

Level \ Type	Discounting the stimulus	Discounting the options	Discounting the responsibility
Discounting the existence	1 I don't see that there is a downturn in sales from looking at these figures.	2 There is a problem here in terms of sales, but there aren't any options for us to solve it.	3 None of this is my responsibility.
Discounting the significance	2 There is a downturn in sales, but it is not significant – we don't need to do anything.	3 There are ways in which we could solve this problem in falling sales, but none of them are worth looking at.	4 I can't see how I need to do anything more about this than I'm already doing.
Discounting the specific relevance	3 There is a downturn in sales, it is serious, but there's nothing that can be done – it's the way the market is at the moment.	4 None of these options is going to make any difference to the situation – they are not viable options.	5 This is happening everywhere – not just on my patch.
Discounting personal ability	4 There is a downturn, it's serious, and something could be done about it; however, I don't have the skills to analyse the situation or do anything about it.	5 I do recognize the fact that there are several viable options we could go for which could solve this problem, but I'm no good at following through and acting on options.	6 If they wanted someone who could do more about this, they should have appointed superman.

Table 8.3   Discounting: Example – Speeding

Type / Level	Discounting the stimulus	Discounting the options	Discounting the responsibility
Discounting the existence	1 I wasn't speeding.	2 There is a problem here in terms of speeding, but there aren't any ways for me to solve it.	3 I'm not responsible for making sure I keep to the speed limits – I've got too many other things to deal with.
Discounting the significance	2 I was speeding, but it was not significant – because I am able to judge what is safe.	3 There are options for what I could do to solve this problem of me driving above the speed limit, but none of them are worth looking at.	4 Wasting time checking my speed when I'm driving is irresponsible and unnecessary.
Discounting the specific relevance	3 I was speeding, it was serious, but there's nothing that can be done – it's the way we have to drive in terms of lack of time.	4 None of these options is going to make any difference to the situation – they are not viable options.	5 These speed limits are just for rough guidance – I don't need to take particular notice of this one.
Discounting personal ability	4 I was speeding, it was serious, and something could be done about it; however, I don't have the skills to manage my time to avoid having to rush around.	5 I recognize there are several viable options I could take that would make me a safer driver, but I'm no good at following through and acting on options – after all, I never keep my New Year's resolutions.	6 They should make the driving test more rigorous if they want me to drive with this level of sophistication.

The Route to Accounting (Macefield and Mellor, 2006)

When someone is discounting, the focus needs to be on the stage before the level they are discounting. It may even be necessary to go right back to the level of existence of information before they can progress to options or responsibilities. The eight steps in the diagram below show the varieties of routes to the outcome:

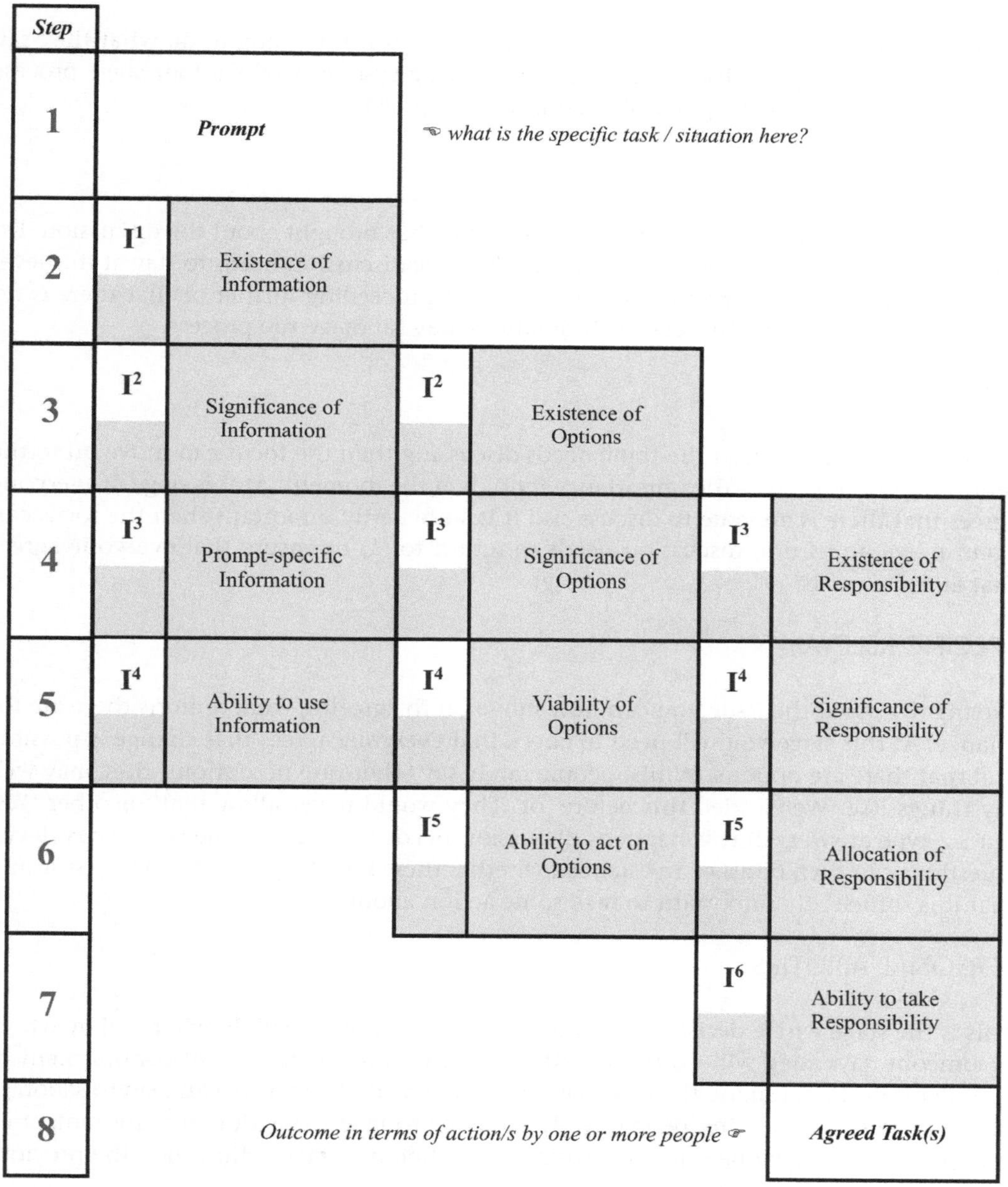

Step						
1		*Prompt*		☞ *what is the specific task / situation here?*		
2	I^1	Existence of Information				
3	I^2	Significance of Information	I^2	Existence of Options		
4	I^3	Prompt-specific Information	I^3	Significance of Options	I^3	Existence of Responsibility
5	I^4	Ability to use Information	I^4	Viability of Options	I^4	Significance of Responsibility
6			I^5	Ability to act on Options	I^5	Allocation of Responsibility
7					I^6	Ability to take Responsibility
8		*Outcome in terms of action/s by one or more people* ☞				***Agreed Task(s)***

Figure 8.1   Route to Accounting

Source: Macefield and Mellor, 2006.

Instead of discounting you need to fully acknowledge, or as we say, account, the situation, in other words to notice the stimulus, realize that it may require action, know that there are options and know that we, as individuals, have responsibilities and can carry them through.

Getting Decision-Making at Work to Result in Action

People often leave a meeting wondering if everyone is really going to do what they say they will do. Using the discounting and accounting system here is a four stage process which enables the checking out of what has been agreed:

EXISTENCE

First there is a need to clearly outline the issue that has brought about the discussion. Do all parties agree that there is an issue? If not then the discussion needs to stay at this level to ensure either that everyone is on board before proceeding further or that there is no issue. Without ensuring this clarity, individuals may sabotage the process.

SERIOUSNESS

Once everyone agrees that the topic needs discussing then the focus can move on to the seriousness of the issue – the importance it holds at the moment. At this stage, if everyone agrees that there is an issue to discuss and it is sufficiently important then the focus can again move on. If not, discussion needs to return to (1) to ensure that everyone agrees that an issue exists.

SPECIFIC RELEVANCE

Having discussed the issue you can now move on to agreeing what options there are for change. At this stage you will need to check that everyone agrees that change is possible and that there are options. Whilst people rarely say 'There are no options' they may well say things like 'We've tried this before' or 'They would never allow that' or other 'Yes, but …' type answers. If this happens discussion needs to return to the seriousness level. Questions can then be asked to establish whether there is still agreement on the issue and that it is sufficiently important to take some action about.

PERSONAL ABILITIES

This is the stage where decisions need to be made about who will do what and by when. If someone says they will do it, but without conviction, their level of commitment or confidence in undertaking the task needs to be checked. Reluctance can lead to sabotage of the process, so ensuring people really do agree to take the action and are motivated is important. If individuals are not willing or confident to take action then the previous levels will need to be returned to.

This will take time to do, but time invested at the outset repays itself with greater likelihood of success. Rushing forward prematurely can give the illusion of progress, only to find that action is not taken because everyone thought someone else was doing it, they had other priorities, they did not believe change was possible or that they had the ability to do it. Taking time at the meeting is better than waiting six months to find out that nothing has happened.

All of these levels need to considered and discussed in a non-threatening way, enabling people to share their views.

Summary

By acknowledging and accounting the existence, seriousness and possible options in a situation you can sometimes avert difficulties. If you focus on the present and are Mindful of the current situation you will be accounting. Here is a breakdown of the process to show what you need to do at each stage:

- Notice the signs of a situation requiring action or a potential difficulty
- Realize that these signs have a cause and attention needs to be paid to this
- Understand that this is something that could become an actual difficulty or problem if you don't pay attention to it
- Accept that there is a possibility that the situation can be changed
- Consider what options there are
- Acknowledge that you have the ability to act differently
- Recognize that difficulties in general, and this one in particular can be dealt with effectively
- Accept that people *generally* can solve problems and that specifically includes *you* being able to do
- Decide what action you are going to take – including who will take on various aspects of responsibility

EXERCISES

EXERCISE 1

Take an example from your work situation where something didn't go right and in retrospect, having read this chapter, you feel that you might have been discounting. Alternatively, you could choose an example involving someone else – though you will probably get more benefit in terms of your understanding of this concept by using something you were involved in.

Don't feel that you have to fill every one of the 12 boxes, but put statements that fit for you in as many as feel right for you. You may well notice that statements from boxes that have the same number are actually different ways of stating the discount. For instance, discounting the significance of a stimulus (box number 2 in the first column) is a different way of stating that there is a discount of the existence of a problem (box numbered 2 in the second column).

Table 8.4   Blank Discounting Exercise

Type / Level	Discounting the stimulus	Discounting the options	Discounting the responsibility
Discounting the existence	1	2	3
Discounting the significance	2	3	4
Discounting the specific relevance	3	4	5
Discounting personal ability	4	5	6

FIFTY EXCUSES FOR A CLOSED MIND

You may have seen this list of reasons not to do anything, the source of which is not known.

Table 8.5   Fifty Excuses for a Closed Mind

	Excuse	Area being discounted	Level of discount	Comment
1	We tried it before			
2	Our place is different			
3	It costs too much			
4	Leave it until we are not busy			
5	We don't have the time			
6	Our place is too small			
7	It's too big a change			
8	The staff associations will scream			
9	The staff will never accept it			
10	We've never done it before			
11	It's against department policy			
12	Run up our overheads			
13	We don't have the authority			
14	We like change – so long as it does not involve alterations			
15	That's too 'ivory tower' [theoretical]			
16	Let's get back to reality			
17	That's not our problem			
18	Why change it – it's okay			
19	I don't like the idea			
20	You're right but …			
21	We are not ready for that yet			
22	You can't teach an old dog new tricks			
23	It isn't in the budget			
24	Good thought – but impracticable			
25	Let's hold it in abeyance			
26	We'll be the laughing stock			
27	Let's give it more thought			

Table 8.5   Continued

	Excuse	Area being discounted	Level of discount	Comment
28	My mind is made up, don't confuse me with facts			
29	Not that again			
30	We'll lose money in the long run			
31	Where did you dig that one up from?			
32	We do all right without it			
33	That's what you'd expect from the staff			
34	It's never been tried before			
35	Let's form a committee			
36	Client's will not like it			
37	Has anyone else tried it?			
38	We're all too busy to try it			
39	It will not work in our place			
40	Who's trying to teach me my job?			
41	That may work in your department but not in ours			
42	I'm not convinced			
43	Let's sleep on it			
44	Think of the disruption it will cause			
45	It will make our equipment obsolete			
46	It cannot be done			
47	It's too much trouble to change			
48	It will not pay for itself			
49	I know someone who tried it			
50	We've always done it this way			

9 *The Games We Play*

Introduction

'I've been here before' or

'Why does this always happen to me?' or

'I know where this is all going.'

At some time or other you are likely to have been in situations where you end up making such statements. In TA we might call these types of situations a *psychological game*. A game is a set of transactions (see Chapter 4) between two or more people that follows a familiar pattern of behaviour and has a predictable outcome – which invariably involves bad feelings. When you play games, energy is used non-productively and time is wasted on tensions and conflict. This chapter explores what games are, and why we 'play' them. It gives tips on how to stay clear of games, moving towards a more productive use of our time.

You play psychological games outside your awareness, with the aim of meeting your needs, but they are not a successful way of doing this. Very often people only realize that they have been in a game after it is over. This chapter will look at some of the warning signs to enable you to be more alert to them.

An Example of a Game

Philip: Jarvis, where did you put that file? I had it yesterday and now it's not here. **Jarvis:** It is on the top of the filing cabinet where you left it! **Philip:** Please don't talk to me in that tetchy way. I only asked you where it was, I have been really busy lately, my PA is away and I can't keep on top of everything.	*Philip's tone of voice is tense and he appears to be saying that Jarvis is the one who has not put the file in the right place. Jarvis is feeling aggrieved. He picks up the tone in Philip's voice and believes he is being blamed.* *However, neither Philip nor Jarvis say what is really going on in the process between them. They often get into these situations and, one or both of them end up feeling annoyed but without any resolution since nothing is ever said directly.* *In this particular situation Philip starts off Persecuting Jarvis and then moves to experiencing himself as a Victim as he has so much work to do, and in a defensive way is intimating that he is having a hard time so he cannot be blamed for being accusatory. None of this is said, only implied.*

In this example both Philip and Jarvis are giving out two messages at the same time. Both may see themselves as being Mindful. However, behind the factual content of what they are saying to each other is a tone of voice which arguably comes from Criticizing Mode. It is likely that internally they are saying something like:

Philip – *'He is always moving my files.'*

Jarvis – *'He is to blame because of his lack of organization and filing.'*

So their exchanges are examples of ulterior transactions (see Chapter 4). There will be give-away signs in tone of voice, facial expressions and body posture which will convey this psychological level message to the other person.

This pattern of behaviour between them is a repeating one and has a predictable outcome. Commonly there are a limited number of roles that people play in games and we shall look at these later in the chapter, with the Drama Triangle.

These situations can also happen between teams, departments and between different agencies.

Examples of Games

1) George has been with the company for sometime. He is in a bad mood and is talking to Jane about an interaction he had with Jack, a colleague. 'Jack and I always get into this. He came up to me this morning saying that I was late with my stats. He is not my boss but he tries to boss me around. He knows I get angry when he does this and yet he is always finding fault. I always get into saying something like 'So what!' Then he gets stroppy with me and tells me not to get on my high horse and he is only trying to help. I then stomp off saying, like hell he is, and to mind his own business. I then feel angry for the rest of the day and get little work done. I don't know why he is like this with me!'	*Jack will also be feeling bad and he might genuinely believe that he was only trying to help Jack by reminding him about his stats. Alternatively, Jack might have been having a go at George, with the ulterior message being something like: 'You're lazy', which is why George reacted like he did as he responded to the psychological level of the message. Given the repeating patterns of behaviour with both men it is likely to be the latter. These are not Mindful transactions and are non-problem-solving. Now the repeating pattern has been recognized by George he is actually in a position to deal with it with Jack.*
2) Alan feels he is struggling with an aspect of his current project. He tells John about it and asks for help. John makes a suggestion about how Alan could resolve the issue. Alan tells John that this wouldn't work. John comes up with another suggestion. Alan tells him he's tried that already. This process goes on several times more, and then suddenly Alan tells John he's no help at all and stalks off, leaving John feeling mystified.	*In this example Alan is feeling hopeless and even though he asks for help he is closed to receiving it. By experiencing John as unhelpful Alan can reinforce his Life Position of I'm Not OK and You're Not OK. This keeps life predictable and Alan can also reinforce his frame of reference. In this situation John is being invited to try harder and harder. If this were John's weakness then the two of them could continue to get into these situations. Instead John needs to relax, take account of the situation and say something like: 'I'm sure you will be able to work this out for yourself', thus releasing him from trying hard to solve Alan's problem.*

3) Jean is known as a really caring person who takes on other people's hurts. She is approached by Sally who tells her all about Janice being nasty to her. Janice is seen as a high flyer, and has just been appointed as a project leader. Sally went for the post as well but did not get it. On hearing Sally's story Jean becomes concerned. She has known her for a long time. She decides to go to see Janice to see if she can support Sally. Janice is very annoyed with Jean, she has no idea what she is talking about and was not even in the office on the day in question. It appears to her that Sally is trying to set people against her.	*Jean's 'weakness' is her rescuing nature. Sally wanted some recognition as she was feeling low and guessed that Jean would have time for her and listen to her. 'Poor me' is Sally's hook for Jean's rescuing nature and so she tries to intervene in the relationship only to find that she is persecuted. Jean's initial response to Sally needs to have been different. Rather than intervening on Sally's behalf she needs to listen and empathize and then perhaps discuss with Sally what she can do about it.*

The Drama Triangle

Stephen Karpman (1968) devised a simple diagram for analysing the 'games' that people get into with each other. He uses three roles as in a play or drama – Persecutor, Rescuer and Victim. These are spelt with capital first letter, to distinguish them from the ordinary use of the words. For example, if we say that someone was a victim of a car accident, we would use lower case, whereas if we say someone was in the Victim role, we would use upper case.

For example, you may be one of life's *Rescuers*. You may rush to help someone without checking with them first. They may not need or want your help, or may not want as much as you give. The role of Rescuer always discounts someone else's ability to problem-solve, such as in the scenario above with Jean, Sally and Janice. If you are in the Rescuer role you take over the other person's thinking and do more than 50 per cent of the work and either put or maintain the other person in the Victim role. This relates to the interfering Mode of OK Modes model (see Chapter 3).

Because people don't like feeling a Victim they might look for ways to get out of it. In the Sally scenario it is likely that Sally would get angry with Jean for going to see Janice, thereby moving from Victim to Persecutor, and inviting Jean to move to Victim. The Persecutor role feels a far more powerful place than the Victim role, which is why people often make that switch.

If you are in the *Victim* role you act as the long-suffering person and look for someone to Rescue or Persecute you. You act as if you do not have the capability to make decisions and solve your own problems. As there is less power in the Victim role it is likely that you will move up into the Persecutor role when your Rescuer does not do something well or you experience them as letting you down. You might therefore move from the Over-Adapted Mode on the OK Modes Model, up into the Criticizing Mode.

If you are in the *Persecutor* role you will believe that you need to control the situation and others. You make others Not OK and want to punish them. This is the bullying position and your transactions will come from the Criticizing Mode.

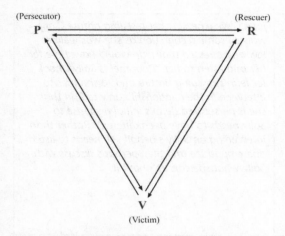

(Persecutor)   (Rescuer)

P ━━━━━━━━━━━━━━━━━▶ R

V

(Victim)

Figure 9.1   The Drama Triangle
Source: Karpman, 1968.

All of these roles involve discounts – of yourself, others or the situation you are in. Involvement on the Drama Triangle will lead you to believe that you are incapable, think others are incapable or hold others responsible for not looking after you properly. Once in any of the three roles – Persecutor, Rescuer or Victim – you can keep going round the triangle indefinitely. There is no Mindful Process anywhere on the triangle as each role is an ineffective mode (see Chapter 3).

There may be one role which you take up more than any of the others and by becoming aware of this you can start to change it.

In this model the triangle is on its point and game players can move to any role on the triangle. Although there are three points on the triangle, a game may involve just two players – since not all three positions need to be occupied at any one moment. There may be more than two players – such as the example with Sally, Jean and Janice.

Predictable Outcomes

People play different games as they have all had different families and different life experiences. People adopt games as strategies to maintain their beliefs about self, other people and life. In this way the world can remain predictable. If you tend to view the world from a Persecutory position it is likely that you will play games with someone who views the world from the position of Victim and thus each perspective is reinforced. You give off a signal to the other person or people who are about to play the game that you are looking for someone to play a game with.

Without being aware of it, you send out messages to see if someone will play your game with you. These are like hooks looking for fish to bite. Some hooks are tempting for some fish, whilst other fish will just keep on swimming until they see more tasty bait. This is how you get to be fly-fishers, sea fishers, and so on. In other words different people have different invitations to play different games that correspond with specific types of people.

There are four degrees of games:

- First degree – players willing to play in social circle
- Second degree – players would rather not make public
- Third degree – games which are played for keeps, end in hospital, in court or the cemetery
- Fourth degree – games where the outcomes could affect whole communities, cities, countries or the world (this last degree is the authors' addition)

The fourth degree takes account of the current realities of world politics, where the actions of one or more world leaders can have consequences for whole communities, or the whole world. This means that there is an increase in the seriousness of the outcomes. Thus large scale fraud affecting an organization, takeovers in the guise of 'rescuing' the company only to ensure it goes into liquidation and riots and wars would all fall into this fourth category.

There is a link with stroking patterns in organizations. Where employees perceive that there is an inequality of stroking by management they will react in a number of ways:

- endure the distress
- demand compensation
- retaliation
- psychologically justify and rationalize the inequality – for instance, 'I don't work as hard so I don't deserve as much.' (or, I'll work a lot harder, and *then* I'll get the recognition I deserve)
- withdraw

(Clavier, Timm, Wilkens, 1978)

All of these are non-problem-solving behaviours and as such have the potential to discount the options available. As all games start with a discount (see Chapter 8), this has the potential to start the game process.

Early TA writings focused on individual moves and the roles of the players. In organizations you need to look further than this. In organizational games you are concerned with intra- and inter-group dynamics.

In organizations there are some classical games which are played. Games are often given names in TA as a way of giving a flavour of the dynamic which is involved. For example:

Lunch bag: You bring your lunch to work so that you can continue to work through the lunch break. Others are going out for lunch and you offer to take phone calls. The phone never stops ringing when your colleagues return to work you regale them with what you had to do on their behalf. You feel self-righteous and they feel guilty and in this way you have moved from the Rescuing role to that of Victim, and then Persecute the others.

Now I've Got You: This is a typical game in an organization involving power plays. It occurs when you find ways to put one over on someone or catch them out. When you are successful at this, the other person is then likely to look out for an opportunity to get you back (or vice versa). This can sometimes be to the point of ensuring someone loses their job. An example of this would be when a manager has cause to discipline a member of their team. This person may then look for ways to 'get the manager back' and, at the first mistake, take glee in making a complaint about them rather than discussing the issue first. It can sometimes take years for a person to fulfil the Game by getting back at someone.

Uproar: This can be played by setting others up to argue, and then withdrawing and watching the 'fireworks'. You can then say to passers by 'I was just asking X' or 'I was just interested in what they thought about Y'.

Games can continue and follow on from each other – with each player's 'fish hooks' interlocking with another person or with other people.

Berne's Six Advantages of Games

We play Games because they offer advantages – benefits – to us. For example, let's take Jack and George in the scenario above. George knows what Jack is like and yet he still gets into the familiar pattern of behaviour. He had other options such as thanking Jack saying he was aware that he was late with his stats. and was dealing with it. This would be within the Mindful Process and using his Structuring Mode. In this way he does not take Jack's hook, does not pick up on the ulterior message and instead responds to the social level message, thus crossing the transaction.

There are six prime reasons why we play Games and here is an easy way to remember them:

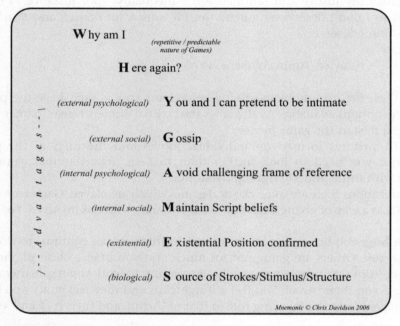

W hy am I *(repetitive / predictable nature of Games)*

H ere again?

(external psychological) **Y** ou and I can pretend to be intimate

(external social) **G** ossip

(internal psychological) **A** void challenging frame of reference

(internal social) **M** aintain Script beliefs

(existential) **E** xistential Position confirmed

(biological) **S** ource of Strokes/Stimulus/Structure

--Advantages--\

Mnemonic © Chris Davidson 2006

Figure 9.2   Why Games?

To outline the above table a little further, Games:

- Offer the opportunity to pretend to yourself that you are being open. You experience that getting close to another person carries risks and isn't safe. Pretending to be close may feel safer in these circumstances. Berne referred to this as the *external psychological advantage.*
- Give you something to talk about with friends and get strokes by telling the story. Berne referred to this as the *external social advantage.*
- Are ways of avoiding situations that challenge your Frame of Reference and so avoid anxiety. Your frame of reference is the overall way in which you see yourself, others and the world. Berne referred to this as the *internal psychological advantage.*
- Are a way of avoiding memories of pain you experienced earlier in your life and maintaining the script belief (see Chapter 10) that this is the way to get attention

even if the result is that you get hurt. You believe you will experience less hurt this way. Berne referred to this as the *internal social advantage*.

- Reinforce your basic Life Position – in other words your overall attitude to yourself, others and the world. This will be one of the 'Not-OK' positions – either you, or others, or everyone, is Not OK. Berne referred to this as the *existential advantage*.
- Are reliable ways to get strokes, even if they are negative. Berne referred to this as the *biological advantage*.

Games and Ethics

Maintaining an ethical stance when working in organizations helps to prevent games. When you maintain an I'm OK/You're OK position (see page 15) you are more likely to remain in the Mindful Process, be straight in your communication and say what you mean. This will free up your energy (that would have been bound up in past events and patterns) to use your intuition and consider any hidden agendas there may be and assist you in avoiding any underhand and manipulative politicking. Clear, detailed written contracts will also assist this, as they help to prevent assumptions and discounting behaviour, including exploitation.

A game can often start when someone oversteps a boundary. For example, someone may regularly be late for work. When this is not addressed by the boss or colleagues, resentment starts to build up. This sort of behaviour will lead to game playing as a time boundary has been discounted along with the implications of that person's lateness on other people's work.

In addition, you can respect the organizational culture even if you want to change it. By acknowledging where the current culture came from – with its advantages and disadvantages – you are more likely to find ways to move on that fit with ethical behaviour.

Success in Organizations

Sometimes within organizations, one team being successful can be experienced negatively by other teams. For example, Team A meet, and go beyond, all their targets for which senior management praise them. Other employees feel inferior as their own output is only 60 per cent of what is required. Instead of experiencing the difference as motivational and a challenge, they turn against the achieving team. Therefore Team A, with the highest productivity in the organization, can suddenly find themselves Victims – Persecuted by others for their success. Managers might also Persecute failing teams – out of their inability to motivate the teams to achieve such high productivity. One possible outcome of this is Team A lowering their output to meet the lower level of the others.

How different it would be if instead the leadership challenged the jealousy and encouraged leaders of the jealous teams to learn from the leadership of the effective team. Instead of other team managers and team members playing 'Now I've Got You' with the successful team they might have found ways for everyone to be motivated to improve.

On the other hand it may be that everyone is working to full capacity but because some jobs take longer those further down the line cannot cope with the outstanding paperwork for those goods being produced. The primary focus in this instance would be the organizational systems and structures – to do with managing the logistics. However, this too could lead to game playing if there is lack of dialogue between those affected.

For an organization to be successful it needs to find ways to keep everyone OK and use the competition in a healthy way rather than find ways to stop it. Unhealthy competition needs to be challenged so that organizations can go from strength to strength with the workforce enjoying what they do, finding creative and motivational ways to improve their output.

Financial Games

Edmunds (2003) has written about how people play investment games. He notes that a person's behaviour with real estate, bonds, stocks or other investments could involve them in sabotaging their own, and other people's, futures.

Another example of games being played around money would be with a person who might reasonably be regarded as rich but who may not be willing to accept themselves as such. Perhaps their family of origin believed that rich was bad and poor was virtuous. Thus, they may be good at making money but also be good at spending it and losing their fortune, proving that the family was right all along. Edmunds calls this game 'Poor Little Rich Girl or Boy'. These people also play *Why does this always happen to me?*

Games are frequently played in organizations – whose members have their own issues and frames of reference about money. When organizational changes are instigated, anxiety and hostility can ensue and this can then increase the likelihood of game playing. As part of their defence, employees can project their fears onto management and, if management retaliates, the whole process can escalate. Also when there is insufficient recognition of people in the workplace it is easy to see why they might play games as a way to obtain greater attention – even if this attention is negative.

When games are played between groups or teams they can be distinguished by:

- being played repeatedly and as a matter of course between members
- being 'rewarded' within the group itself, that is, attention being given to the game and the people who play it, thereby giving the behaviour recognition
- being supported by the group culture
- opportunities being provided within the culture for justification and advancement of the game

Dealing with Games

You can avoid getting into a game by recognizing the discount which will occur at the opening of the game so that you do not get hooked or alternatively put out the hook yourself. It takes a bit of practice to notice the hook, but once you do you will be able to deal with it from the Mindful Process. One way to do this is to notice your intuitive feeling that something is not right – even if you don't know what it is. Your intuition enables you to be more hesitant, to ask questions and to consider your responses. Alternatively you can practice listening for discounts and respond appropriately. Even if you only notice half way through that you are in a familiar process you can still decide to do something different and get out of the game.

Another way to consider games is to answer a number of questions devised by James (1973):

- How does the repetitive pattern start?
- What happens next?
- What is my secret message to the other person?
- And then?
- What is the other person's secret message to me?
- How does it end?
- How do I feel?
- How do I think the other person feels?
- What keeps happening to me over and over again?

Ways to Deal with Games

There are various ways to stop a game. We can:

1. CROSS THE TRANSACTION

Crossing the transaction means that you respond from a different Mode than the one the stimulus is designed to hook. For example:

On asking John for assistance Alan keeps responding with 'Yes, but ...' instead of continuing to offer suggestions John says: 'I am sure you will work it out, Alan.'	*This crosses the transaction and keeps them both OK. John does not need to keep trying to help which releases him from the invitation to try harder.*

2. DEAL WITH THE ULTERIOR OR PSYCHOLOGICAL MESSAGE

You can deal with the ulterior rather than the social message. For example:

Susan to Mary: 'I can't do this, I'm useless.' Rather than saying 'Let me do this for you' Mary responds with 'It sounds like you have a problem. What would you like me to do about it?' (Said from the Mindful Process and inviting clear contracting.)	*This keeps Mary out of the invitation to do something for Susan without a clear contract. Susan is invited to contract clearly and does not pick up on the 'I'm useless' statement which could be another way to invite Mary to Rescue her.*

3. NOTICE THE OPENING DISCOUNT

The opening message in a game always entails a discount. There are further discounts at each stage of the game. By detecting discounts you can identify game invitations and defuse them with options. (A discount is when you minimize, maximize, or ignore some aspect of a problem which would assist you in resolving it. For example, you say in a whiney voice 'This is too difficult for me to do', putting out an invitation for someone to help.) In the above vignette Susan's comment of 'I'm useless' is an example of this.

4. REPLACE THE STROKES

Games are a way to obtain strokes (recognition). Therefore you need to replace the strokes that you and/or the other person obtain by playing games. People get a great many strokes from games, even if they are negative. However, if you don't obtain sufficient positive strokes, or give yourself positive strokes, you may well go for quantity rather than quality of strokes and play games in order to get them. When people play fewer games, there is a loss of a source of strokes – and also a loss of excitement that the game has previously generated, so ways need to be found to replace these in positive ways.

5. DEVELOP AWARENESS AT ANY STAGE

You can still change your behaviour from your usual pattern even if you don't notice the pattern until you are part the way through the process. Once you do something differently the other person will not be able to act in the same way either.

If you do get all the way to the end of the process:

1. You can decide not to pick up the bad feeling at the end of the game.
2. You can debrief what happened and find ways for all parties to change their communication processes.

6. CONFRONT OR IGNORE THE GAME

When you become aware that someone is playing a game or you are involved in a game you have the option to confront or ignore it.

Confront the game – this needs to be undertaken from the position of *I'm OK and You're OK*, staying within the Mindful Process of the OK Modes Model. You might say something like: 'I am aware that you and I often get into this and I wonder what we might do differently in order to avoid doing so in future. Are you willing to discuss this with me?'

Ignore the game – you can decide that you will ignore the game invitations but remain aware of the potential for the other person to escalate as you stop playing the games you used to play.

Summary

Changes can be made at any stage of the game. You need to keep off the Drama Triangle since each of the positions involve being in one of the *ineffective modes*. Whilst you cannot make someone stop a game, you can stay out of the game yourself. You can also maximize the chance that you will invite the other person out of their game. You also need to ensure that you keep your stroke bank stocked up and remain Mindful.

It is not usually helpful to inform somebody that they are playing a game as they are unlikely to know what we are talking about. If you were to do this it is likely that you would do it in such a way as to use TA to metaphorically 'beat the other person up'. Rather, you need to consider what your part might be in the game playing process and make the necessary changes.

When you are operating from Mindfully you are able to stay in contact with others, seek to understand them, take responsibility for your actions and volunteer how you are feeling whilst staying potent. For example, Sally might have gone to Jean to talk with her. Part the way through the process Sally realizes she is inviting Jean to Rescue her. She therefore stops and informs Jean of her realization and agrees that she will take responsibility for her relationship with Janice. Sally recognizes that she is hurt by the way Janice talks to her but think it possible that Janice feels awkward because they both went for the same post. Sally decides to go and see Janice to find a way to improve their relationship.

The Drama Triangle is drawn with the Victim position at the bottom, symbolizing that it is precarious and unstable. The following diagram is a pyramid with the four corners on the base representing the different actions we need to undertake to be effective in our communication. It can serve as an aide memoir to effective communication.

In the model, being potent means that you are remaining Mindful and staying assertive. This point also represents the positive energy that occurs when you are staying in contact with the other person or people, seeking to understand them as well as acknowledging and sharing your own thoughts and feelings whilst taking responsibility for your own actions. When you do this you are also encouraging the other person to be potent.

The corner entitled 'Acknowledging and Sharing how I feel' is about sharing your feelings but remaining potent and assertive. For example, 'I feel … (*angry/hurt/sad/scared/ disappointed, and so on*) right now and would like to talk with you about the effect your

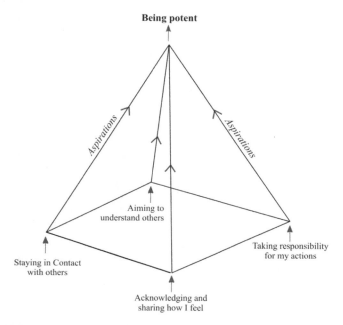

Figure 9.3   The Winners' Pyramid

behaviour has on me. Are you willing to do this?' In this instance you are taking responsibility for your own feelings and contracting with the person to discuss the situation.

Taking responsibility means accepting responsibility for your own actions and feelings rather than blaming others.

The importance of this diagram is the relationship with the other person or people and the other two corners of the pyramid take this into consideration. Regardless of what has happened it is important to understand what was, and is, going on for the other person. Staying in contact with that person increases the possibility that a resolution can be achieved. Usually when you Mindfully ask questions about what was going on for them when they did X or Y, you develop an understanding about the other person's motives. Conflict can then be resolved more easily. You might do this from the Structuring Mode perhaps with the aim of being able to move into the Co-creative Mode.

The arrows to the top point on the diagram are termed *aspirations*. Sometimes the term for this in TA is *physis*, the thrust of life itself. The upward edges of the winners' pyramid represent the positive energetic force that occurs when all these aspects come together.

To be effective and healthy in your communication processes you need to ensure that you obtain strokes in healthy ways, rather than through game playing. You need to keep the Winners' Pyramid in mind as a way of thinking about relationships with self and others. Having become aware that you play games you need to ask yourself what the aim is and consider how you might get your needs met in healthy ways which relate to the present, rather than some past time.

EXERCISES

EXERCISE 1 – THE GAME DIARY

The following exercise will enable you to think through your own game processes. When you get that 'same old feeling' then this is the time to bring out the diary and consider what occurred. By doing this you will become more finely attuned to the process and find ways to stop it earlier on, and eventually not get involved at all.

This is based on Game theory. By identifying the predictable points in arguments, you are able to see how, and where, you can intervene in processes and change the outcome.

What to do

Work through a recent event. Choose one that you seem to repeat again and again and where you also experience feeling or thinking something at the end which is familiar.

Draw the chart landscaped out on a piece of paper, with sufficient room for making notes within each box.

1. Chart the steps on a diary like the one below by answering the questions at the top of the page.
2. Over time, after perhaps two or three occurrences, a familiar pattern with a predictable outcome may appear and this will indicate a Game.
3. Identify the familiar feeling which will probably accompany the end of the process.
4. Continue to work through similar incidents as they occur.
5. Consider any patterns and themes that you notice.
6. Where could you do something different? What options do you have at each stage?
7. When you realize how you hooked someone else into a game, or were hooked yourself, consider what you could do differently in the future. For example, if you are one of life's Rescuers consider what you might do to remind yourself that you are OK as you are, without having to look after others. Alternatively consider how you could notice your own, or someone else's opening discount that might start the game.
8. Where will you get your need met for recognition in healthy ways in future?

EXERCISE 2 – SECRETS

Consider the last time you were involved in game playing and then consider:

1. What was your secret message to the other person or people?
2. What do you think their secret message to you was?
3. How could you deal with this differently in future?

Table 9.1   Games Diary Table

	What started it Time How I felt	What I did	What they did	What happened	The payoff, or how I felt when it ended
Sunday					
Monday					
Tuesday					
Wednesday					
Thursday					
Friday					
Saturday					

Source: Mountain, 2004.

CHAPTER **10** *Telling the Story*

Introduction

All organizations have stories about their origins, the founder(s) and the people within them. These stories can be positive or negative and have a strong influence on the workforce's views of the organization, what is good (or bad) about it and how it became successful. The organizational story will also be a large determinant of people's understanding about what can or cannot be done there. It can be given a title and many will resonate with it. By knowing and understanding this particular story we can know how to make appropriate interventions. In this chapter we will explore this aspect, starting with the individual and then extending this to organizations.

From Story to Plan

In Transactional Analysis this 'story' is called the *life script*. This is effectively a *plan* which you developed in childhood, about who you are, how you relate to other people, the way you should live your life, and how, for instance, you see fate or destiny leading you to certain outcomes, or preventing you from others. Although in adulthood this plan is most likely to be outside your awareness, it nevertheless will exert great influence on who and how you are and what you do or do not do. There will be themes contained in the plan – for instance about success or failure, trust and betrayal. This life plan will have been influenced by the messages you received from significant others, as well as cultural influences. You will have made your own sense of these when growing up and developed a set of beliefs and decisions about yourself as a result. These beliefs and decisions then influence the strategies and actions you take throughout your life.

EXAMPLES

1) Fred is successful at his job and in his career. He is in a fulfilling relationship and has several satisfying hobbies which occupy his spare time well and give him a real contrast to his working week. However, to talk to Fred, you would not guess that any of this was true. He describes himself as unfulfilled and a failure. He looks forward to the time when he can 'make it' in his life.	*Fred discounts his present circumstances and therefore his achievements. His early decisions are about 'trying' to be successful and he does not feel free to enjoy his successes. Instead he waits for a time when he will be fulfilled, thus he lives for tomorrow, not for today. His life appears to be about striving but not enjoying.*

2) Jenny is a very able professional. She gets excited about new projects, but is not able to sustain her enthusiasm for very long. Her company work around this, making sure they always have someone else on the project who has the staying power to follow through to a conclusion.	*Jenny has to try hard to achieve things but then gets bored before the task is completed. Her script is slightly different to Fred's in that she tries hard, gets excited about new things to do but does not have any internal messages about it being important to complete things. So her script is more about starting but not completing.*
3) Jeff is plagued by the conviction that things always go wrong for him. He plans meticulously, but life has taught him that however much he does this something will happen that means he fails or is disappointed in some way.	*Jeff is rather pessimistic and does not get excited about things. When things go wrong he uses this to reinforce his script saying that this always happens to him. His early decisions would have been 'I have to work really hard to get the detail perfectly right and then perhaps, just perhaps, nothing awful will happen – but of course it always does'. With this frame of reference it will be difficult for Jeff to enjoy life.*

Creating Your Script

You start developing script decisions in your earliest years – at a time when you had little ability to deal with abstract concepts or understand events from an adult perspective. Whilst you will have revised your script decisions to some extent as you progressed through childhood, many aspects of these beliefs and decisions survive with you into adulthood, despite their severely limiting and distorting qualities.

Kolb (1984) described learning as the 'transformation of experience'. Generally, the product of learning is an increased sense of the world and, with regard to life, to make it more predictable. If we see learning as our attempt to make sense of the world then as small children we are using our experiences to make meaning for ourselves, others and the way the world 'works'. This is largely from our biological instinct to survive and belong.

Once you have made decisions about self, others and the world, new experiences are interpreted to fit these. In this way you can make the world relatively predictable. You recall only what you chose to notice and, moreover, you remember it in a way that is shaped to fit your beliefs and decisions about what is important. Gregory (1970) argued that perception is 1 per cent what you see and 99 per cent what you construct.

Some examples of script are:

- Where your, or another person's, actions seem stuck in a repetitive, often self-destructive, loop. The same kinds of things keep happening, which get in the way of being effective. Particular examples of this might be arguments or conflicts which have the same pattern.
- Where your perceptions of yourself and others seem at odds with the facts. For example, you might consistently under-recognize (or overestimate) your abilities or stereotype managers as 'all being the same' even when the evidence does not fit.

Script can be illustrated by showing how your parents or primary caregivers have influenced you as a child. Although the messages that are given to children by adults are powerful, it remains up to the child as to what sense is made of these messages and whether and how they are taken on board. Scripts include, or at least closely relate to, most of the other TA concepts we have covered in previous chapters.

In the smallest of your actions and decisions, you are likely to see the patterns of your lifelong script being played out moment by moment. So the overall, lifelong pattern of your script is reflected in miniature in the smallest of your actions.

It was Berne who developed the idea of scripts – analogous to a drama with central characters, including heroes, villains, a plot and an ending, which may have tragic or happy themes. Just as a play has a predefined 'script' at the start, so people write their own script which they then live out.

Substitution of Feelings

The term 'racket' was introduced by Berne for what we call 'substitute' feelings. Berne's term came from the days of prohibition, when a business, which was, for example, ostensibly a laundry, may have been a cover for an illegal distillery. The term 'racket' is pejorative, and not self-explanatory, hence our term, 'substitute'.

Stewart and Joines (1987) defined this type of feeling as:

a familiar emotion, learned and encouraged in childhood and experienced in many different stress situations, and maladaptive as an adult means of problem-solving.

We can experience a substitute feeling in response to independently occurring stress situations, ones which we have not initiated.

The substitute system, also called the *script system* (Erskine and Moursund (1988) from an original article by Erskine and Zalcman (1979)), is therefore a process we used as children, and may still use as adults, to cover one feeling with another. An example of this might be that you feel hurt by someone's actions but because you don't allow yourself to feel this sort of pain, you move quickly to feeling angry which you can rationalize as necessary. With this shift you ignore, and invite the other person to ignore, your hurt feelings and then do not get your needs met. You then develop a whole system of beliefs and actions around this substitution and subsequently go on to reinforce these beliefs by interpreting situations in a way that justifies them.

EXAMPLES

Martin worked with Tina, a woman who was disabled from birth. Her parents felt guilty for having a disabled child and Tina learnt not to show sadness but instead to smile all the time and pretend to be happy. This situation only came to light when Martin was working on a project with her and mentioned how she always smiled regardless of what was happening. Tina explained about her parents and also said that her smile covered how lonely she felt inside.	*In this instance Tina is substituting the feeling of happiness for a range of other feelings that might be more appropriate. These might, for instance, be feelings of sadness, anger or fear.*

Suzanne seemed to respond to situations with the same feelings all the time. If her boss came in and asked her to do something, instead of saying that she could not take on the work right now as she was busy she would get angry. When her friend and colleague was ill, Suzanne snapped at everyone else in the team and gave them a hard time. When her dog got run over she came to work angry and volatile. If someone asked her for information she would become angry.	*Sometimes there are feelings which we don't allow ourselves to have. For example, Suzanne may have felt sad when her dog died, but anger was her learnt way of responding. She covered up her sadness with anger and so never actually resolved her sad feeling. People respond to her angry feeling by withdrawing from her. She is doing this outside of her awareness. This is likely to have started in childhood when expressing feelings generally, or it may have been the case that expressing sadness in particular was not allowed in her family.*

Resolving Substitute Feelings

When you feel a different feeling from the one which might be appropriate to the situation, you will have difficulty reaching a resolution so that you can 'let go'. In this way substitute feelings are non problem-solving. For example, Suzanne seems to become angry in a variety of situations, even though anyone else might feel sadness or hurt. The belief behind the decision not to show certain feelings might be something like 'I will get angry instead of hurt so that others will not ridicule me'. Eventually Suzanne has become so far removed from the original feeling that she is not even aware of it and now just displays the learnt feeling of anger. This then translates into *I am OK and You're Not OK*. Moving to a resolution of these feelings then becomes impossible because the real need is not being met. So however many times this is repeated, this will still be the case. One way of describing this is 'we never get enough of what we don't need'.

Whilst we all need to take account of our own feelings it may be appropriate to consider what you can do if one of your colleagues seems to be expressing the same emotion in a variety of situations, and this tends to lead to non problem-solving behaviour. If you have a good relationship with the person and can agree with them how you might support them, raising this aspect could be helpful in their development. It might be an aspect for attention within an appraisal process where change is considered necessary.

The script system is useful as a way of considering a variety of situations at home and at work. The following example outlines the substitute thoughts and feelings that might occur for Jeff at work (Figure 10.1).

This is a looped system. Jeff ignores his here and now feelings and in an attempt to be accepted he tries to please other people. This system works for him to a degree, but when he believes that he is not able to please people, Jeff feels low. Each new experience at work is seen by Jeff through this frame of reference. When asked for his own opinion he does not know what he believes as he considers other people's ideas and thoughts more relevant than his own.

Most of us develop our own specific substitutions system. In this instance Jeff's manager would need to let him know that he is important and that he can think for himself. He needs to be asked if he can manage extra work and what support he requires.

You can have substitution systems for a range of situations and aspects. This might include what you do when you make a mistake, when you feel overweight, when you don't understand something and so on. In these instances you go into a self reinforcing

Script System

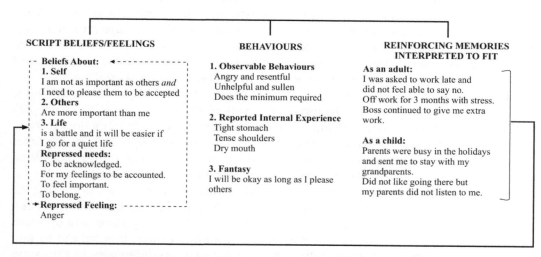

Figure 10.1 Revised Substitution System (Script System) for Jeff

loop and believe that this is how things have to be and that there must be something wrong with you or with others. You need to recognize that these are beliefs, and that beliefs can be changed. You need to establish what your beliefs are, how these affect you and what new belief you can develop in order to change things. (See Chapter 15 on Stress, pages 222–224 for exercises related to this.)

Organizational Scripts

Organizations are founded by individuals – so in one sense we could see an organization having a 'parent' or parents who 'bring it into the world'. That individual's script beliefs are then likely to be lived out in the organization. Just as each of us has made decisions about how to be in the world, you could argue that organizations do likewise. Whilst an organization is not a living creature it does develop an energy and identity of its own. You can experience this when you go into two different organizations undertaking the same task. Take for instance two different doctor's surgeries. In one, the receptionists sit behind glass and are not welcoming and you have to wait to get their attention. It takes three weeks to get to see the GP of your choice and some of the doctors are surly and brusque. When it is your turn an electrical printout of your name comes on the overhead display calling you to the GP's room. In the other surgery the reception area is light and open. The receptionists sit behind a curved administrative desk with no glass panels separating them off from the patients and chat with you when you go in. At the allotted time the GP comes to get you.

These two surgeries undertake the same task and yet they feel very different. The energy in the second is relaxed, pleasant and caring. If you were to take a look at who set the surgeries up you would find very different people and it is them who influence the organization and the organization's script.

Other influences on the script are the community and the culture within which the organization is situated. The cultural influences include both the local and national cultures, and in the case of GP surgeries, the government will also have an influence – by the policies that they introduce, and by the way that the health service is referred to in political discussion. These different influences help to form the frame of reference of those who developed the organization about how the organization should be.

The culture of an organization is closely linked with the script. When things go in a particular way within the organization it will often be interpreted to fit people's expectations and opinions. For example, management may stereotype shopfloor workers and say 'They don't know what it's like to …' or 'They never cooperate.' On the other hand, shop floor workers may stereotype management by saying things like 'What else would you expect?', or 'They asked us our opinion and didn't listen', or 'Fat cat management, making money at our expense.' When this happens, you are not seeing the actual person (or people) but have made them like objects (or are talking about them as if they were an object). By objectifying them in this way, individual qualities and opinions are not acknowledged. In order to develop open communication, it is helpful to find the areas where people *do* connect rather than simply focus on differences and the ways in which they discount each other. You can also challenge the Frame of Reference (for instance – *They never cooperate*) by asking such questions as:

- 'When was the last time they didn't cooperate?'
- 'What was going then?'
- 'What was the context/situation?'
- 'What did you do to resolve this and cooperate with them?'
- 'How will you deal with this process now so that everyone can move forward?'
- 'What options do you have?'

All of these questions together with the positive focus suggested above are designed to encourage accounting rather than discounting. When you challenge words such as 'never' or 'always' you are encouraging open communication.

High-Pressure Sales

There are organizations whose founder had a high level of competitiveness to the point of being aggressive. This would create a very particular organizational script. Let us take sales for example. Many sales people are set off against each other. The sales person who achieves the most sales is likely to be paid big bonuses and big rewards. This can often lead to manipulative and coercive sales techniques with the buyer agreeing to buy when they might not actually want to, which in turn, is likely to lead to a cancellation of the agreement within the 14-day cooling-off period. This process can cause stress for both parties to the contract, the buyer and the seller. Should a complaint be made about a sales person the organization may well blame their employee when, all along, they have been rewarding such behaviour by celebrating the high sales figures the individual has achieved.

Fortunately, not all sales representatives get trained that way these days. One international training organization emphasizes the importance of relationships with prospective clients. The more this happens the greater the likelihood of change and the development of a positive organizational script. As those with the newer styles and approaches show an increase in sales they are likely to become influential within their organizations so the culture will change.

We can draw the script matrix of an organization. A matrix for an individual consists of messages from significant other people. These messages are represented through the Structural Model of Ego States (See Chapter 3) to the Parent, Adult, Child of the individual. With an organization the Parent, Adult, Child model could be representative of the community, the founding leader/s, the government, or perhaps HQ. In this way you can start to understand the messages that were involved in the setting up of the organization. (You cannot of course be sure where the messages come from, but for our purposes here we are using the Structural model because we are not talking about individual people.)

Social Services departments are frequently the subject of government enquiries, investigating the reasons someone has died where social services might have been expected to take action. However, they are also frequently on the receiving end for criticism from the media for the occasions when they do take action. Therefore the mixture of messages might be illustrated in this way:

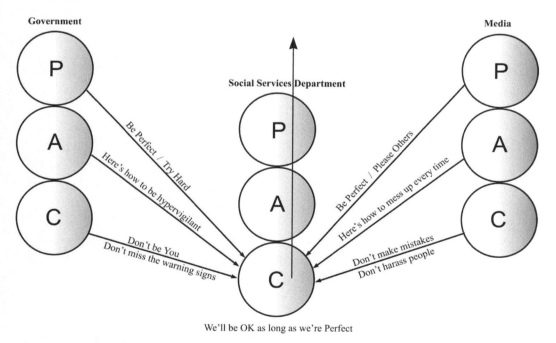

Figure 10.2 Organizational Script Matrix

When considering interventions in organizations you could ask such questions as: How will things be if you go on as you are? How will things be if they get worse? How would you like to be? What would you need to do to get there?

Script Theory can also be used in planning for the future. One creative way forward is scenario planning – which contrasts with the way you have developed your life script, based on past experience. With scenario planning, a variety of possible futures are explored in depth – considering what would happen if things go on as they are and what would happen if they changed. Jaworski (1996) used this approach in examining the global situation.

Summary

The script is a way of considering how you, as an individual, or an organization, has developed. By exploring the different influential messages that have been incorporated into an organization, you can see how you, and the organization, arrived in the current position.

If you then consider the future in the light of this new awareness you can then extrapolate what might happen in the future if things go on as they are. If this outcome is potentially damaging for the organization, then attention can be focussed on what would need to change in order to correct this future pathway.

EXERCISES

The best place to start to understand script is with yourself.
  Consider what you believe about:

- your abilities
- what you will end up doing/becoming
- what you deserve
- what beliefs about others you notice in yourself that get in your way of being able to function as well or efficiently as you might? For example:
  - do you trust other people?
  - how do you see others in comparison to you?
  - are other people important to you?
  - life – is it exciting, dull, depressing?
  - the world – is it an exciting place with opportunities?

What repeating patterns and outcomes do you notice yourself being caught in? For example, are there patterns to arguments/disagreements you have with others, or patterns to the feelings, thoughts or responses you have to things that happen in your life?
  Are these beliefs supporting you to lead a happy, healthy, confident life? If not what will you do about that?

ORGANIZATIONAL SCRIPT

You may be curious to know what the themes are in the script of the organization you work with or for. This exercise gives you the opportunity to increase your understanding of this by taking a step back.
  Consider the organization you work for, or if you are a consultant, an organization by whom you are commissioned:

1. Take a look around the room you are in (you don't have to be within the organization premises to do this) and find examples of objects that reflect different elements of that organization.
2. Think about what the entrance hall or reception area is like and then what is it like as you walk through the building. How do people respond to you and to each other? Find an object that represents that.
3. Now consider what the structure of the organization is like – is it rigid or flexible, formal or informal? Find an object to represent that.
4. How do people communicate and what are the dynamics between different departments. Choose something to represent these aspects.
5. How would you represent the leadership of this organization?
6. Continue locating objects for the different aspects and put them in relationship to each other, including perhaps an object for yourself.

What you have produced is known as a *sculpt*. Each object symbolizes how you see a particular aspect of the organization. The ways you have physically placed these objects show how you see them in relation to each other in the real organization. The purpose in doing this is to approach the way you see your organization from a different standpoint – very often unexpected – and significant – insights arise from doing this kind of exercise. So, bearing that in mind:

- What do you realize as you look overall at this organizational sculpt that you have made?
- What is the 'feel' of the objects you have found?
- Are they hard, soft or malleable, and what kind of relationships do they have with each other?
- What, if anything, in your view, needs to change?
- Is this something that is within your influence or control?

You could do this exercise with others – which then gives the opportunity of comparing notes – the perceptions you have in common, the differences between you, and so on. The important consideration when doing this is to be open to having a dialogue about those differences.

Either way, make notes of what you have learned, and make a contract (with yourself and with others) about what you will do, by when and the support you will use to achieve that.

11 The Relationship between Individuals and the Organization

Introduction

This chapter is designed as a guide to the way TA sees the formation and structure of an organization, how its culture develops and the subsequent leadership processes that come into play. Change in an organization is harder to achieve without an understanding of its history and development – and the influence this has on the present and the future. Ensuring an organization is 'fit for purpose' can be a difficult task at the best of times as organizations are made up of people, not just machines, equipment and buildings.

Berne (1963, 1966) developed diagrammatic ways to understand how groups work and how to enable organizations to be more successful, and this work will form the basis for this chapter. An organization has a range of different interrelated facets and influences that can be illustrated. Diagrams also enable a large amount of information to be condensed. These diagrams can then become tools for assessment, analysis and action. We have kept with Berne's conceptualization of the different aspects of an organization and in addition have added some of our own developments and understanding.

The Organization's Past

In terms of the history of an organization, the founder/s (or to use Berne's term 'Primal leader/s') play a crucial role in determining the culture and preoccupations of an organization. As the organization develops, it builds its own culture, which can be a conscious activity, or one that occurs without much awareness on the part of people within the organization. Part of this culture will be a reflection of the personality of the founder and part will be the written documents, policies and procedures of the organization (known as the 'Canon') which set out what the organization does, how it does it, and why.

The Organization in the Present

The current structures of the organization, the nature and style of leadership and authority within it, are directly observable properties. The interpretation of these is likely to be different from an insider's and an outsider's perspective.

The nature of the roles of people within the organization is another aspect of the current functioning of the organization:

1. Roles *as laid down* (which Berne called *etiquette*). These will usually be contained in manuals about procedure, who can talk to who in the organization, and so on. In some organizations these will be implemented rigorously – which would result in (2) below being identical to the official line. However, in other organizations, there may be little resemblance between the official rules and what happens day by day.
2. Roles *as actually performed* (which Berne called *technical*). These will be ascertained by watching what people do and how they interact with each other *in practice*.
3. Roles as people fulfilling them *perceive* them to be (which Berne called *character*). These are likely to be less accessible, since people will not often openly talk about these internal thoughts and feelings. Examples here might be hidden fears of redundancy, or being discovered as incompetent, and secret hopes about, say, promotion, or getting revenge for the time a particular person upset you. Whilst these perceptions are hidden, they will affect the way a person fulfils their role – enthusiastically, with resentment, half-heartedly and so on.

Finally, and linked to this last, internal, aspect of roles, is what Berne called the private structure of the organization – the internal pictures, beliefs and perceptions of each of the people who work within it. Whilst not immediately apparent, these exert an influence on the organization at what Berne described as the *psychological level*. He referred to these 'pictures' as imagoes and we will look at these in detail later in this chapter.

The Organization in the Future

At an individual level, Berne talked about *physis* – the force of life – which propels us – and indeed all living things. By extension, successful organizations also need to have a continuing momentum which drives them forward.

Authority and Organizations

Berne was keen to examine authority in organizations and establish its sources. This is important, since the way that authority is exercised will either inhibit or encourage certain activities, and in general, determine the extent to which people can operate effectively. Since the 1960s there has been a tendency to see authority as something which is unhelpful, but positive exercise of authority is vital to the healthy function of any organization. Authority is likely to originate from a number of different sources, including:

- The way power is exercised and the style of management and leadership
- The body of theory and practice into which a person has been trained and in which they have built experience. This informs what they see as important and the ethical stance they take

- The body of rules, procedures and 'custom and practice' that have been developed over time within an organization
- Important figures in an organization's history and their personal style

What was important historically may now be exerting an unhelpful influence on the organization.

We will now look in more detail at the elements of Berne's model.

Historical Influences

Each organization has a history which begins with an individual or a group of individuals who were the founders. Berne referred to the founder as the primal leader, who, once dead, is referred to as the Euhemerus. Naming the dead leader after this ancient Greek thinker had a particular significance. Euhemerus regarded the Greek myths as versions of actual past events which had been reshaped by their retelling and infusing with cultural additions and influences. The deceased founding person – the Euhemerus – will have an identity which has been reshaped through the history and development of the organization. They continue to exert an influence even after their death, and are likely to become idealized. (For Ford Motor Company the Euhemerus is Henry Ford, and for Transactional Analysts worldwide it is Eric Berne.)

The primal leader/Euhemerus is the person who sets the original organizational structure, canon, policies, practices, culture and values, which form part of the organizational identity. These leaders tend to have stories told about them as if they were heroes and they can take on a magical quality. Should the primal leader choose to move away and then return years later, it is likely that some of the workforce will be disappointed because this primal leader is likely to be experienced as a more ordinary person who does not live up to the stories that have been told about them. However, it is this founder (or founders) who will have had the greatest influence on the organizational culture. Others may come later who change the culture and they will also have stories told about them by later generations. However, they are unlikely to have the same level of influence as their earlier counterparts. We can tell a lot about the organizational culture from the myths and legends that are told by the work force. These stories also help to maintain and reinforce the psychological contract (see Chapter 6).

The Founder and the Identity

Another way to consider the organizational identity is to take a look at the organization's name. For example, most people in the western world are aware of the Virgin label, no matter what that label is attached to: music, trains, planes or cosmetics. This label is synonymous with primal leader, Richard Branson, as he has a certain reputation for success, fun, risk-taking and caring. Branson has managed to be the brand and that brand, and indeed Branson himself, are, on the whole, seen in a positive light. Despite not realistically being able to be involved at all levels with all the different facets of the Virgin label, somehow people experience him as being so. Therefore the organizational script (see Chapter 10) for Virgin is one about success, possibility and aspiration (physis).

One of the reasons Virgin is successful is because of Branson's belief in achievement. For example, in his late teens he did not 'follow the rules' when setting up his first university newspaper (Branson, 2000). He wanted to interview famous musicians and, despite being an unknown student, he did not stop himself calling them up and getting them to talk with him. Generally he achieved what he wanted because he did not entertain the idea of failure.

Branson also has a belief that work can be fun, that people have great ideas and that these ideas should be listened to. In this way the culture of his organizations is about 'can do'. Of course, this is an outsider's perspective and may not be experienced in exactly the same way inside, because, as mentioned earlier, stories will be told about the organization and its leader and these will influence the internal culture.

Figure 11.1 shows in brief the elements of Berne's organizational theory. We have drawn these as a time line from past to present to future.

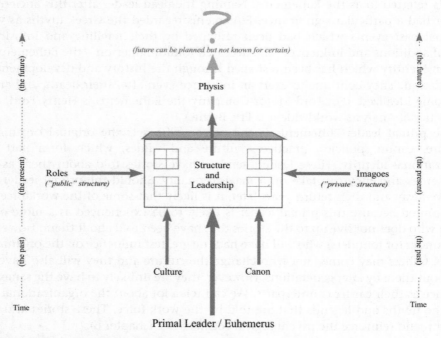

Figure 11.1 The Elements of the Organization

An Example: Railways in Great Britain

So, let us take a look at how we can illustrate the history of an organization, using the case example of railways in Britain. Berne (1963) tabulated this into five areas: Cultural, Historical, Personal, Organizational and Manuals. By looking at the origin of the areas we can assess how the organization has developed and therefore what we need to consider when deciding on programmes for change.

This example has been chosen since it will be readily familiar to many British readers. Readers from other countries will be able to look comparatively at their own railway system.

Table 11.1 Formal Authority Diagram: Railways in Britain

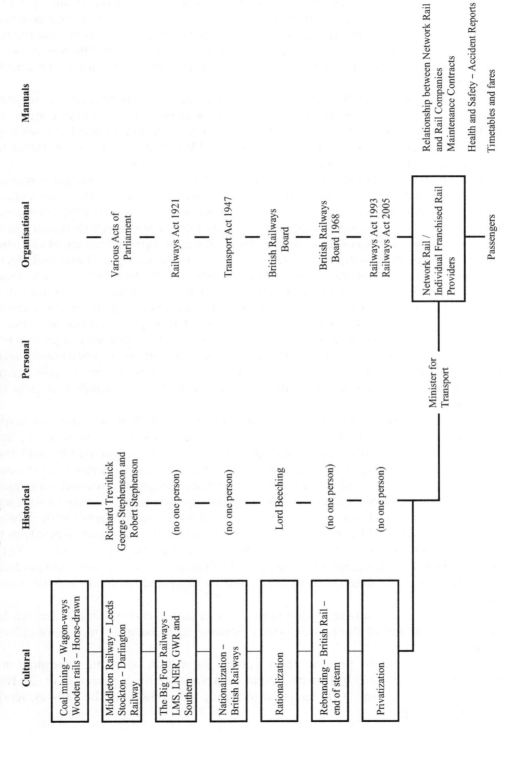

Cultural	Historical	Personal	Organisational	Manuals
Coal mining – Wagon-ways Wooden rails – Horse-drawn				
Middleton Railway – Leeds Stockton – Darlington Railway	Richard Trevithick George Stephenson and Robert Stephenson		Various Acts of Parliament	
The Big Four Railways – LMS, LNER, GWR and Southern	(no one person)		Railways Act 1921	
Nationalization – British Railways	(no one person)		Transport Act 1947	
Rationalization	Lord Beeching		British Railways Board	
Rebranding – British Rail – end of steam	(no one person)		British Railways Board 1968	
Privatization	(no one person)		Railways Act 1993 Railways Act 2005	
		Minister for Transport	Network Rail / Individual Franchised Rail Providers	Relationship between Network Rail and Rail Companies Maintenance Contracts
			Passengers	Health and Safety – Accident Reports
				Timetables and fares

The passenger railway system in Britain has its origin in the mining industry, where, as far back as the seventeenth century, wooden track was used for horse drawn wagons to move coal or extracted ore. The development of the first steam engines around the start of the nineteenth century began purely as an improvement to this. The first passenger lines came slightly later. Initially, there were numerous small companies, each running local lines.

After the First World War an Act of Parliament of 1921 rationalized this situation, leading to the 'Big Four' companies – London Midland and Scottish (LMS), London and North Eastern Railway (LNER), Great Western Railway (GWR) and Southern Railway – based on regional operation. After the Second World War, the railways were nationalized, and British Railways became a unified, state-owned organization.

As road systems improved including the building of motorways, car-ownership increased dramatically. This led to the decline of the railways and by the 1960s concern developed that an unprofitable railway system was not sustainable. The British Railways Board commissioned a report by Dr (later Lord) Richard Beeching which resulted in the cutting of large numbers of unprofitable lines and a substantial trimming of the whole system. Later in the 1960s, the transition from steam operation to diesel and electric was completed, together with a rebranding as 'British Rail'. Finally, the whole system was privatized in 1993, with ownership of the track network being separate from about 25 franchised companies which had responsibility for operating the trains. Thus the history of passenger train service in the UK which had began with the operation of many small companies, now returned to a similar system, albeit with a greater level of government oversight. Since 2005, analysis of accidents since privatization raised concerns about maintenance and safety, and the track network once again became owned by the government. This history immediately elicits a number of facts (see Table 11.1).

We can see that in the origins of the railway system there was not one central authority, and that there were not, in fact, clear primal leaders in its history. The most recent developments return the system to this multiplicity – at the end of 2010 there were around 27 companies running the services. The famous characters from the early days, such as Trevithick and George and Robert Stephenson, were involved in designing trains and building lines, rather than running the organization. This may explain why, when people are asked to come up with a name of someone connected with railways, the name of Lord Beeching so frequently comes to mind. He came fairly recently to the railways in terms of their long history, and his unpopularity (whether justified or not) is arguably what fuels his fame. However, he was chairman of the British Railways Board for a relatively short time (1960 to 1965) and he produced his report on the Board's commission.

So a useful question here is what influence this lack of clear primal leaders has had on the development of the railway system, strategy and clarity of purpose of railways in the UK.

Whilst we tend to see the train system in Britain as being predominantly about passengers, its origins lie with freight, and post-Beeching, a number of surviving lines only carry freight. This fact is interesting too. Whom is the railway service primarily serving?

Throughout its history there is a greater degree of specific government legislation relating to railways than would be expected in other organizations. This is despite the fact that the railways were nationalized for only 50 years of their 170-year history.

There has always been controversy over the swingeing cuts recommended by Beeching and implemented by government. One commentator (Hondelink, 1965) pointed out that Beeching's criterion for cuts was unprofitability. He did not consider options that might have made these lines profitable. Neither he, nor the government, considered the view that a railway should provide a public service, regardless of profitability. And Hondelink argues that he did not look at the whole transport system, including the far greater cost of the road network.

By plotting this history, the disparate nature of railways in Britain becomes clear. There is a lack of joined-up thinking and little apparent communication between the companies, who after all, are in competition with each other. Penalties for late arrival of trains charged to companies mean that they are not willing to 'hold' trains where someone needs a connection, and where their first train (probably run by a different company) is running late. This actually results in a poorer, not a better, service.

So the authority diagram provides us with one way to examine the structure and authority of an organization over time. And if consultancy were being commissioned to address some of the difficulties this analysis would provide an important foundation on which to build a new system which links the various rail networks as well as the road system thereby provided an integrated transport system that would be both nationally beneficial but also ecological.

Boundaries

The interplay between an organization's internal world and the external environment can be illustrated and assessed. As mentioned the internal world also has boundaries. These boundaries can be between:

- board and the senior leadership team
- senior leadership team and managers
- managers and the workforce
- different groups of the workforce

Naturally all these will vary depending on the nature and culture of the organization and the culture of the country in which the organization resides. The former will be influenced by the primal leader, or Euhemerus, and the latter by history, legislation and market forces.

We tend to feel threatened when organizations are restructured, re-engineered and undergo fundamental change and this is due to our fear about a change of identity. At these times we start to ask ourselves:

- Will there be a place for me in the changed organization?
- If there is, who will I be in that changed world?
- How does this affect me in the wider world?
- Will I fit and do I want to fit?

Historical continuity enables people to find their place and have a secure base. When they don't have a secure base, people have difficulty in making strong relationships with other people. It is as if all the pieces have been thrown up in the air and everything is in a state of flux, which many people find threatening. This happens at international, national as well as organizational levels.

The perimeter of the organization's environment, that is, of both the building and its grounds create a psychological boundary as well as a physical one. Boundary crossing in an organization occurs in a number of ways. Those who retire, are made redundant, or resign, cross the boundary in an outward direction. Those who come in to 'troubleshoot', or are elected to the board or are a new recruit are crossing the boundary in an inward direction. Even when invited to join an organization, colleagues with whom a new recruit works, may not be willing to engage with them. This will depend upon the organizational culture in terms of language, personal style, gender, sexuality, race or creed. For example, how would it be if a popular internal candidate for a position did not get appointed but someone else did? Even without intentionally doing so the team may well give messages to the new recruit that they are not welcome to cross the psychological boundary.

Berne developed a range of diagrams for organizations so that the organizational authority could be noted, as could the way in which individuals see their group (whether a team or a department) and the dynamics that go on between people. Through these diagrams we are also able to explore the relationship between the internal and external boundaries.

Organizations can be broken down into what can be seen and what cannot – what goes on inside the heads of the members of the organization. Berne called what can be seen the 'Public Structure' and what could not, the 'Private Structure' and developed diagrams for each.

Public Structure and Dynamic Diagrams

The Public Structure can be drawn using simple diagrams designed to show the:

- boundaries, both internal and external, and by doing this, to show the
- relationship of individuals to the leader and to each other

Dynamic Diagrams

Berne used these diagrams to assess the way a group or organization operated. Using circles to represent the overall structure (inside the circle) and its boundary, the influences on this boundary and the dynamic between people, the external environment and the various elements within the organization can all be shown. The outermost circle represents the *major external boundary* between the organization and its environment, and the innermost circle, a *major internal boundary* between the leadership and the rest of the workforce. At its simplest, this can be illustrated as follows in Figure 11.2.

So using this diagram creatively, the size of the innermost circle can be adjusted to illustrate the influence or size of the leadership in this group/organization. The thickness of the lines can be adjusted to show how rigid or closed a boundary is – either between

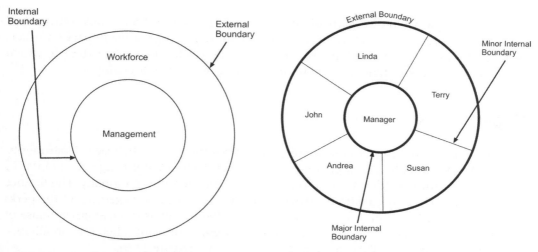

Figure 11.2 Simple Structural Diagram

Figure 11.3 Internal and External Boundaries

the organization and its environment (for instance an organization which operates with little or no interest or interaction with the world around it) or between the leadership and the rest of the organization (for instance a leader or leaders who cocoon themselves in their offices and are rarely seen). Conversely, the lines can be drawn thinner or even dotted, to show that the boundary is not being clearly kept (for instance, a manager who spends a deal of their time demonstrating that they are 'one of the gang' – leading to people being unclear who is running the show).

The boundary between management and the workforce is the major internal boundary. When looked at in more detail, the workforce are likely to have minor internal boundaries between themselves – here between individuals (Figure 11.3).

The same diagram could equally be used to illustrate departments (see below). The diagram can be further adapted to show the existence of subgroups within a group – in this case to show that Sue and Tom are a recognizable subgroup (Figure 11.4).

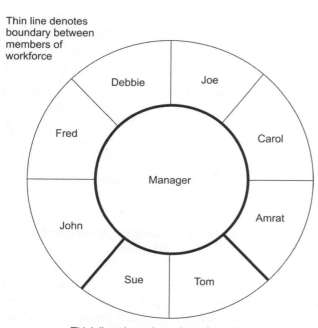

Thick line shows boundary of a sub-group within the workforce (Sue and Tom have a relationship outside work and always sit together)

Figure 11.4 Major Internal Boundary

This example would be particularly important, if Tom and Sue's relationship had no official status in the organization, and furthermore had a negative impact on others working around them. Indeed, many organizations place limits on the extent to which people in these circumstances would be allowed to work closely together.

Departments

Instead of individuals, the following diagram shows the process between departments. Let us take an example of a large not-for-profit organization employing consultants. To do their work, the consultants need to travel nationally and internationally. The finance department and the administrative department see the consultants getting all the perks and spending all the money. In contrast, they see themselves as the real powerhouse of the organization – more important than any other group or team. Therefore an alliance develops between them. This could be drawn as follows (Figure 11.5).

The examples to this point have been at the simplest level. Figure 11.6 below illustrates a more complex organization – where there are two people – Partner 1 and Partner 2 – in the leadership position, but without them having clearly demarcated line responsibilities. In these circumstances, people might well experience contradictory direction from the two managers, or might play the two off in a manipulative way:

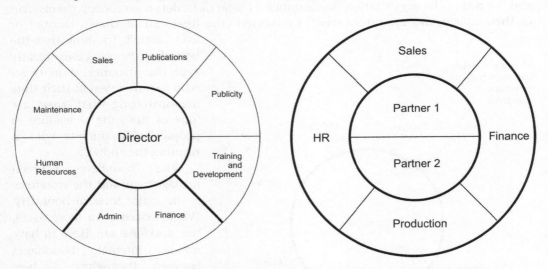

Figure 11.5 Example Structural Diagram

Figure 11.6 Complex Structural Diagram

The process of drawing the organization in these ways sometimes points out explanations for difficulties which had not previously been apparent. For instance, in our experience, this kind of issue frequently emerges in small family run businesses – where roles have been found for various family members, without a clear rationale. This then leads to a lack of clarity, and a ripe atmosphere for conflict.

So far, we have concentrated on the smallest, simplest organizations, with a single level of management. An organization with several layers of hierarchy – which Berne

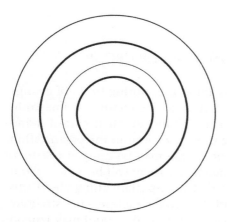

Figure 11.7
Compound Structural Diagram

termed compound – needs to be illustrated in a way which distinguishes between the levels of the hierarchy. Each concentric circle here denotes another level of the structure (figure 11.7).

This series of circles denotes different levels of the workforce in relation to the level of power they exercise. For example, in some organizations the CEO may develop a culture in which they hold most power, and their leadership region could be drawn much larger. Each subsequent circle radiating from the centre would represent the different level of power held by that section of the workforce. A typical organization might have a senior management team in the next circle, then divisional managers, department heads, team leaders, and so on to the outer edge of the circle. The senior management team's second circle would have a width representing the amount of power they were seen to have and similarly for each role up to the cleaning staff at the outer edge. As has previously been suggested above, the use of thinner or thicker lines can be used to show the extent of the internal boundary between levels. Sometimes the two upper levels of the hierarchy separate themselves off from the lower levels who have a closer relationship with each other.

These diagrams could be used in conjunction with the private structure (see below) in that people will perceive their position differently. They can also be linked with the concept of psychological distance, which was described in Chapter 6 (Micholt, 1992). The main benefits will come if creativity is used when drawing a diagram for a particular organization. The elements described here represent the suggested building blocks.

The Private Structure

To recap on the beginning of this chapter, our place in an organization has three aspects:

- the actual role assigned by the organization
- the way this role is enacted – which is observable
- people's feelings and responses to the first two

This last aspect includes people's perceptions about themselves and others within the work environment, be it the team, the project group, department, division or organization as a whole.

Imagoes

THE PRIVATE STRUCTURE OF AN ORGANIZATION, TEAM OR GROUP

The *private structure* of an organization is particularly important during times of change or new appointments. By private structure we are referring to the picture (or imago) in each person's head of the organization as a whole. This will include their part of it and to a greater or lesser extent – depending on the time they have been in the organization – other individuals. In this picture, whole groups of people may be lumped together, alliances seen (which may or may not actually be there), and there will be a view about power and the way the person thinks it is distributed. The important thing about this internal picture is that it may not actually tie up with the 'real' structure – the structure on paper. However, because it is a strong influence on each individual, and may remain unspoken, it represents a 'psychological' level of the organization which is ignored at the organization's peril.

Imagoes represent the individual's developing pictures of themselves and others in the organization, team or group, taken at different points in time. As mentioned above, this is part of the private structure of an organization, in that it cannot be seen, other than possibly in the resulting behaviour of an individual. These individual perspectives will all have their impact on the dynamics and processes that occur within the group. Because the psychological level is more powerful than the roles and structures, any lack of safety is likely to be played out through games (Chapter 9) and substitute feelings (Chapter 10). An example here might be a team agreeing to a course of action which some members don't, in reality, agree with, resulting in failure despite their apparent commitment.

Our internal picture will be more generalized in the earlier stages – lumping people together into recognizable groups (for instance *all men* or *all women*) but will show a greater recognition – termed 'differentiation' – of individuals as time goes on.

The following diagrams are a useful way of illustrating our internal pictures of a group, teams, project groups, or committees. Berne's diagrams show our internal pictures of the group and will be different for different members at different times. We have adapted these diagrams and names for ease of reference.

Stages of Groups

All groups go through different stages. An understanding of these is useful to enable group development to occur as quickly as possible.

We have called the first diagram *Who Are They?* This illustrates the fantasy, or image, that we have in our minds before we meet anyone in the group. If we know the manager, and perhaps one or two others, they will be in our picture. This would also hold for other groups we join, such as project groups, action learning sets or training courses. In this case we draw the key figures within an oval, which represents the boundary between the team and its environment. The raised bump at the top of the diagram represents what Berne (1966) called the *leadership slot*. This is important, since especially in the early stages of a group, the leader is one person who is clearly identifiable, and who has overall responsibility for the group.

At this stage our major concern is ourselves and how we will fit in. We know that the leader is an important power figure and therefore they are the only person we have differentiated. The questions individuals might be asking themselves here are likely to be:

- Who am I in this team?
- Do I want to be part of this team/organization?
- Will I be accepted?

The *Who Are They?* imago looks like this:

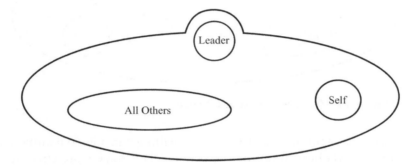

Figure 11.8 Imago: Stage one

The second imago created is when the individual has arrived in the group and feels comfortable with some members. At this stage they are making connections with certain people whilst others are still unknown. They will also be observing the leader and watching how they operate to see if they are trustworthy and meet their expectations – positive or otherwise.

This adjusted image is called: *Some Are OK* imago and looks like this:

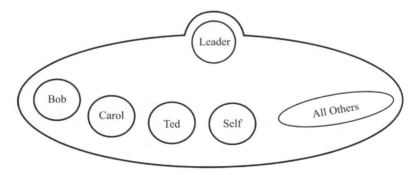

Figure 11.9 Imago: Stage two

Then the individual may start to get into conflict with the boss or leader. Perhaps they are not how the individual would like them to be or their behaviour is not what they expected. This may reinforce previous experiences including, perhaps, in their family and they might think 'Typical. Here we go again. This always happens to me'. At this point, they may react by withdrawing, storming out of the room or getting into conflict with the leader. Those people who are important in the group imago will be the ones who are involved in the conflict with them, and all others may pale into insignificance. This diagram is called the *This Is Me* imago and looks like this.

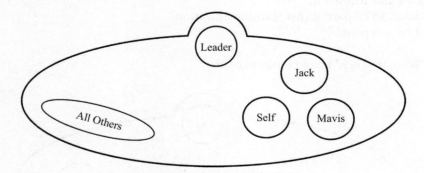

Figure 11.10   Imago: Stage three

At this stage it is important that the leader is willing and able to maintain an OK–OK position and keep level-headed during the conflict. This stage represents the individual working out if the leader is strong enough to ensure group stability, to develop a trusting environment and stay OK–OK with themselves and others.

Next we have the *Get On With* imago. This is where other people are recognized and accepted, even if there is not always agreement. This means that each individual is experienced as an individual – *differentiated* from others. This is the time in the group where people get on with the task, discuss differences and achieve results that are greater than any individual might have achieved on their own. This is the time when people feel safe enough to be really productive. Productivity will increase since less energy is being spent on establishing reliability and trust. The Get On With imago looks like this:

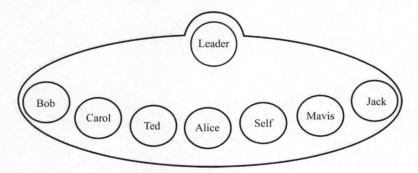

Figure 11.11   Imago: Stage four

When a new member comes into the group, or someone leaves, the participants may well return to an earlier stage and repeat the other stages until they feel safe again with the new person and the changed group.

Summary

All of the diagrams in this chapter can be used to assess how people think the organization, division, department or team is at the moment and where they would like it to be. The diagrams can be used as a basis for discussion and ways found to consider how to make the changes required to achieve a shared vision.

EXERCISES

EXERCISE 1

The Influence of the Primal Leader

If you are a leader, consider if your style of leadership fits with that of the primal leader – this is the person who makes decisions that cannot be vetoed by others. Do you experience them as having any influence on the organizational culture? Are you happy with the congruity or incongruity between the primal leader's style and your own? If not what will you do to change this? or...

If you are the primal leader, what is the evidence that the workforce are as productive and co-creative as they could be? What do you think might be your responsibility in this? If this could be improved, what could you change in terms of your leadership style? What support do you need to do this? How will you monitor the changes? What evidence will you look for?

EXERCISE 2

Dynamics

1. Consider your department or team and draw one of Berne's dynamics diagrams in a way that reflects the boundaries within it.
2. Is it how you would like it to be?
3. What could you do to change it, or maintain it if you think it is working well enough?

EXERCISE 3

Initial Imagoes

1. Consider when you went to a meeting, a conference, or joined a new team, and knew no one. If you are unable to think about a past situation perhaps there is one you will be going to in the future.
2. Does your internal image reflect that of the first group stage above – Who Are They?
3. If it does, is there anything you needed prior to arrival for you to be at your most confident? This might include more information about the event, including who is going to be there, the aims and objectives or your role.
4. If it does not reflect the first image consider what is different and why this might be? Is this of benefit to you and how did it, or will it, affect your relationships with others in the group, including the leader? Or, if you are the leader, how will this affect you?
5. If you are exploring a past event, what could you have done differently? If you are considering a future event, then what will you do now in the light of this new awareness, if anything?

12 *Integrative Leadership*

Introduction

Leadership and management roles require a range of skills, expertise and a 'leadership attitude', that is, positive, principled, professional, and decisive. The ability to integrate the needs of the organization and, at the same time, take account of the workforce and make effective decisions, is highly prized – and much sought after. In one way this whole book is about acquiring insights into these skills but this chapter aims to explain specific aspects of management and leadership. Our term 'Integrative Leadership' reflects the need to 'integrate' organizational goals with the people skills available and underpinning this with a strong value base. It is necessary to focus on the range of aspects that leaders are required to integrate in order for their style to be congruent.

The Landscape

In general a manager's role is to establish and maintain order, structure and predictable certainty within a business or a team in order to achieve objectives, deadlines and budgets. This is a far more practical role than that of a leader. The leadership task is to bring about learning and inspire, or maintain the inspiration of followers to contribute to the visions and goals of the organization. These days, with leaner organizations it is important to have people who can be both managers and leaders who can inspire the workforce as well as be strategic. They also need to have the facility to be led as well as lead when the situation calls for it. Linking both functions can enable greater understanding about resources and structures and promote effective realistic practice, whilst still permitting calculated risks. For the purposes of this book we take the perspective of an integration of these roles and functions.

Leaders exist at all levels of the organization and Berne (1963) noted three type of leader: responsible, effective and psychological.

If you are the *responsible* leader you are the one with whom the 'buck stops'. You stand or fall by your decisions and those in higher authority expect you to account for yourself should things go wrong. You need to be working with others to align the organizational goals with the values, behaviours and commitment of the total workforce.

If you are the *effective* leader you will be seen in the thick of what is going on – involved first hand. You will be listened to by others and have your opinions and suggestions heard and acted upon. You will have proved yourself over time and, even if you are not the responsible leader, you are trusted to make decisions.

In smaller organizations it is possible to be both the responsible and the effective leader. However, the norm is for you as responsible leader to create an operational leadership role beneath you. This operational leader is the one who is effective with day-to-day matters but the responsibility still lies with you as their boss. As long as the operational leader fulfils their role, all will be well, as this releases you to deal with strategic and political matters.

As the *psychological* leader you can benefit or harm the team or organization. The psychological leader sets the tone, attitude and culture and great things will be expected of you for example to be perfect and healthy and wise all the time. You will be looked to for guidance about agreeing or resisting actions. This will often be observing your response to what is being proposed, rather than necessarily asking you. The psychological leader is part of the private structure of the team (see Chapter 11). You will not usually be overtly recognized as a leader but will, even when you are not aware of it, be influencing others. There will be benefits for the organization and game playing will be minimized when you keep yourself and others OK.

Let's take a case example to illustrate these three types of leader:

Ali is a newly appointed director. He enjoys the challenge of developing people's skills and talents so that they can enjoy influencing the organizational development, enabling it to go from strength to strength. The senior management team are aware that he means what he says and says what he means, so they are reluctant to get into the political manoeuvring that they used to engage in with the previous director. Because of this some of them feel safer than they used to and are less stressed. The work environment feels lighter and there is an air of camaraderie.

Samantha is the deputy manager; she is efficient and competent and makes good decisions. She was acting director before Ali came but did not want the post long-term and so did not apply, even though she was invited to do so. As she had a good reputation prior to Ali taking up the post he knows that she can be trusted to continue to make good decisions now. They made agreements about this in some detail so that Samantha is aware what sort of decisions she can make. The workforce trust and like Samantha and know that she will support them in new ventures. Amongst the workforce there is good leadership at most levels.

Within the senior management team there is one member, Ray, who tends to influence the group. He has set the level of joking and banter as well as the commitment to do a good job and on time. He has good boundaries and does not over-commit himself or those who report to him. If anyone should make 'You (or They) are Not OK' comments, including those that are racist or sexist, Ray will find ways to confront them whilst also managing to keep the individual OK.

This case study shows that Ali is the responsible leader, Samantha the effective leader and Ray the psychological leader. It is quite possible that Ali could become both the responsible, effective and psychological leader and in large organizations these roles often need to be shared between more people. The more capable someone is, with a Life Position of OK–OK, the more likely they are to be all three types of leader. However, leaders are required at every level of the organization so that even where someone is not the responsible leader it is important that their potential to move into the other types of leadership is recognized. This is particularly so when they have the potential to become a psychological leader with negative consequences. The responsible and effective leaders will then need to decide how they will respond to ensure the workforce use their energy positively.

The following case study, based on an actual situation, outlines an example where the psychological leader used her influence negatively:

Dot was a new team member, in her mid twenties, quite noisy and who liked to be the centre of attention. May, a long-established team member, received accolades for her work and was invited to an award ceremony where she would be recognized as the lead person of a research project that had attracted substantial funding for the organization. May's work frequently took her out of the office and whilst she was out Dot would find ways to stir things up amongst the team. Some of the team were afraid of Dot as she was bright and articulate and thought that their lives would be easier if they went along with her, even when this meant agreeing not to talk with May when she came in. May became stressed about the situation and one or two of her colleagues would say 'hello' in whispered tones and then stop as soon as Dot came in. Eventually May took out a grievance against Dot and sought counselling support, paid for by her organization. An investigation ensued but when each team member was interviewed they were so afraid of Dot that they blamed May for being arrogant and not talking to them.	*Here the psychological leader is acting in detrimental ways to the team and therefore to the organization. The organization could not believe that everyone could be wrong and so they found no evidence for the grievance May took out on Dot. May left the organization and they found themselves without a talented researcher whose previous track record with people had been exemplary. Eventually the truth about the situation came out as another team member was losing sleep and went to see her boss about what had happened. However, by this time they had lost a valued member of their staff.*

When a psychological leader's actions are detrimental to the organization the leadership needs to find ways to get a grip on the situation. Without this the responsible leadership will not be effective and the organizational culture will be unsafe and there will be a lack of trust. In the situation above with Dot and May there appears to be a lack of leadership as there was no management awareness of the shunning May had experienced. Had there been awareness through the supervisory process it could have been addressed early on and it is unlikely to have developed into a grievance procedure and someone leaving. The wider organizational culture may also have required analysis to see if there was general collusion with bullying and therefore lack of emotional safety.

Responsibility

Responsibility is an important issue in an organization. Responsibility involves solving problems instead of blaming. At all levels people can only respond if they have the resources to do so. These include authority, qualifications and abilities. This links with Chapter 16 – Concepts for Thriving – since you will only take responsibility when you feel safe.

EXAMPLE

Let's look at the following examples in terms of responsibility:

1. Maria's department is made up of one other woman, Fiona, and eight men, including her boss. The department deals with a lot of internal and external calls. Fiona experiences being sexually harassed by Ted, one of the men in her team but has only informed Maria about this. Every time someone calls, Ted comes off the phone and is rude about the caller. Very often this tirade includes a lot of swearing and if the caller is female Ted makes sexist comments, all of which Maria finds offensive. She goes to her boss and tells him that she finds Ted's behaviour offensive and is told to deal with it herself. This stresses her as she is quiet by nature and does not wish to upset anyone or 'rock the boat'.	*Maria's boss is right to encourage her to be assertive; however, he too needs to take some responsibility for the culture of his department. Maria needs his backing to deal with this issue, which in fact is one he needs to address himself in the first instance. Without doing so he is colluding with Ted's behaviour. He is not taking account of his own role and responsibilities as a manager and fails to appreciate the effect of Ted's behaviour on the atmosphere of the department. Where leaders collude with negative and sexist behaviours it is even more difficult for women to assert themselves as they are unlikely to be supported should the assertive behaviour receive further aggressive responses. This is not the sort of environment where a 'do it yourself' approach is likely to work.*
2. Jarvis is the leader of a group of sales staff. He comes across as an angry man who has a tendency to want to catch others out in some way. His bosses send him on a managing conflict workshop as an attempt to change his behaviour. Jarvis does not engage with the process saying that being angry works for him. In fact his team make sure they are out of the office as much as possible in an attempt to avoid him. Productivity is average for this team and does in fact go down when Jarvis is away, which only serves to reinforce his view that his style works.	*Management appear to be putting the responsibility onto the consultant to change Jarvis' behaviour. Jarvis has no investment in changing – he is in Criticizing Mode and his behaviour is usually from an I'm OK, You're Not OK position. There are no management interventions so Jarvis does not experience a problem. However, Jarvis' analysis of the situation is based on somewhat skewed thinking. It is true that the workforce do work when he is angry as this is a result of being scared. When Jarvis is not there, they rebel in safety by doing very little – 'when the cat's away the mice will play'. Jarvis is using a coercive style of leadership which is based on fear. The way in which he is using his power means that there will be less creativity and less effective problem-solving as energy is spent on survival. If Jarvis were to change, productivity would go up as people would feel safe (see Chapter 16 on Concepts for Thriving) and would pull together. Management also need to take their responsibility and supervise and manage Jarvis.*

3. Sarbjit is a head of service who stands by her team and considers their views and their workloads. She is being pressured by her manager to pass on more and more paperwork to them but she resists doing so as she knows they are already overloaded. Instead she looks for alternative ways to deal with the problem, which include consulting with staff about the situation, looking for where savings could be made and where funding could come from to employ extra staff so that the increase in administration could be taken up. When her staff come to her for help she listens and encourages them to solve the problem as they know their job better than anyone else. Whilst some management members find Sarbjit's assertiveness frustrating they respect her for setting boundaries and for finding creative ways to deal with issues rather than just complying and becoming stressed.	*Sarbjit consults as well as protects her team. She largely uses her Mindful Process to consider her options. She wants to encourage her workforce to take responsibility as she is aware that those doing the job usually know best. Her team therefore respond to her and respect her as she is not afraid to express herself and be creative and she in turn respects them. She is able to keep her eye on the organizational goals and find ways to maintain her team's direction within these goals. Her team feel safe and productivity is high. Sarbjit uses her power, competence and knowledge and takes into account other people's personalities, competence and skills and encourages others to be creative and take responsibility. In this way her team feels valued and is therefore more likely to value themselves and others.*

In the Maria case study the manager is using the Inconsistent or Reckless Mode of behaviour (see Chapters 3 and 4) and does not take responsibility. Instead the manager needs to consider the situation from his Mindful Process and decide whether to:

- Use the Structuring Mode and see Ted during one-to-one supervision and require him to change his behaviour. If Ted's response is dismissive then the manager would need to decide at which level Ted is discounting (See Chapter 8) – it is likely that he is discounting at the level of existence of a problem, and might blame Maria for being 'over-sensitive'. If this were the case the manager would need to find ways to get Ted to accept that there is a problem, which at the very least is distressing Maria who has a right to work in a supportive environment. In addition the fact that he puts people down in their absence is not-OK behaviour. Regardless of Ted understanding the reason for changing his behaviour, the manager needs to set the boundary which he can do from the Structuring Mode, informing Ted that his behaviour needs to change as he will not tolerate it in his department.

- Other options for the manager might be that boundaries are set via the Playful Mode, such as: 'Okay Ted, let's see how long you can go without putting someone down when you come off the phone. You never know you may be able to have a happy day because of it!' This option would of course be the first step in the process and if Ted's behaviour did change then no further interventions would be required.

- If staff challenge Ted, the manager would need to come in and support them. It is important to start with lower level interventions to see if they work before going down the route of grievance procedures to put in boundaries. If the culture is one that has permitted aggressive behaviour, for instance the male colleague making sexual approaches to Maria's colleague Fiona, then this may change once the leader changes. However, it is always Maria's right to take out a grievance procedure, particularly if the manager himself does not seem prepared to challenge Ted and there is a culture of aggression within the department – and possibly the organization.

In the Jarvis case study, the management need to acknowledge the impact of his behaviour on team members and therefore productivity. They are discounting information (Chapter 8) at the level of personal ability. They know there is a problem, but believe that a Managing Conflict course will sort it out. They are not taking their responsibility as managers and appropriately supervising the situation. Productivity will remain low and respect for leadership will lessen leading to an alienated workforce.

In the final case study, Sarbjit demonstrates effective Integrative Leadership. She is willing to acknowledge other's expertise whilst at the same time taking responsibility for decision-making. She is well respected by her team as well as by the management and her team work well even when feeling overloaded as they know Sarbjit is working to support them.

These case studies highlight both the managerial and individual levels of responsibility and uses of power. If we are out of touch with a sense of our own power we may attempt to obtain this through power *over* rather than power *with* others. Therefore the way we use power as a manager and leader will affect the success of the organization. Managers and leaders need to have the capacity to create change despite resistance (and by extension the ability to resist unwanted change).

You learn to discount your ability to solve problems in early childhood if you are not given the opportunity to learn from making mistakes. Later, when you go to work, your ability or lack of ability, to make decisions is influenced by this early life experience. You may have decided not to take risks as you believe that risk-taking is dangerous. Alternatively, you may have found that if you take control of situations you feel safer – even if this means being a bully. Whatever experiences you had as a child they are likely to influence the way in which you use power now. This is what is called 'transference', where you carry over some aspect of the past into the present, which may be helpful or unhelpful. Thus, when you work for an organization you can find that the leadership style may reinforce or clash with the way in which you believe leaders should be.

Sharing Power

When people develop new organizations they are often enthusiastic, creative, risk-takers. As these new structures develop those who started it all off need to remain open to new ideas as this is good for individuals as well as productivity. Unfortunately the primal leaders sometimes make it difficult for others to come alongside them as they enjoy the elite status they have achieved. Managers and leaders in this position feel too threatened to encourage autonomy and rarely delegate decision-making. Morale will decrease if you are a leader who resents the workforce acting as if they are equal and in these situations politicking and game playing will ensue and productivity will go down.

If you are one of the founders or primal leaders you need to ensure that the organization develops in a healthy way by recognizing that there are stages to growth and allowing other people to come alongside you, sharing their thoughts and aspirations. When this happens you are more likely to be using the Mindful Process in the OK Modes model.

A good example of this is Frank Gehry, the famous Canadian architect who designed the Guggenheim Museum in Bilbao. His way of working is to create the design for the building in the way an artist would, by sketching and then making models of the structure. Eventually Gehry was persuaded to use computer-generated designs and, whilst he had not been an advocate of computers, he followed this suggestion and other people found ways to convert his models into computer designs.

Gehry recognized the need to develop with the times and to use the resources that were available. He is not threatened by others who have the skills to do what he cannot. Instead he employs people to do what he cannot do, or is not interested in doing. Gehry was also not too proud to go for help to enable him to release his creative talents when he realized that he was stuck.

As a leader you will need to keep an eye open for your own egotism and be aware when you are enjoying the status more than the process of being a leader. This may be the time to find a good coach, and question values, beliefs and processes.

Your Attitude is Catching: The Change Process

During any period of change, the primary task for leaders is to decide on their attitude. Beliefs about change being problematic and detrimental promote the development of hostile pessimistic attitudes to the process. Hostile attitudes will pass throughout the team, department and organization where others will reinforce this negativity, creating fragmentation, games and conflicts. In contrast, seeing change as an opportunity for growth and development will develop an attitude of optimism which is more likely to be enabling.

Change is part of life and you need to grow with it rather than fight against it. As a leader it is important to develop resilience (see Chapter 2) so that the workforce can be encouraged and supported when they are struggling.

During the 1914 Trans-Antarctic Expedition Sir Ernest Shackleton showed great resilience. The ship he and his crew were on became trapped in the ice and remained for 634 days in Antarctica at sub-zero temperatures (Perkins, 2000). Shackleton faced extraordinary demands on his mental and physical endurance while at the same time he was determined to get the crew home safely. During this time he made personal sacrifices for his crew, giving up such important items as his boots, gloves and biscuits to those in greater need. He also took the longest watch, as he was concerned about the physical and psychological health of the men. He inspired unswerving loyalty and his attitude kept everyone going. Had his attitude been one of defeat and negativity the expedition would not have reached safety. Of course, there are lessons to be learnt by the failure of the expedition to reach its goal, but in this instance we are making the focus Shackleton's positive attitude. Whilst today's organizational difficulties cannot be likened to the life and death situations faced by Shackleton and his crew there is learning here regarding issues of resilience and leadership.

In today's computerized world it appears that many exaggerate risk and have developed low frustration-tolerance. For example, how many people do you see sitting in a traffic jam and hitting the steering wheel because they are frustrated? Does it get them through the traffic any faster? No. Does it get them hyper-aroused, agitated and therefore stressed? Yes. Good leadership is about remaining calm, acknowledging the difficulty, creating options and taking the appropriate action.

Panicking about a situation leads to less thinking which might even delay a process. Staying calm within the situation promotes clear thinking and accounting. Taking the traffic jam example the following questions may be helpful:

- Are you able to change the situation?
- Is it something you can influence?
- Can you call someone and let them know you are going to be late?
- Is there something that can be learnt from this situation? For example, the road is notorious for hold-ups and you had previously considered using a different route. You could have looked up to see if there were any road works on that stretch of the motorway and any warnings about long delays.
- Did you leave sufficient time for the journey in case there were any hold-ups?

Whatever the learning, right at that moment you are still in the traffic jam and, as you are not in control of the difficulty, then you may as well relax and wait for the problem to be resolved – and, if it is an accident, be concerned for the victims and relieved that you were not involved.

Whilst this example concerns traffic the same is true at work. Very often you can become stressed about things you have no control or even influence over. At work you might like to consider the following questions:

- Where it is possible to control or influence are you expressing your opinion in an OK–OK way?
- What ways are you using to get yourself heard?
- Are you being open in discussions?
- Are you listening to other's perspectives and considering them and updating your beliefs and opinions?
- Are you keeping your sights on where you want to go and then deciding on how you are going to get there?
- When there are obstacles in your way how do you deal with them in general and then specifically for a particular situation?
- Do you see difficulties as challenges or problems that overwhelm you?

Someone who sees challenges rather than problems is likely to be more resilient. The person who says 'This always happens to me' or 'They never listen' is less likely to be effective than someone who acknowledges the situation, considers it, decides what they are responsible for and takes action.

When there are long-term objectives – for example when planning a journey from Brighton on the south coast of Britain to the Outer Hebrides off the north-west coast of Scotland – you may also need to focus on some shorter term objectives and take several breaks and celebrate when you get to those. Resting and celebrating are important and often get lost in times of change. You are usually so busy dealing with the day to day issues that celebrating achievements often gets overlooked. When this happens stress will increase and morale will decrease, thereby causing friction and game playing.

As managers and leaders you have an important role to play in every day working relationships as well as during change. However, during times of change, recognition and support need to be maintained and, in some cases, increased. Information needs to be shared regularly and as fully as possible. When organizational restructuring has taken place, account also needs to be taken of the need for inter-team building. In addition those whose behaviour is oppositional and/or hostile need to be engaged rather than ignored.

You also need to be a role model for how to manage change. You need to instil optimism and confidence based on the reality of the situation. You also need to consider what different individuals need as the change process continues as this is likely to vary dependent on their position on the competence curve (see curve and chart on page 228 and 229).

Issues which Affect Leadership

Your past experiences affect how you are as a leader and a follower.

If you are someone who seeks other people to provide the Structuring Mode for you, and then the organization downsizes or reorganizes you are likely to seek someone else, or another structured organization, to fill the gap. If you are unable to find this there is a danger of not managing. (For diagrammatic ways to consider this take a look at Chapters 3 and 4.)

The way you have internalized your past experiences influences both your Structural Parent Ego State, and your Child Ego State. This in turn will affect how you are as a follower and how you are as a leader. The other influences in the Parent Ego State may include the national culture, our subculture, and the organizational culture.

This concept is useful when considering leadership and the way you are able to be led yourself as it shows the different messages that you may automatically play in your head. As discussed in Chapter 3, some of the people whose attitudes and behaviours you have internalized without realizing may be detrimental and some may be useful. You need to be able to turn the volume up on the useful ones and down on the harmful or negative ones.

It is possible, and important, to incorporate new positive Parent messages as you go along and particularly so when learning new ways of managing or leading. You might see someone in the organization that you would like to emulate in terms of leadership style. The way to incorporate this person's behaviour is to consider what they might say in different situations and what they might do. For example, when on an outward bound course you see Jo, a manager from another department, who is in your team. A difficult decision has to be made and Jo has taken the lead. She is clear, concise and encouraging. As a leader Jo is excellent at setting boundaries to ensure safety and is great at celebrating achievements. You think, 'I'd like to be like that' and you find opportunities to watch Jo in different situations. Back in the workplace you aim to emulate Jo's skills, choosing to turn the volume up on the new messages you wish to incorporate into your Parent Ego State and down on previous negative self-talk from other aspects of your Parent Ego State.

When in difficult situations at work you can then ask yourself what Jo would have said and find that you are making clear rational decisions, taking on board other people's comments. Eventually, Jo's voice becomes your own as you have incorporated her positive behaviour and values and you are now congruent with how you wanted to be. Of course, in reality, Jo's voice was always your own but this process enables you to integrate new behaviour more easily. Once you are operating more naturally with these new skills, you will have integrated these new Parent messages into your here and now, Integrating Adult Ego State, making it your own.

You may use different people for different areas of your life. For example, when outdoors walking on rough terrain you might draw on an experienced walking friend and imagine them saying to you 'Watch where you put your feet', and this keeps you safe. Whilst at work you might hear your coach saying 'You are a national expert on leadership. It is not appropriate to lose your temper in this situation. Calm down and think.'

As this is an internal or intra-psychic process you can use the Structural Ego State Model to think about this because you are in effect, intentionally growing a new Parent Ego State that you can then integrate into your Integrating Adult Ego State. This is a staged process: first you need to recognize the need for a new positive message yourself and then look for people you can use to help you do this. When in difficult situations consider what that person (or people) would do, say or think in this situation. Eventually this new way of being is integrated within you and you talk to yourself naturally in this way, taking care of yourself and others in ways that are appropriate to the situation.

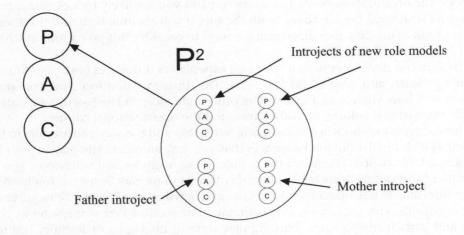

Together these constitute the Parent Ego State

Figure 12.1 The P2 Diagram

Energy and Motivation

To understand energy and motivation we need to understand both the personal and the social areas of our lives. This is where the breadth of the organizational TA approach is most effective.

Motivation is a complex issue, influenced by many variables and having many different theories. TA has its own perspective on the subject. Although it has often been reduced to 'seeking strokes', Berne's theory recognized the complexity of working with both the individual and the social. He did not speak specifically about theories of motivation, instead he offered ideas about how we structure time, which he termed 'hungers' (Berne, 1972). (see also Chapter 15 on stress.)

CASE EXAMPLE

When Miranda started her new job she was enthusiastic and keen to learn new skills and develop the learning she had acquired. Her team leader had a Please Others Driver and had difficulty making decisions herself and let others make decisions from a desire not to 'rock the boat'. Miranda had some ideas about how to streamline systems and would go to her team leader and make suggestions about how to improve things. Unfortunately, the team leader was reluctant to let Miranda make these changes as he was concerned that this would affect the way others worked and thought it best to leave things as they were. Miranda started to become demotivated and stopped making suggestions.	*In this case Miranda needed a team leader who would listen, acknowledge her creativity and decide if the organization would benefit from these changes. Her job would be to find ways to consult with those whose work might be affected and to decide if, and how, the changes could be implemented. This would have maintained Miranda's creativity and encouraged her to come up with ideas. It would also have sent out a clear message to other employees that the organization was open to new ideas. Productivity would have improved as people became increasingly motivated.*

Theories about motivation developed in the 1920s and 1930s. They led to the awareness that:

- people are motivated by social needs
- rewarding relationships are important at work
- individuals are more responsive to pressure from work colleagues than from their managers

Taylor (1912) promoted *scientific management* which required workers to undertake tasks according to a scheme which purported to be scientific, and in return they would be rewarded with an increase in pay. This theory was uni-dimensional, with employees being seen as economic beings. (This had correlations with the Skinner experiments with animals.) Today we can see that the terminology 'Human Resources' also has an implied sense of employees as economic beings as they are *resources*.

McGregor (1960), on the other hand, believed that people want to learn. He believed that people want the freedom to do difficult and challenging work by themselves. From this perspective, a manager and leader needs to dovetail the human wish for self-development into the organization's need for maximum productivity.

Today modern theorists recognize the need to take social needs into account. This is one of the considerations when organizations consider out-working because people receive fewer strokes (recognition) when working from home. This is one reason why out-workers are often encouraged to go into the workplace at least one day a week.

The environment, including the layout of the working environment, also needs to be considered in order to ensure a balance between technical needs and social needs. Open plan offices are a difficulty for many. Whilst they tend to be economical on space they can be disruptive for those who find noise difficult to deal with. If you are in a leadership position and need to talk confidentially to others on the telephone you can find open plan layouts compromising.

You will find environmental issues more or less important depending on your personality type. Those of you who prefer peace and quiet in which to concentrate will be demotivated and increasingly frustrated by open-plan layouts, whereas those of you who have the ability to concentrate whatever the situation will be unlikely to understand this.

Motivation levels determine the effort we put in and it affects the standard of the output.

Motivation consists of:

- aspiration (or *physis*, the thrust of life itself)
- drive (being keen and enthusiastic)
- inspiration (having a sense of being stimulated)

We are motivated by:

- having a purpose
- being stretched or challenged
- receiving positive recognition or strokes
- making a difference to someone or something
- taking or being given responsibility
- a sense of achievement
- being in a position of leadership *or*
- leadership that is integrative and fair

Although many people start a new job motivated, somehow the processes and systems at work can be demotivating. Given that employees are the organization's greatest assets, more needs to be done to maintain motivation rather than try and re-kindle it once it has declined, as in the above case example of Miranda.

Lack of motivation affects business through lowered productivity, increased sickness levels and the sabotage of the organizational processes. If you are a dissenter and are defined as difficult and dealt with by being discounted then you are likely to feel resentful and withhold ideas. If as a leader you are threatened by dissent the rest of the workforce is likely to take note.

The way in which power is used helps to develop trust and trust promotes motivation. If you use your power in ways that are coercive or over-controlling then the workforce will become demotivated. Instead as a leader you need to use the power that derives from your formal position to ensure there is clarity about decision-making and that there are sufficient accountability procedures. Further, when you offer the appropriate level of guidance and support for people at all levels of the organization trust will develop.

Table 12.1　Fret Diagram

- **F**eedback
- **Re**cognition
  - soon
  - sincere
  - specific
  - positive
- **T**rust

To the left is a mnemonic to help you remember strategies for increasing your own and others' motivation levels. The mnemonic of FRET, as in a guitar fret, helps to recall the strategies to increase motivation, you can then 'play' the energy as if it were music.

The word PACKAGE is an easy way to remember some of the important elements that go into effective motivational strategies:

Table 12.2 Package Diagram

• **P**ositive reinforcement	There needs to be a culture of positive recognition and reinforcement of positive actions and effective work.
• **A**ccounting	Everyone needs to account realities and take action to deal with any difficulties.
• **C**ontracts and communication	Making effective contracts that detail aims, responsibilities, and realistic deadlines. Communication is open and is from the effective modes of behaviour.
• **K**eeping OK–OK	Everyone respects each other and even when disagreeing stays OK–OK.
• **A**chievements	Achievements are recognized at all levels at individual, team, department, levels, etc.; e.g., targets are published and when achieved or surpassed are acknowledged.
• **G**oals	Goals are clear and widely shared. The rationale for changes and developments are communicated to the workforce.
• **E**xpectations	Expectations are shared as part of the contract making process so that there is clarity and no hidden agendas. Any differences in expectations can then be addressed.

When people have ideas, suggestions and challenges that are considered by management everybody wins. Leaders are challenged to analyse the current product, working procedures or structures; those offering the ideas experience being valued; and the organization as a whole develops a vibrant co-creative culture. This Integrative Leadership style has space and place for dissenters. If you are an Integrative Leader you will look for the positive in what they are saying and consider whether there is any merit in what they have to say. This means that you are open to members of the workforce taking the initiative to offer ideas and solutions rather than believing you have to do everything yourself.

Symbiosis

EXAMPLE

The MD of a stockholding company had taken over as head of the family business. The old ways of doing things maintained impermeable boundaries with only the MD (the current incumbent's father) making the decisions. The new MD wanted to change this process and developed a strategy for the development of management and senior staff. To some of them making decisions and initiative was seen as 'crossing a boundary' but the new MD wanted to encourage leadership at all levels. Once the senior management team started to make decisions and take responsibility, both productivity, and the profit margin increased. (Berne drew diagrams to enable the understanding of boundaries within organizations and you can read about these in Chapter 11.) This MD had broken what is called the symbiotic chain.

In TA psychotherapy symbiosis is seen as occurring between two people who are not fully utilizing their structural Integrating Adult Ego States. One result of this is that one person uses only their Parent Ego State and the other, only their Child Ego State in their interactions. Organizational symbiosis tends to develop in those organizations that are authority based and autocratic, or benevolent. They tend to create a hierarchy where, at each level, the person expects compliance from those below and in their turn they are compliant to those above them. As mentioned, we can think of this using either the Structural Ego State Model because this way of operating is transferential that is, carried over from the past, or the OK Modes model. For our purposes we have chosen to use the latter model to illustrate the symbiotic chain:

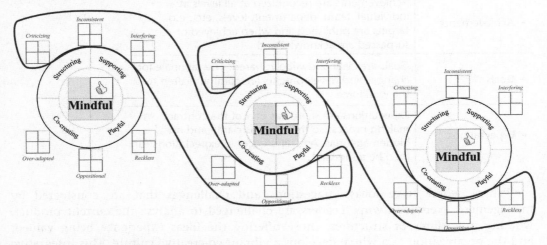

Figure 12.2 The Symbiotic Chain

Let's take an example of a boss who talks down to the manager below him. This manager is then likely to be punitive and dismissive of those below him and so this process is continued down the hierarchy. Each person engages their Over-Adapted Mode in relation to the person above them, and their Criticizing Mode in relation to the person below. Thus, although the chain of authority seems clear, each level adapts to the level above and behaves in an authoritarian way to the level below. The outcome of this is that the workforce engage limited Mindfulness and little critical thinking occurs. Those who have been treated like a child will experience very little power so that when they are leading others they are likely to exert their power through their Criticizing Mode to those below them, thus replicating the unhealthy system and lowering productivity as people feel disempowered and energy goes into maintaining the position rather than dealing with the daily tasks.

Consultations within this symbiotic system will be difficult, if not a waste of time, as employees will still operate within the passive process and be reluctant to express themselves. When someone is promoted from within the organization the symbiotic chain is in danger of being maintained. If someone is appointed from outside the organization those interviewing can, outside of their awareness, choose someone who will fit into this symbiotic process. On occasions when this does not happen and the appointee shows autonomous thinking, they will need to find ways to obtain support in order develop and maintain effective leadership, break the symbiotic chain and maintain reasonable relationships with those above them.

For the people left in the chain below this will be a time of flux and anxiety. Many may escalate their symbiotic processes – for instance being dependent, in an attempt to maintain the homeostasis (the way things have always been), whilst others may rejoice in their new found freedom and enjoy the space to make their own decisions.

Skills

As an Integrative Leader you are not only aware of power that comes from your position but you are also in touch with your personal power. This ensures that you are able to be effective and more likely to manifest Crossman's three P's – permission, protection and potency (1966, 1977).

Permission – you offer permission through trusting others and encourage autonomous thinking, delegate, accept challenges and ask for ideas.

Protection – you defend your team when with others whilst at the same time you are willing to listen for the grain of truth in what may be said. You will also facilitate others to fully consider issues and actions and so prevent future difficulties.

Potency – As a potent leader you will be able to maintain boundaries; be prepared to change – based on sound rationale; be open about your thinking and in your communication, and remain OK with yourself and others.

As an Integrative Leader you also need to develop facilitation and coaching styles so that you encourage others to deal with the day-to-day difficulties of self-managed project groups and teams. This requires new behavioural norms, which need to be supported by the organizational culture. If you work with people who are used to the more traditional systems of leadership they may find this threatening and attempt to create impermeable boundaries as a way of preventing the new structures. Dependent on their sphere of influence they may be successful in this or at least be able to delay progress. However, with sufficient support most people will develop and enjoy your new leadership styles.

Being Effective

One key to effective management is effectively managing yourself. You need to ensure that you obtain life balance, give yourself positive recognition, learn from mistakes and seek support from others when needed. If you are a good leader and manager you model the Winner's Pyramid (see Chapter 18) and, at the same time, you are willing to take risks and be congruent in thoughts, feelings and behaviour, being true to yourself. Where your values and goals are not congruent with those of the organization in which you work then the situation needs to be acknowledged and options considered. For example the questions to ask yourself could include:

- What brought you into that organization?
- Are the values and goals so vastly different that you experience difficulties?
- How serious are these difficulties?
- What needs to change within the organization for you to feel comfortable?
- When considering the above changes, which are you in control of, which can you have influence over and which are you unable to influence at all?
- Are you prepared to change your values and goals and if so at what cost?
- What action will you take and by when?

When you want to be heard and have your opinions acknowledged it is particularly important for you to consider your communication style. Your style will be affected if you are threatened or anticipate that you will be threatened, and it is likely that you will become defensive. In the work place any defensive behaviour takes up energy and detracts from the task in hand. Inevitably production will be hampered if you are giving mental time to how you might win, dominate, impress, avoid someone finding out something, or if you give substantial time to how you might avoid being attacked. At such times instructions may go haywire. If you do not address a difficult relationship you have with someone you are likely to become increasingly defensive, this in turn, will lead to more difficulties.

As an Integrative Leader you are able to create supportive climates to work in rather than defensive ones. When the organizational culture is one of evaluating or judging, people go on their guard. Therefore the creation of supportive cultures is affected by *how* you talk to someone, as much as what you actually say. In earlier chapters we discussed how the same thing can be said in different ways and the content of what you say is altered by the tone and inflection of your voice, the speed you say it and its audibility. These aspects will also be affected by the country and region you come from and whether you are male or female.

Tannen (2001) suggests that this latter point is to do with the way females are socialized: '(*women*) who are in some way superior are expected to downplay rather than flaunt their superiority'.

This is true too when those from different cultures come together as their backgrounds will influence their perspectives and if the climate is a supportive one then each person will be willing to acknowledge different perspectives and build on them. The key is to listen and acknowledge different approaches, regardless of gender and culture, rather than be dismissive. You need to consider what you can learn from the differences and what you can do to develop and grow. Again the Winner's Pyramid (see Chapter 9) is a useful diagram to keep in mind when relating with others.

This is very much in keeping with Peck's (1987) stages of community:

- Pseudo-community – where people are conflict-avoiding and act as if they are a community that all get on together.
- Chaos – where people are attempting to convert others to their way of thinking. The aim is to hold on to particular prejudices, stereotypes and frames of reference. This is in keeping with Berne's statement about the need to get rid of all the trash in your head that you have accumulated since coming home from the maternity ward (1972, page 4). People are also wishing to avoid the next stage which would mean changing our frame of reference.

- Emptiness – at this stage people put down all their prejudices and stereotypes and actually see who is there, rather than whom they *think* is there. They stop trying to covert others and are prepared to hear them, even if this challenges their frame of reference. When here people are open rather than defensive.
- Community – this is the stage where people are conflict resolving. Trust has developed in order to do this and they start to understand how others may have different views. There is understanding that everyone comes from different backgrounds and that this enriches, rather than threatens, development. This is where the work will get done.

Whilst organizations are not 'communities' in every sense of the word, many aspects are the same. Teams work better together when there is an understanding of other people and their perspectives. Then, when consulting with others and problem-solving, your views are more likely to be provisional rather than set, allowing for increased communication as people feel valued and accounted. At the final stage teams and departments are more likely to accept necessary unilateral decisions made by leaders because they know that they are valued and their views are sought.

You need to become aware of the linguistic differences for men and women as well as for different cultures. In this way those who have something to say will be heard, even if they say it in a way that does not fit with the cultural norm of the work place.

As the workforce feels acknowledged and valued they will develop a sense of belonging with the freedom and autonomy to contribute and make a difference. The overall culture will benefit from this as will productivity since less energy will be spent on stress and more on the task in hand.

You also need to be aware of the stroking culture of the organization at both the macro and micro levels. To do this consideration needs to be given to:

- How is *success* defined in this organization/department/team and how is it recognized?
- How is *failure* seen here and how is that recognized?
- How is the good enough person recognized? (Hay, 2009)

These questions are important as highly successful people often get rewards, for example through bonuses. In addition, those who are experienced as failing also get recognition (stroked) but through increased attention through coaching and mentoring or capability processes. The person doing a good enough job may not be interested in reaching the heights that those who are successful achieve, and this often means that they may not get very much attention and so feel discounted. They are probably also doing the best they can and it is just not within their ability to be 'brilliant', or perhaps they are not interested in doing the necessary overtime because they want a life outside work. In these situations they may resent not being stroked and, subconsciously, could end up doing less or taking time off sick, or messing up in order to get some recognition. Therefore managers and leaders need to keep in mind the overall stroking culture to ensure equanimity.

Summary

Integrative leadership and management demands a range of personal and professional skills. In order to be highly functioning leaders need to take time out, ensure they obtain sufficient recognition, are assertive and set boundaries whilst at the same time be willing to be flexible. Remaining in *I'm OK, You're OK* on the OK Corral and within the Mindfulness process on the OK Modes model will greatly assist with the leadership task both at the personal and professional levels.

You need to ensure that you pay attention to those who discourage but spend the majority of your time with those who are encouraging. This includes developing your own positive self-talk and ability to remain Mindful. Organizational goals need to be kept in focus so that you are moving toward something rather than spending time holding on to the past. The risk if you do not is that you will stay stuck in limbo, somewhere between the past and the future but not even in the present.

Ensuring you keep a balance between goals, tasks, people and self, underpinned by a strong OK–OK value base with clear contracting, will lead to effective Integrative Leadership.

EXERCISES

EXERCISE 1 – LEADING TO CONGRUENCE

Consider your own organization and answer the following questions:

- Is there congruence between the espoused values and philosophy on the one hand and management and leadership styles on the other?
- Where this is not the case is this due to the individual or to collusion by leaders with more aggressive tactics?
- Is there equity in the way leaders obtain resources?
- What is the stroking culture? What is success and how is it stroked?
- What is failure and how is it stroked?
- How is the worker doing a good job, neither highly successful nor failing, stroked?
- How do I give and receive strokes?
- Do I feel accounted and do I account myself?
- Are any changes needed?
- What strategies could you use to do this?
- Who will you get support from?

EXERCISE 2 – PLAYING MY PART

Have a look at these statements and decide what behaviour or action you need to change, what will you stop doing, continue to do, start doing? Who do you need support from? Do you need any extra training? How will you know when you have achieved your goals? What will be different? Be specific.

professional development questions	Circle number (5 representing most true for you)				
I am clear about the organizational and team's vision and values	1	2	3	4	5
My own goals and values fit with those of the organization	1	2	3	4	5
There is congruity between all aspects of the organization	1	2	3	4	5
I tend to be reticent about sharing my opinion with colleagues	1	2	3	4	5
I feel safe to share my thoughts and feelings with colleagues	1	2	3	4	5
I need to be more structuring to ensure the group is effective	1	2	3	4	5
I have a good Integrating Adult Ego State and this enables me to support the team/department/organization, to be effective	1	2	3	4	5
I am able to relate to a range of people and tend to get myself heard and to hear others	1	2	3	4	5
I have become weary and disenchanted	1	2	3	4	5
I really believe change is possible	1	2	3	4	5

I am prepared to lead from behind so that others feel good about themselves and develop	1	2	3	4	5
I have got the courage to challenge and still support others/the leader, even if I don't agree	1	2	3	4	5
I have earned the trust of others and in turn I trust others and there is open communication	1	2	3	4	5
I have the communication skills to challenge others in OK–OK ways	1	2	3	4	5

Source: Developed from Chaleff (2003).

EXERCISE 3 – THE MODE GRAPH

One way to consider our leadership style is through the use of a Mode graph.

This is a concept that enables assessment of how much energy and time you spend in the different Modes of behaviour (see Chapter 3). The Mode graph is drawn like a bar graph with each bar representing the amount of time spent. The Mindful Process has four different modes and they have been separated out so that each one can be illustrated separately. In this way the authors are acknowledging that we all have different strengths a weaknesses and that some may not yet have full and equal access to all of the Modes – Structuring, Supporting, Playful and Co-creative.

The bar graph below is black and grey, symbolizing effective and ineffective modes respectively (black represents green; grey represents red).

Make a judgement (this will inevitably be your subjective impression) of the amount of time and energy you spend in these Modes using the following diagram. Complete the bar graph, using red (for grey – ineffective) and green (for black – effective) as with the above example.

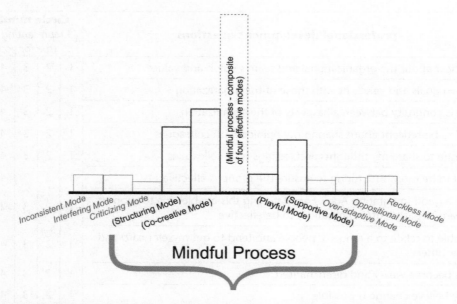

Figure 12.3 Modes of Behaviour Graph: A Completed Example

If your Mode graph is not how you would like it then consider what you will do to change. As there is only a fixed amount of energy, if you concentrate on raising the positive aspects then you will automatically have less energy for the ineffective Modes.

- Are there any differences in the way you treat others and the way you treat yourself, or are they the same?
- Are these ways effective for you in terms of establishing good relationships, getting work done, and enjoying what you do?

You might also like to ask other people for their assessment and ask them to draw their Mode graph of you. If other people's assessments of you are consistent with each other, but not with yours then you could take the opportunity to understand their perspective and decide if you have an investment in changing.

You can also complete one of these for each member of a team to see if everyone agrees with each others perspectives and if there is balance in the team. This would be a useful contribution to 360-degree feedback.

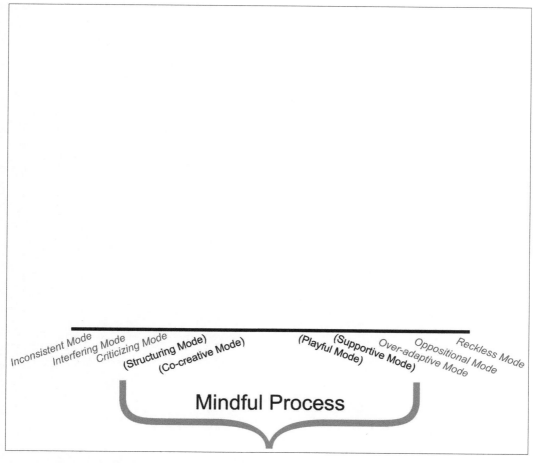

Figure 12.4 Blank Modes of Behaviour Graph

CHAPTER 13 *Culture*

Introduction

In order to make the most of our increasingly globalized economy we need to consider the culture of an organization and the way it sits in this context. How does this culture impact on the individual and the community – and vice versa? In this chapter we will explore how, dependent upon your sphere of influence, your individual perspective can affect the culture as well as how the organizational culture can affect you.

Culture can be defined as a shared set of customs and traditions, values and beliefs, rules, experiences, expectations and behaviours developed and maintained by a group of people. This group of people could vary in size from a nation or race, to a community or a small group or team. Characteristically, this shared experience is learned rather than innate and is transmitted by stories and symbols.

Cultures offer us guidelines by which to live. Life would be impossible without having the broad framework for making decisions mapped out in this way. Whilst we are always left with a level of free choice about how we act and think, having to do this for every single detail in every single moment of our day would be exhausting and grind us to a halt. At the social level, without culture, we would have to be spending all our time negotiating and renegotiating the way forward.

However, the cultures in which we find ourselves may, or may not, be positive in relation to individual or organizational development. Further, we are part of many cultures in our lives: family, work, community, social networks, hobbies, and so on, any or all of which may clash with another one.

AN EXAMPLE

As with most of the case studies we use the following is taken from a real example:

Millie works in an organization with 80 employees. A new director has recently been appointed who has managed to alienate all the middle managers and has restructured the organization, appointing new team leaders who have little experience or skill in management. There have been no consultations with the employees over the changes and no apparent concern about the impending redundancies of the experienced middle managers. This situation has left the staff feeling insecure. The union representatives are blaming one of the middle managers for 'selling out', not realizing that he was one of the people being made redundant. There are an increasing number of factions throughout the organization and people begin to dislike coming into work. One day Millie receives a telephone call from the new director demanding she come into her office. Once there Millie finds another colleague, Sam, who is also involved in the project and an external consultant who the director wanted to be removed from a project as she was inept (something Millie had agreed with). Millie had been given the task of contacting this consultant and terminating their contract. However, the director is now demanding to know who made this decision as the external consultant has come in to find out what the problem is. Sam says that she made the decision and takes full responsibility for it. Millie is amazed at the director's accusations as it was she who initiated the process, and, on hearing Sam take responsibility, cannot work out what on earth is going on. On leaving the office, Sam tells Millie that she is quite happy to take responsibility as the director is obviously too weak to do so. In doing this she believes that she has shown the director how strong she is. The director also has regular meetings with the new team leaders. One day one of the team leaders cannot go and Millie attends as a deputy leader for her team. At that meeting she asks questions about a decision and the new team decides to rescind an earlier decision based on these further considerations. Subsequently the director stops anyone other than team leaders attending the meetings.	*In this example the developing culture is defensive and blaming. The director is coming from the Life Position of I am OK and You're Not OK. Her behaviour is from Criticizing Mode and she appears to be adopting a bullying approach to her directorship. She has appointed people into key positions who are unlikely to disagree with her because they have little experience or skill in managing. This whole process alienated staff and led to a disintegration of the organization. One or two strong personalities are willing to take responsibility and to question the new regime but this is at a cost. Eventually, the morale is at an all time low and even new employees decide to leave.*

Cultural differences are particularly relevant to global organizations – and 'Global Estates' is a hypothetical example of this:

The construction company, *Global Estates*, have developed a site in a Far East Asian country and, as an international organization, they expect the workforce to operate in the same ways as the workforce at UK headquarters. This frame of reference is damaging to the interaction with the local workforce and the local community since their expectations are different. This causes difficulties with motivation and with the retention of employees.

If an international organization imposes a value base without learning about the local culture, and without considering the implications of that imposition, they are discounting at the level of existence of the problem (see Chapter 8). Developing loyalty and motivation is therefore likely to be more difficult. When working in a diverse world, we need to educate ourselves about other races and cultures. Another interesting example is HSBC advertisement in Russia, (seen on a visit in 2010); they have the strap line 'the World's local Bank' – in English – a language not all Russians can be expected to speak or understand and yet calls itself the 'local bank'.

As a generalization, western cultures tend to be individualistic, whereas those of the east tend to be collectivist. The former emphasize the individual, and might benefit from learning from eastern cultures about groups and communities, whilst on their part, collectivist cultures might obtain benefit from nurturing the individual rather more. There are strengths in both as they complement each other.

Culture is reflected through things like:

- beliefs
- values
- myths
- rituals
- language
- slogans
- inside jokes

Organizations need to develop a positive, strong, identifiable culture to which people can belong as this will be helpful to its growth and development. Organizations need to be willing to learn from clients and customers, employees, new directors and board members and yet retain their essential culture. Organizations need to be distinctive yet adaptive.

The concept of the 'Learning Organization' invites organizations to ask 'How can we create learning systems that promote our culture?' Training and performance improvement need to take account of the organizational culture when developing learning and communication systems. In this way positive cultures can be supported, or more negative ones enabled to change (Silberman, 1999).

Organizational Socialization

At the individual level we all bring our own particular frame of reference to the workplace. These different perspectives will have an influence on our work and on how others see us. Sharing a common culture makes it easier, but not necessarily easy, to communicate. When we come from the same country, race, gender, and speak the same language, we can forget that our family of origin, the neighbourhood and school all have their own cultures and these will have their effect on us. We then take our experience of these cultures into our work environment and expect there to be a fit between the organization and our own previous cultural experiences.

Krausz (1986) noted that behaviour is reinforced through socialization and in this way the organization's cultural values and ideologies are imposed on newcomers. These values and ideologies prescribe relationships between individuals and the organization. These specify goals, patterns of behaviour, define forms of control, and direct which qualities and characteristics are rewarded and sanctioned. Naturally through interaction there will be a modifying influence between the organizational members and the organizational culture.

Examples

The following examples highlight how individual leaders can influence the organizational culture.

1) Jane lives for her job. She has no interests outside work. She lives on her own and has few friends other than work colleagues – who she only sees in work time. She is absolutely wedded to the values and goals of the company.	*Jane is likely to get 'burnout' if there is no balance in her life. If she were a leader she may well promote the development of a culture that reflects her 'workaholic' frame of reference. This is then likely to lead to high productivity in the shorter term but high staff turnover and high sickness levels in the longer term.*
2) Victor really only works to earn money. His family and his sailing are the centre of his life. He goes along with what he needs to say and do in his work, but there is always a sense for his colleagues that he is not truly committed to the company.	*If Victor were the primal leader he would need to appoint an operations manager. Unless he has other primal leaders who are partners in founding the organization the culture is likely to be insufficiently competitive to thrive. The benefits of Victor's frame of reference are that he will get less stressed than others because his priorities are elsewhere. The type of organization may also be significant. For example if he established, or works in, a sailing school this might maintain his enthusiasm for work!*
3) Valentine Dyall is the founding director of the Wringtone Corporation, which in its thirtieth year of operation has a turnover of £40 million and employs over 500 people. He does not understand why the strategy team seems to be failing to influence the sales team. The sales team seem to be unaware of the goals and values of the company and seem to go their own way. Valentine rarely brings the teams together and offers very little direction. Goals are not broadcast to the workforce and there is little understanding of each department's relationship with each other.	*This organization requires direction and goal orientation. It would appear that, as the founding director, Valentine needs to be implementing strategies that bring people together as his organization appears to be fragmented. An assessment needs to be made about the psychological distance (Micholt, 1992, Chapter 6) between the different departments, the departments and the management, the management and the board of directors. Goals need to be clear and the workforce needs to understand the relationship between theirs and other's roles.*

In the very Beginning

An organization is developed by an individual or group of individuals, and it is from them that the culture develops. As the organization develops and takes on more people, the sphere of influence any individual has on the culture will depend on their position within the hierarchy – the higher up, the more influence.

We have designed a diagram to show the cultural influences on each of us as individuals. We refer to these diagrams as culture clouds – a pictorial representation of our cultural influences, the relative strength of these and the way that they relate to each other.

The outer circle represents our overall life/personality, value base and culture. The *clouds* within this are aspects of that. If there is a distance between clouds, this indicates that there is no connection between the two aspects. Where clouds overlap with each other, there is a level of influence between them – to the extent of the overlapping. A cloud will influence one which it partially covers and be influenced by one which covers it. If the shading of two or more clouds merge then this signifies that they influence each other equally.

In Jane's culture diagram the overall culture or value system is represented by the outer circle. Work is Jane's sole interest in life and that forms the largest cloud within this circle. She is highly wedded to the company values. She lives on her own, and does not have any friends other than work colleagues. She is no longer in contact with her family of origin, but they instilled in her many of the values that drive her in her work today.

Below is Victor's very different culture diagram. His work and family of origin overlap as it was through his father that he originally got his job, and his father still works for the company. He vows never to let work invade his family life, so although his work cloud overlaps with his family cloud, he takes his family values and beliefs to work with him. His present-day family occupies the largest cloud. Still exerting an influence on present day life is his family of origin, since his mother visits frequently and has views on how children should be brought up, which influence Victor. All of these clouds fall within the pale grey circle – which is the prevailing culture of the country where he lives. His hobby, which is international sailing, takes him to countries all over the world, and leads him to be influenced by all of the different cultures he has experienced.

Given that different aspects of our lives influence us as individuals it is also likely that some may clash with each other as the value base, philosophies and expectations may differ and cause stress.

When we obtain work in organizations we aim to get a 'fit' between our culture and that of the organization. If we are the founder of the organization then our own culture will affect the organizational processes, even outside of our awareness.

Organizations are made up of human beings and therefore constitute living structures. The social patterns, values, traditions and rules that guide their functioning provide a set of formal and informal patterns of behaviour, a frame of reference that defines the relationship between individuals and groups in the organization.

Figure 13.1 Jane's Culture Diagram

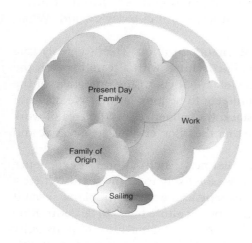

Figure 13.2 Victor's Culture Diagram

The Wringtone Corporation

The imaginary Wringtone Corporation (see example 3 above) is a medium-sized company whose founding director Valentine Dyall still works for the firm. However, he is semi-retired, and his presence is not as influential in the company as it once was. He has been a prominent figure on the UK business scene with outspoken ideas, and so in the diagram this is represented by the fact that the UK culture cloud and his own cloud merge to some extent – they have influenced each other. The UK culture figures very largely – all the current ideas and values about how to do business, and so on, will form part of this aspect of culture. Valentine nowadays only meets regularly with the strategy team, who enjoy the fact that they have this privileged contact with him. So although his continuing influence means that his cloud still figures quite largely in the company culture – and overlaps with the present day leadership cloud – there is some separation between them, as shown by the line being visible at the point they cross. Finally there are the cultural influences of the economy and government policy and legislation. So, in the Wringtone company, the present-day leadership's influence on the culture is somewhat dwarfed by these other influences.

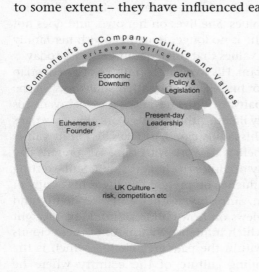

Figure 13.3 Wringtone Culture

Developing a Positive Culture

As we saw in Chapter 11, when considering an organization's culture we need to consider the founder of the organization, their values, ethics and philosophy as well as the context and era the organization was established. Are these still relevant in today's world? What, if anything, needs to change and why?

We also need to consider the general 'feel' of the organization. This is equally true when we are working with one person undertaking coaching, with a team, or with the whole organization. If we only look at the micro view we discount the influences of the macro on the micro and our interventions are unlikely to be long lasting. We may not be able to intervene at all levels but if we understand the influences on the area of work we are involved with we are more likely to ensure that the interventions are effective and long lasting.

Perhaps the culture we are working in is a defensive one. In such cultures we experience being evaluated or judged and when this happens we are likely to be on guard. Where a number of people in different departments have experienced accusation, blame or fault finding, then a defensive culture will develop. This type of culture tends to be controlling with little delegation or consultation. This leads to people taking little responsibility for their actions, or for negative outcomes. In TA terms this is a culture of symbiotic relationships, with some people being in the Criticizing Mode and others in the Over-

Adaptive or Oppositional Mode. The Criticizing Mode tends to be adopted by those in senior positions and the Over-Adaptive or Oppositional Mode by those who report to them. However, as the culture generally promotes the use of these more negative Modes of behaviour it is likely that this will happen between all levels as the workforce attempt to exert what little power they believe they have.

In such situations it is easy to see that change strategies need the development of awareness at all levels, starting with the board and working down. Those at the top would need to be convinced of the necessity for change as they have a vested interest in the way they use power.

Playing Games

Psychological games are more likely to be played within cultures where people try to 'cover their backs'. This in turn leads to a lack of positive recognition and a great deal of criticism, with people being played off against each other. In such situations trust is lacking and people do not feel safe. In this environment we are more likely to over-adapt or be oppositional – perhaps using criticism as a defence. There is little energy left for thinking and autonomy, therefore decision-making is likely to be defensive and lead to less productivity. There is also less interest in supporting others or celebrating achievements and so employees tend not to put themselves forward as experience has shown them that they will not receive positive recognition. In fact, in such a competitive atmosphere they may even be put down for achieving.

In contrast, supportive climates are those where there is more interest in solving problems than in blaming others. The workforce is therefore more willing to take responsibility for mistakes, and creativity, spontaneity and diversity are valued. This diversity is experienced as enabling and therefore equality is accepted as part and parcel of every day life. There are no cut and dried solutions to problems and consultation is a high priority, with those at the top being willing to set boundaries as and when necessary. Managers and leaders are willing to delegate and ask those doing the job what their views are. Because this is a supportive culture, people tend to be empathic with each other. This empathic response encourages potency and responsibility and this leads to the organization being more powerful. As this culture favours individual autonomy it is more likely that there will be leaders at every level of the workforce.

The country and region we come from and whether we are male or female will affect how we say something as well as our perspective on situations. Whether we are heard will be affected by the tone and inflection of our voice, the speed we say it and its audibility. Positive thinking, a belief in abundance – a glass half full rather than half empty mentality – and a desire to understand others first, will all affect the way in which we use language. In this way language influences behaviour and therefore relationships. Language is one way in which we give status to ourselves and others. If we talk down to others then we are saying they are not as good as us. If we do not give others time to end their sentences before we rush in to end them for them, we are saying they are not as important as we are.

The Organizational Culture and Productivity

There is a clear link between the organizational culture and individual beliefs, feelings of self worth and confidence, behaviour and communication. Inevitably this dynamic influences the outcomes and productivity of the organization.

We can think of this as a cycle, which can be negative or positive. Where the organizational culture is one of criticism employees are likely to be over-adapting or oppositional. When this occurs the workforce will tend to develop in the following way:

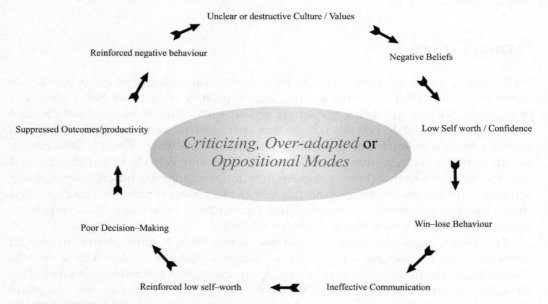

Figure 13.4 Destructive Culture Cycle

This negative cycle results in feelings of low self-worth and lack of confidence and therefore employees will think less because they are likely to be operating from Over-Adaptive or Oppositional Mode. In these circumstances decision-making will be delayed for fear of making a mistake and being blamed for it. Employees at all levels are likely to feel got at or want to 'get' others before they are 'got'. The management expect and espouse a certain set of values whilst their behaviour is not congruent with this. In this Machiavellian environment decision-making will be for the good of the individual rather than for the good of the company and when decisions result in mistakes, attempts will be made to cover them up.

If the cycle is positive (for instance the culture and values promote positive regard, problem-solving rather than blaming, with the person doing the job being recognized as the expert in that job), then employee's beliefs tend to be positive. The individual's self-worth and confidence will be high and the behaviour that goes with this will be supportive, creative and good humoured. This will lead to effective communication which, in itself, improves self worth and confidence, and 'outside the box' decision-making is encouraged. In turn this will lead to high productivity and more effective outcomes. This will be a congruent organization that invests in its employees as well as in its products.

A positive cycle would look like this:

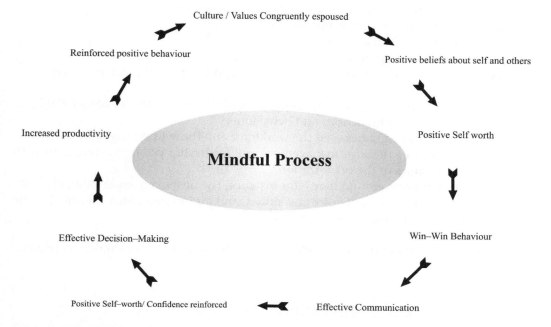

Figure 13.5 Positive Culture Cycle

Nature of Relationships in an Organization

In order to ascertain the nature of relationships in an organization, department or team we might consider the following questions:

- When was the company founded?
- Who is the organizational Euhemerus and what is their legacy and canon?
- Are these founders reflected in the way the organization operates today?
- What are the values and philosophy of the organization now?
- Is there a written 'manual' about these values and philosophy?
- Does the organization function differently now than it did in the past and, if so, how?
- What governmental rules and regulations impact on the organization's functioning (for example, health and safety)?
- To what extent does the authority and personality of the founder/s influence management and leadership?
- Is this positive and supportive?
- What stories and myths are told about past 'heroes'?
- What formal and informal relationships exist?
- Where can good relationships be built on and poor ones improved?
- Do the relationships reflect the organizational values?
- Are there clear underpinning values?
- Is there openness and willingness to confront difficulties?

- Is there trust and support between employees at all levels?
- Are conflicts resolved?
- Are relationships with other groups, teams, departments sound?
- Are people prepared to review the way they operate?
- Do efforts match values and purpose?
- What kind of culture is desired?
- How does the present culture reflect the values, philosophy and actions of the founder?
- Are these relevant, appropriate and supportive of the organization's goals today?
- Are they congruent with actions and behaviours?
- What is the relationship between the workforce and those in management?
- Is the behaviour of those in management and leadership positions congruent with the espoused values of the organization?
- How are things done around here – for instance, the unspoken expectations that are transmitted through tone of voice and stories, and for instance being informed of the good news and only implying the bad news?

The answers to these questions will facilitate decision about the most appropriate interventions.

Cross-Cultural Communication

Since the second half of the twentieth century the workplace has become increasingly diverse. Understanding communication differences and acknowledging these differences will lead to effective relationships. No matter how much knowledge a leader has, if their communication skills are poor then the workforce will have little trust in or respect for them.

Very often our language and the phrases we use are inherited and second nature to us. We might use stereotypical language without realizing that we are violating cultural rules. If we are to operate in OK–OK ways, we need to update ourselves and ensure that we give consideration to these differences.

Stereotyping tends to lump everyone into one group rather than see someone as an individual – 'He is always late, but then (ethnic origin) always are'. The reason we do this is so that we do not have to challenge our frame of reference and the world can remain the same as we thought it was. Therefore we maximize the differences between people rather than looking at the similarities.

We might also stereotype by qualifying our statements when we don't need to. For example: 'The articulate (ethnic origin) worker', implying that certain groupings usually have low verbal skills.

The way in which different cultures listen to each other varies. Some experience constant eye contact as a violation. In some cultures it is also acceptable to interject with a viewpoint and this would not be seen as discounting the other person, as it is in other cultures including the white British culture.

Cultural expectations will also need to be considered when we want to give someone recognition (a stroke using TA terminology). If there is a difference between what different cultures find acceptable we can offend. For example, if it is natural and usual for us to give recognition to a colleague for receiving an award then we are likely to be surprised and perhaps offended if they don't respond with a similar recognition if we receive one. Worse still if we don't receive a response and then ask our colleague what they thought we might be even more offended if they tell us chapter and verse about what they actually think when we only expected or wanted 'You are great and deserve it'.

When considering communication we therefore need to take into account cultural expectations. Even when we do this communication can easily go awry and this is where Transactional Analysis can be helpful. If we inadvertently make a mistake in another culture embarrassment can lead to awkward and difficult relationships. When we remain Mindful, we can consider options for resolving and easing the difficulties.

We (the authors) have rather an amusing example of cultural expectations. Prior to undertaking voluntary training in Armenia we read up about the culture. One thing we learnt was that the Armenians were more formal than we are and tended to dress well for work. The day after our arrival we were taken out round the city of Yerevan before going to a meeting in the evening with the team of translators. Just before her departure our Armenian colleague said to us 'Go home, get dressed, and I will collect you to go to the meeting at 7.00pm'. For us this confirmed our research about being well dressed. On arrival at the meeting we were somewhat surprised to meet the translators who were dressed casually. Again, given our learning, we then thought that this must have been a cultural expectation that the consultants must be well dressed.

At the end of our three-week trip the same colleague was with us and, on departure, before meeting us again in the evening, she said to us 'Go home, get rest and I'll see you later'. It suddenly dawned on us that she had said the same thing three weeks earlier but, because we were not then tuned into her pronunciation of English, we had heard it as 'Go home, get dressed ...' Later, when she told everyone what had happened, the group said that they had thought we were used to formality and had chosen to dress so smartly.

This mix-up, though minor, shows how expectations can affect how we hear something and how we adjust what we find to fit this expectation. In this instance we could all laugh about it but that may not always be the case.

Summary

Culture is an important aspect of working life. It develops from the initial, and subsequent, primal leaders and can have a negative or positive effect on the workforce and on production. If we want to change the culture we first need to understand it and decide what we want and why. Then we can consider the changes and developments that need to take place in order to achieve the desired outcomes.

If a global organization is sufficiently flexible and reflective of the local culture it is more likely to achieve its aims and objectives as the workforce will be more in tune.

The culture of the organization is then like a fugue in an orchestral composition. It is the central theme that runs throughout the organization, and whilst some parts may move away from this theme, they all need to harmonize with each other for a positive outcome.

EXERCISES

EXERCISE 1 – ASSESSING ORGANIZATIONAL CULTURE

Think of an organization you work in or with and consider the following questions:

- What would you say are the characteristics of the culture of the organization? Draw up your own Culture Cloud Diagram, showing the various cultural influences, as described on pages 192–4.
- Which of those elements are important in retaining employees and customers?
- Which of those elements tends to impede performance?
- How can you maintain both the values and styles that are the foundation of its identity and success, and still develop a learning culture in which people and teams grow and through which the organization learns, innovates, experiments, and thrives?
- How can the potential pitfalls of distance and diversity and size best be overcome and turned into opportunities?
- What should the organization's learning priorities be?
- Which policies and practices regarding communication and learning will promote a distinctive culture and excellence in performance?

EXERCISE 2 – THINKING 'MARTIAN'

- What stories, myths and legends are told in your organization?
- How do these stories reinforce the culture?
- Imagine you are a Martian; what would you see if you were looking in at your organization and what sense would you make of this?
- As that Martian, looking in from the outside, what changes would you suggest?

Introduction

The focus of this chapter is bullying as a phenomenon within organizations, rather than the psychopathology of bullying behaviour. If organizations ignore bullying by tolerating it or blaming the victim, this will have serious repercussions for the whole organization not just individual victims. The focus should not be on tolerating the behaviour but stopping it.

In order to understand the process of bullying behaviour it is appropriate to develop some understanding of those who bully. Understanding bullying behaviour can lead the potential victim to be empowered through responding, rather than reacting. Understanding often makes it easier to respond appropriately without taking on the damaging outcomes of bullying behaviour.

Definitions

The Oxford Dictionary defines a bully as:

A person using strength or power to coerce others by fear.

Different definitions of bullying abound and include:

- Unwanted behaviour whether physical or verbal which is offensive, humiliating and viewed as unacceptable to the recipient.

And the following one:

- The misuse of power to intimidate somebody in a way which leaves them feeling, hurt, angry, vulnerable or powerless.

Bullying can take many different forms. It can be blatant or subtle. Even the terminology 'bullying' is difficult as some people believe that this only happens between children and young people; because of this some people prefer the term 'workplace abuse'. The authors will keep the term bullying but wish to emphasize that it takes many different forms, including racism, taunting, undermining, sidelining, sexism and so on.

The following case studies highlight some of the nuances of bullying behaviour.

In this first one there is an issue with a director joining in with belittling behaviour by his reports which carries with it the pull to be accepted in the group by putting down someone else.

Clive, a new director had recently been appointed to the board. He had previously met his CEO at national meetings and appreciated his value base and was therefore keen to work for the organization under his leadership. During one meeting a woman director needed to leave early and, on her departure, the group began to make fun of her and deride her abilities. Clive confronted this behaviour saying he felt uncomfortable that someone was being spoken about in a derogatory way and who also was not in the room. After the meeting he approached his boss saying that he was shocked and surprised that he had gone along with the derisory process in the meeting. He had previously experienced him as expressing a set of values that he would have thought would have been incongruent with this behaviour and would not have expected this of him.	*This situation invites those involved to take part as a way to be accepted and belong. Whether or not the boss shows bullying type behaviours in others areas of work, this is an example of group bullying. Even though the woman being talked about had left the room the derisory comments are likely to be picked up by her at an ulterior level and will be harmful to her, as well as to culture of the group, department and of course to all those involved in the process. It takes great courage to confront the process in a situation such as this. Experience suggests that such a challenge at an early stage is likely to act as a protection to Clive. Once confronted, those who bully tend to leave the challenger alone.*

Bullying is not always obvious. When you make someone's situation difficult, minimize or overload their work these are also forms of bullying that are more difficult to deal with than up-front *I'm OK* and *You're Not OK* responses. The following is an example of this:

Martha experienced the goalposts being shifted by her boss, Tania. One minute she thought she knew what Tania wanted and yet, despite checking this out with her, Tania would later deny ever saying it. Martha was exhausted with the constant changes, with the ever increasing demands on her by Tania and the lack of appreciation for anything she did. Her areas of responsibility were being gradually eroded and she started to feel vulnerable and isolated.	*These types of situations are particularly difficult for individuals to deal with. It is necessary to confirm decisions in writing to ensure that there is clarity about the process and something to refer back to. Tania is inviting Martha to move into a Not OK position and Martha will need to remain OK–OK in order to deal with this. She also requires support both within and outside the organization.*

Contrast these two processes with the following one about much more direct aggressive bullying behaviour.

The team manager, David, had been experiencing difficulties being assertive with his reports. Many of the team members had lost respect for him as he appeared to be favouring one woman, Erin, in the team and giving her the 'best' bits of work to do. This situation arose because David had allowed Erin to be openly sarcastic and facetious to and about him. She had also shouted at him on a number of occasions in the office and this also meant that no one else would challenge her.	*This is an example of overtly bullying behaviour. The team leader has not challenged Erin and therefore her anti-social behaviour has been reinforced. His lack of leadership leads other team members to feel emotionally unsafe and therefore team members move into passive behaviour and do nothing except 'keep their heads down'. Work therefore becomes a stressful place to be and sickness levels increase.*

Bullying behaviours can be seen as on a continuum between more subtle and tactical to the more outright and aggressive. It can take place on a one-to-one or group level and every time the organization will suffer as energy goes into survival rather than creativity and productivity.

There is clearly a link between bullying behaviour and the use and abuse of power and authority. If you believe that having power gives you the right to control, judge or prohibit the actions of others the way in which you exercise your authority will be from the Criticizing Mode of behaviour and from the *I'm OK and You're Not OK* position.

Alternatively if you believe that power with authority means that you have the ability to influence, guide and direct others toward the organizational goals then the style of leadership will be different. It is likely that you are approachable, willing to take responsibility and also willing to delegate and reward others. You are more likely to maintain the *I'm OK and You're OK* position and remain Mindful.

For some people, power also involves a sense of spirituality; power in this instance is more about having a sense of who you are, a connection with an energy that is greater than you are, and about the intrinsic value of life itself. This is of course, compatible with the above *I'm OK/You're OK* leader.

The way in which you perceive power and how this is used will have a direct influence on how you are with others and how you manage bullying behaviour, whether your own or other people's. This links with Steiner (1987) who considers power as 'the capacity to produce change which flows from seven different sources: grounding, passion, control, love, communication, knowledge and transcendence'.

Understanding Bullying Behaviour

The development of bullying scripts begins in childhood with one-up or one-down transactions from significant others. Put simply, the frame of reference within these scripts is that power equals control and that someone has to win. Where parents exercise authority and do it from physical strength and/or manipulation, then the child can become resentful and in this state there can be a sense of power albeit from a not-OK position. Naturally, the bullying that the victim receives may occur in the playground, rather than at home. However, regardless of the context, if this situation endures the feelings of rejection and isolation that come from the hostile threats and violence offer few choices about how to survive. With limited life experience on which to make sense of the world, it is likely that, outside of conscious awareness, the child may decide either to become a victim or a bully. They may also switch between these two – at home the victim, and outside the home the bully, or vice versa. At least with the latter they experience more power. As time goes on they are likely to find others who are like them and therefore achieve a sense of belonging. This will meet their need for relating to others and the bullying behaviour will be reinforced.

Whilst this outlines the development of bullying behaviour in childhood this behaviour does not just stop in the schoolyard but continues into the workplace.

There are different stages to the development of bullying behaviour. Manning (Sydney, 2001) uses graphics to show this process and uses different stages:

Victim   Bully

Figure 14.1 Development of Bullying: Stage 1

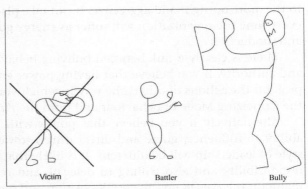

Victim   Battler   Bully

Figure 14.2 Development of Bullying: Stage 2

Stage 1: The child is a Victim of the bully and experiences helplessness.

Stage 2: The child decides to fight back and resist the bullying.

Stage 3: Replacing pain with excitement.

The young person finds others with whom to fight the grown ups and experiences all adults as bullying and authoritarian. Finding others to fight with them creates excitement, which can seem to replace the fear so that they experience less pain. They also develop a sense of belonging with the group of peers they have found. Alternatively one may decide to lead the group and keep others subservient in the way they experienced others bullying them.

Stage 4: Becoming the bully.

As they grow up they choose to move to the bullying position as a defence against the Victim position. (There are some people who do not move into the bullying position and stay as Victim on the Drama Triangle (Karpman, 1968).

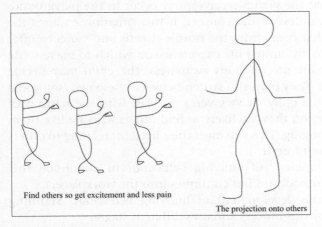

Find others so get excitement and less pain

The projection onto others

Figure 14.3 Development of Bullying: Stage 3

Victim **or** Bully

Figure 14.4 Development of Bullying: Stage 4

WHO'S IN CHARGE?

We do not always know which Structural Ego State is in charge. It could be the introjected Parent, or the Child Ego State, that is, how they were as a child. In an organization it is inappropriate to analyse this aspect as this is unlikely to be appropriate. We have drawn attention to it here to raise awareness.

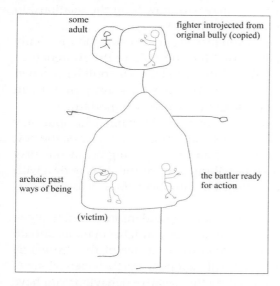

Figure 14.5 Who is in Charge?

Bullying behaviour often stems from feeling fearful. However, this is replaced by acting angrily. That way the bully can feel less vulnerable. In TA terms, the anger is a substitute feeling. The original feeling of fear is covered up and the person is no longer aware of it. Sometimes stopping bullying behaviour can lead to depression if the person has not yet developed other options for dealing with their feelings.

Types of Behaviour

There are some recognizable types of behaviours used by those who bully. It is useful to consider if you behave in any of these and if so what you need to change to believe that others are OK and that you are too.

The types of behaviour shown by bullies. They:

- are overly suspicious
- see their own opinion as the only right one
- will not promote able people
- take credit for other people's good ideas
- blame others when challenged or things go wrong
- alter objectives to cause difficulty
- at their best, can be 'charming manipulators'
- want and expect perfection in themselves and others
- will rationalize their behaviour when confronted, saying it was due to others being out to get them, switching to the Victim position
- do not like showing vulnerability

Bullies know how to wheel and deal and cover their tracks and are very fast thinking. They even get to believe the rationale they use for their behaviour. They often move from organization to organization so that they don't need to deal with the consequences of their behaviour. In fact some organizations actually reward the aggressive behaviour because it is seen as 'go getting', 'dynamic', or 'trouble-shooting'.

Responses to this Behaviour

There are different types of responses to bullying behaviour. As a Victim you might try to adapt and tolerate the behaviour. This might mean that you begin to believe that you deserve it, or that you cannot do anything about it. If you do this you are discounting both yourself and the seriousness of the problem, or your personal ability to do something about it. Eventually when the stress is so great you may withdraw from the relationship which may make life difficult if you need to work with the bully.

It is important to remember that even though you may experience someone as a bully they may not be that way intentionally. It may be that they don't have the awareness or the skills to relate in an equitable way. It could also be that you lack self-confidence when communicating with someone whose style is brusque. You may back away from them instead of confronting their behaviour which while not easy, is very important.

It is important to recognize that some people who manifest bullying behaviour may be doing so for the first time. This may be due to stress and pressure and may be the best they can do in the circumstances. Remove the stress and the bullying behaviour may also cease. If this is the situation, they may then be willing to learn the skills to deal with a variety of situations which previously led to their bullying behaviour. It is here that coaching and mentoring has a role to play.

It is important that you talk with the person who is bullying and inform them that you will not tolerate their behaviour and expect to be treated in an equitable manner. Should the behaviour not stop then it is important to write down evidence of the distressing behaviour and inform the person that, as you are still experiencing their behaviour as bullying you will take out a grievance procedure, citing the negative behaviour you have experienced from them. Throughout this process it is important to find support from colleagues, the union or professional association, friends and family. This will help you to keep yourself OK during the process.

Labelling

There are dangers in labelling someone a bully or a victim as this can, in itself, promote and maintain a system. By separating the behaviour from the personality, a way forward is more likely to be found.

Labelling links with the TA concept of attributions. Attributions are those qualities which are assigned to us by parents and other care givers which define us. These can be positive as well as negative. However, even where they appear to be positive, they can be limiting if you experience *only* having that particular attribute. For example a parent may say, 'Manfred is the clever one' which could be interpreted by the child as not being funny, caring or creative. At work a manager could say 'Mavis is a bully' which might be interpreted by Mavis as that she does not have any skills and that her personality is unpleasant and she is nothing else but that.

Another way of thinking about this is that when we have a negative experience we tend to attribute the cause to other people. When we have a positive experience we tend to attribute the cause to ourselves. When bullying is taking place, both parties – the Victim and the Bully – then blame the other and also blame external reasons. This is where mediation can be helpful to enable all parties to accept some responsibility for their actions. It might be that the person who experienced the bullying behaviour did not stop it straight away and then later had lost so much confidence that it was too late to do anything about it. Whilst the person who is said to have bullied needs to accept that their behaviour is controlling and can be damaging, it might also be that the organization has not taken sufficient action on bullying in the past. In this instance the Victim would not have sufficient faith in the system for anything to be done that could stop the bullying, thus placing increasing stress on themselves.

For many, leaving the organization is the only, and often the best, alternative. Taking the organization to court is so costly in terms of time and emotion that few take this option. Research (Hoel and Cooper, 2000, quoted in Raynor, Hoel and Cooper, 2002) suggests that when a Victim of bullying behaviour deals with this quickly and confronts the bully, a resolution is more likely. Alternatively the Victim may deal with this by what we call stamp-collecting in TA. A 'stamp' is the negative feeling or thought that you collect when someone hurts or angers us. Instead of talking with them about it you collect a 'stamp' and put it in your book to be cashed in later. It may be that someone was patronizing to you and you tell yourself that the issue is too small to deal with. However, you don't let go of what happened and put a stamp, or more, in your book. Then, either someone else comes along who offends you in some way, or the same person returns and you still say nothing, but put more stamps in the book. Eventually you may cash in the book of stamps for a few months off sick or with a huge explosive row when you feel you have taken enough.

Bullying and the Corporate Culture

The organizational focus needs to be on control because, it is better to set clear boundaries than let the damaging behaviour continue. When bullying is allowed to continue this lowers workforce morale and loyalty to the organization as they realize that no one in authority has a grip on the situation. Trust in the leadership's ability or their willingness to take action starts to decline which leads to fewer reports of bullying so the behaviour tends to flourish. If an organization is not dealing with bullying behaviour it is colluding with it. When someone is seen to get away with bullying, those in the organization start to tell stories about what happened and the way in which it was dealt with. If the bullying was seen to have been mismanaged, loyalty diminishes.

The following is an example of organizational collusion:

Jarvis came across as an angry man and had a tendency to annoy people. As a manager he used his position to coerce and threaten people and the team tried to avoid meeting him. Jarvis believed that his way of dealing with team members worked, they did not cross him and were compliant. This meant that he felt everything was under control – his control. It appeared that Jarvis' bosses were scared of him as they did not give him adequate supervision and tried to 'pour oil on troubled waters' when team members complained about him. Eventually, a team member took out a grievance procedure for bullying and harassment, an investigation got underway and Jarvis was suspended. Once this happened other team members came forward to support the grievance. The secretary told investigators that she had done private work for him during office hours and that he had expected her to use the organizational resources. The suspension lasted a year during which time Jarvis continued to attend an ongoing training course which the organization was paying for. When the disciplinary hearing took place the grievances were upheld; however, he was not disciplined and employees were aware that he had undertaken private work whilst suspended and continued with the course. There was speculation about whether or not Jarvis would return to work, which he did not. When Jarvis was not disciplined many of those who had supported the grievance decided that they would leave the organization.

The organization lost good workers because it was seen not to be taking clear action even though a senior manager was culpable. Other employees did not look forward to Jarvis' return. This insecurity meant that productivity went down. Employees across the organization started to say that there was no point in reporting harassment as nothing came of it and it was in fact rewarded by suspension on full pay. This led to an organizational culture of I'm Not OK and They're Not OK, the apathetic position on Wickens quadrant. (See Chapter 2) They began to say that 'It's who you know, not what you know' and the loyalty to the organization lessened. Subsequently morale was low. This incident reinforced people's experience of previous bullying situations that were dealt with poorly thus affecting the organizational culture.

Where workers who have been identified as bullies are given large severance packages rather than just being dismissed the workforce are unlikely to have faith in the process. It is important that the situation is seen to be dealt with fairly rather than negative behaviour being rewarded. This can also lead to a situation where people say things like 'It's OK for him. He got rewarded whilst Jack had to go off sick because of being bullied. In this organization it really is about status. If one of us had bullied we would just have been sacked.'

Bullying behaviour can be difficult to address when the culture is one of banter or teasing. This is the case in situations where people release tension through banter and when this goes too far, or is used with someone who does not like it, the culture itself may make it difficult for the person to confront it. The person is likely to become isolated and therefore more likely to go along with it, moving into the Over-Adapted Mode within the OK Modes Model. This has been known to happen within the military and some incidents have hit the press, but they are not alone in the development of this culture. Good-natured teasing can be affectionate and mean that you belong. However, when the teasing has a 'sting-in-the-tail' then, in TA, we would call this a scorpion stroke; for instance:

'You look good in that outfit. It is a shame you don't usually look very good, ha, ha'.

Where someone's face doesn't fit it may result in others wanting to have a laugh at their expense. The following is an example of this:

A new manager, Andrea, went to work at a sales office. It was a large office and the current sales reps. placed a high value on status and material wealth, rather than on skill and ability. Because the sales reps thought that Andrea came from a different class to them they decided to lay bets on who could get her to show herself up by making a mistake or just by getting her to do their errands for them. The winners would get a case of champagne. Eventually, Andrea became aware of this bet and despite complaining to the manager she was just told to toughen up and no action was taken. She left the organization.	*This was a case of group bullying. The manager needed to put a stop to it. A clear philosophical and value base as well as an anti-bullying policy were needed in order to change the culture and support the manager to confront this behaviour.*

Ways need to be found for people to report bullying behaviour without an immediate escalation of the process. Sometimes a difficult situation can be resolved by getting those involved to talk with each other with a more senior colleague facilitating. In this way grievance procedures may not be required. The aim is to resolve problems using low-key approaches as this might succeed without escalation but there will need to be further steps if these do not work.

Other ways to decrease stressful situations are for employees to be offered assertiveness training, communication skills and managing conflict courses, be involved in mediation or receive coaching. These days most organizations realize that these solutions are not mutually exclusive and grievance procedures may still need to be invoked as a way to maintain control. Sending victims of bullying on courses gives the message that it is their problem. In the case of Andrea above, she was a victim of the organization's culture where everyone in the hierarchy was involved in the process and no amount of courses or coaching would have helped her. This example highlights the fact that bullying is often a symptom of deeper organizational problems. Deal with these and reverberations are likely to be felt throughout the organization including a reduction in the level of bullying behaviour.

Different organizations have different norms. Some organizations develop a 'tough' culture, which is often a bullying culture under another name. This discounts the level of damage being done. Organizations need to remember that they have a legal duty of care, quite apart from a moral imperative to honour and respect their employees.

Individual Responses to Those Who Bully

There are a number of options for dealing with bullying behaviour. If you experience being bullied you need to:

- Remain calm and cross the transactions to maintain Mindful to Mindful channels of communication
- Keep solution focused
- Change your body position if appropriate. What you do will depend very largely on the context. Examples might be to step back not forward, sit down until they have wound down, stand up if feeling too threatened and to keep out of the corner of the room. Relax your shoulders and keep your chin in
- Shout or say their name in order to get attention (but not aggressively)

- Suggest you discuss the matter later
- Check what they are saying – for instance hear them out, look for the grain of truth in what they are saying and agree with them if this is appropriate
- Stay OK with yourself and, with them, but establish a boundary. For example:
  1. 'I do not like the way you're talking to me and I am going to leave. Come and find me when you have calmed down,' or
  2. 'When you … (for example, shout), at me I feel … (for example, scared, humiliated) and I want you to stop'.

In summary remain Mindful then choose the appropriate intervention or action to take. If the bullying behaviour continues, get support.

Developing Awareness

Organizations need to routinely monitor the reasons people give for leaving. Through this Mindful Process – resulting in Structuring Mode behaviour, unreported situations get noticed. It may be that there is a high staff turnover in one department over a short period of time and enquiries may show that this coincides with a new appointment. On interviewing staff it might be discovered that the new appointee is bullying and staff are leaving rather than report the situation. In these instances it is important for the organization to take positive action to stop the bullying behaviour.

There also needs to be awareness that individuals in a team may be too scared to support someone who is being victimized and ostracized. They are likely to be in the Over-Adapted Mode and be thankful that at least the bully is leaving them alone. One such situation occurred when a team of seven stopped talking to one of its members, Sue.

Sue was bright and had a national reputation in her field. A new young team member, Janet, had been appointed and she started to cajole and intimidate the others in the team with the aim of getting them to gang up on Sue, and out of fear, they complied. They stopped talking to her, not even saying good morning or good evening. They were reluctant to work with her and help her, like they did with each other. When Janet was away the rest of the team would talk to Sue. Sue complained to her boss of being shunned. Team members were interviewed and said that Sue was bullying them and not the other way around. Sue stopped being effective at her work and consequently she received fewer and fewer invitations to speak at conferences. The organization could not believe that so many people were not telling the truth and therefore came to the conclusion that Sue must be the problem. Sue eventually resigned from the organization suffering from stress and three other team members went of sick with stress-related symptoms.	*This organization discounted the possibility that Sue was being scapegoated. Team members were in fact so intimidated by Janet, that they went along with her. This Over-Adapted behaviour led to a stressful situation for everybody and particularly for Sue who tendered her resignation. The organization therefore lost a competent, nationally recognized person from their team who developed mental health problems and was unable to work for some time. They also risked legal proceedings for their handling of the case. A great many hours were lost in terms of investigations, low morale and sick leave. This could all have been avoided by effective supervision and leadership.*

Leadership and Responsibility

Effective leadership can be assessed by the extent to which the leader encourages others to make choices and take responsibility using their Mindful Process in the OK Modes Model. There will be leaders who use Criticizing Mode – for instance using authority to pressure people into certain action. In this instance their focus is on getting things done, which can be experienced as bullying.

These days there is greater emphasis on relationships between leaders and others and, therefore, formal power has steadily decreased. This formal power is derived from the contract of employment, company regulations and policies. Today organizations have taken note that they do not get the best from their employees in terms of productivity and effectiveness when this formal power is used. Giving orders, being a disciplinarian, using coercion will tend to promote subordination and, in TA terms, Over-Adaptation. This in turn can lead to game playing (see Chapter 9).

It is often necessary to educate people about good management and leadership, discussing effective and respectful behaviours when relating with others. When you involve everyone in deciding upon the positive behaviours they would like to see in the workplace you are more likely to develop a committed and assertive workforce. These positive behaviours act as permissions to people to compare any actions against those listed and they are therefore, more likely to be assertive. However, should the bullying behaviour not stop then the organization needs to follow through.

All organizations need to have procedures in place for resolving grievances with managers receiving training in these. Many grievances fall down because the process of investigation is flawed. Offering quality training and education in harassment policies and procedures provides managers with the foundation to move forward. It is then the organization's responsibility to ensure congruency between the policies, procedures and behaviours.

A key word when dealing with bullying behaviour is 'responsibility'. You need to ensure you do not bully others and that you maintain respectful boundaries, that is, not to overstep the mark with someone. Those who bully fail to check the impact of their behaviour. The difficulty of doing this in a 'tough' culture is that the very culture itself puts pressure on people to behave in a particular way and individuals come to believe that expressions of feelings are perceived as weak.

It is also important not to blame the Victims. Bullying behaviour hooks the Over-Adapted Mode or I'm Not OK Life Position, and it can be difficult to stand up for yourself. This is where witnesses to bullying behaviour can be helpful, even though they cannot Rescue the victim.

Summary

In summary, a problem with bullying behaviour is not just about those directly involved; it is also about the organizational culture and the responses to bullying. An overall perspective needs to be taken to ascertain whether this behaviour is localized or whether it is symptomatic of deeper issues at the organizational level. Therefore responsibility needs to be taken at all levels, from the micro to the macro. When this occurs the workforce is more likely to develop and maintain loyalty to the organization through a sense of trust in its procedures and processes.

EXERCISES

EXERCISE 1

1. Consider where you are more likely to move to when stressed on the Drama Triangle – Persecutor, Rescuer or Victim (see pages 129–130).
2. What do you need to say to yourself to keep yourself and others OK? Ensure you say this from the Mindful Process and using one of the four Modes as required.
3. How will you ensure that you maintain your Mindful Process and OK behaviour?
4. From whom will you get support?
5. How will you know when you are behaving differently and how will you celebrate these changes?

EXERCISE 2

It is important to develop an awareness of your own body space and need for physical distance between yourself and others. In this way you can develop a sense of what you need to do when this physical boundary is crossed.

This exercise will need to be undertaken with someone else.

1. Use a ball of string and place the string on the floor around you in a circle at the distance you feel most comfortable for someone to come.
2. The other person then walks up to your circle whilst you are inside it. As they do so get a sense of your physical and emotional sensations as well as what you are thinking about this. You can tell the person to stop as soon as you wish to.
3. Some people's string circle will be quite large, whilst others' will be smaller. The circle may also be different sizes in relation to different people, dependent on size or gender or psychological closeness.
4. Now consider the size of your circle in relation to the proximity of others when you are talking. Do you think you allow sufficient space for you to be comfortable with them? Are there some people you will need to take a step back from in future?
5. Consider how you will respond in future, particularly to conflict situations.

EXERCISE 3

1. Be aware of your organization's policy on harassment.
2. Are the behaviours of leaders and managers congruent with this policy?
3. If there is a lack of congruence what influence do you have on this?
4. What positive behaviours are desirable and what involvement of the workforce has there been, or could there be, to decide upon these?
5. What initiatives could you take to develop congruence with your own team, including with your own behaviour?

15 *Stress and Life Balance*

Introduction

Stress is inherent in every healthy form of life. However, the focus of this chapter is to address the undesirable excess of tension which threatens individual and organizational well-being. Taking a macro view, the 13 million working days lost every year in the UK through stress (statistic from the UK National Institute for Clinical Excellence, quoted by BBC News, 5 November 2009) also have an impact on the gross national product.

In this chapter we explore stress from both an organizational and an individual perspective. It is necessary for organizations to take responsibility for the stress they cause people as well as for us, as individuals, to develop our resilience, recognize the triggers that provoke our own stress and be able to respond appropriately.

Different Responses

Stress can be very invasive and if you are not in tune with early warning signs of stress you can often feel as if it has crept up on you. How you deal with stress is due to historical and habitual responses. Responses differ as a consequence of different cultures, experiences, beliefs and personalities. For example, if in a crisis, a report needs to be produced within a day, you might see this as a challenge or you may become stressed by it. You could be someone who enjoys managing 20 staff or be someone who prefers to work at home alone. Ensuring the right person is in the right job acts as a protection for both the organization and the individual.

When stressed you are likely to react in one or more of the following ways:

• make more mistakes
• prefer solitude
• want to go further and further with the challenges, raising your stress levels ever higher
• need to be right
• become over-controlling

Resilience

Resilience is a key factor in stress prevention. Resilience is the ability to recover despite periodical setbacks and problems. Highly resilient people know how to bounce back and find a way to have things turn out well. However, this does not mean developing a 'Be Strong' Driver (see Chapter 7), or setting ourselves up by taking on too much. Siebert (2005) suggests five aspects of resilience:

- Maintaining emotional stability, health and well-being
- Focus outward: good problem-solving skills
- Focus inward: a strong inner sense, high self-esteem, self-confidence, and positive self-concept
- Well-developed attributes and skills
- The talent to convert misfortune into good fortune

Stress can be eased through the ability to make good relationships because then you are likely to believe that you are OK and others are also OK. If you have difficulty in forming relationships you are likely to believe that either, you are Not OK and others are better than you, or that you are better than others. Believing that everyone is OK offers a secure base from which to operate. When this happens attachment to your team and to the organization is likely to increase. One outcome of this is that you will be able to appropriately say 'No' to things whilst still keeping yourself and others OK.

EXAMPLES

1) Molly has been married for 17 years. All is not well within her marriage. At work Molly's *raison d'être* is to please others so that she feels a sense of worth and believes she is needed. The difficulty with this is that she takes on tasks even if she is too busy. She is therefore in danger of becoming burnt out and going off sick. Her manager, Jill, does nothing about Molly's overwork as it helps out the department and Jill receives accolades for the department meeting its targets. Molly, on the other hand, is over-stretched and perhaps avoiding difficulties in the home.	*Action is as important for the organization as for the individual. In this case study the supervisor should have noticed when Molly was becoming overloaded and make the appropriate interventions to prevent this happening.*
2) Jenny has a great social life outside of work. She has a loving family and a network of friends. She enjoys work but knows when she cannot take on any more. On occasions she is willing to stay late and play her part in enabling the team to complete an urgent deadline. However, this is rarely required and Jenny is a well liked and respected team member.	*With Jenny's ability to obtain balance in her life she is likely to be creative, refreshed and be able to deal with difficulties as they arise.*

3) Jack shows no obvious signs of stress. He appears to cope well with his duties, and everything always seems to go smoothly in his department. He does not, however, seem to recognize that other people might be under stress – he seems to take the line that everyone manages the same as he does. This sometimes comes across as indifference to others and his team avoids talking with him about any difficulties because of his somewhat aloof manner. More particularly his team are complaining about how difficult he is to work with as he appears to be able to deal with everything and they feel weak and foolish if they appear not to be dealing with pressure.	*There is a sense that Jack is under pressure but because of his Be Strong Driver (see Chapter 7) the more colleagues approach him about their stress levels, the more evasive and denying he becomes. Dealing with his issues requires a more subtle approach. Jack's supervisor would need to consider at which level Jack could be discounting (see Chapter 8) and then approach the situation at the level before that one. For example, if Jack is discounting the existence of a problem then the supervisor would need to help him understand there is a problem with stress for his staff, even if not for himself. Once Jack accepts that there is a problem the next step would be to enable him to see that this is a serious issue before moving on to consider options for change. If Jack struggles at any stage of the process the supervisor would need to return to the level at which he is accounting and start again from there.*

Good management also entails effective supervision which in turn entails noticing when someone is on overload and doing something about it.

One of the causes of stress on people is the need to multitask. Administrators and secretarial staff have to do this a lot – be it writing a report, answering a query when someone comes to their office or answering the phone. Whilst this is an accepted pressure for administrators it does not mean that it is necessarily any easier for them than for others. The western world tends to see multitasking as good, hence the comments about women being able to do it well, whereas men are often seen as lacking this ability. Whether or not this is a fallacy it does highlight that fact that multitasking is valued. Getting your life in balance probably means doing less multitasking and becoming more focused.

Beliefs and Time Structuring

When you are stressed you often don't make time for breaks, which would enable you to be refreshed and more able to get on with the task. Having tight deadlines usually means you have taken on too much and should not have agreed to it.

All of this relates to your beliefs about self, time and work. If you believe that you are less important than others and that you should be able to do more than you do, you are likely to agree to an increase in your workload. This could mean that the Criticizing Mode within you is constantly pushing you and demanding that you do more and more.

You can use the Structural Ego State Model to consider if you have incorporated within yourself a significant person from your childhood, for example, parent, teacher or aunt, and are talking to yourself from their perspective without even realizing it. This is good if the person you incorporated was positive and encouraging but not so good if they were criticizing and discouraging as this would have been – and still is – damaging to your confidence and feelings of self-worth. If this internal voice is critical you need to ask that part of you if it is willing to be on your side, rather than on your 'case'. If it is not willing to do that then you will need to develop a new part of you that you can use to take care of yourself.

Many of you will have used this negative self-talk for so long that you are not aware of it and think that these negative things are factual. You can actually change this self-talk so that it is positive, including the need to be structuring – by setting boundaries – and being supportive.

Often people talk about *time management*. However, time cannot be 'managed'. Rather, you need to manage yourself and ensure you achieve and maintain balance in your life. This may mean making a new decision about the way you view and use time.

One of the key elements of traditional time management is selling 'time management' equipment as a follow up to time management courses. This is big business. This way of considering time management does not fundamentally change what people do, it just gives them the opportunity to put more into the long hours they are at work.

The way in which you structure time will affect how you obtain a balance in your life. You can structure time in the following ways:

1. Withdrawal – This is when you emotionally or physically withdraw and are mentally removed from others. Daydreams, walking alone, and meditation are all forms of withdrawal. It is usually safe and requires little emotional investment. When you do this there are no strokes from others, though there are strokes from ourselves and by our experience of being in touch with a spiritual part of ourselves, for example, when meditating. Berne talked about strokes only coming from other human beings but for example, the experience of meditation can be so profound that we have decided to refer to this as a source of strokes here.

2. Rituals – These are safe and predictable ways of exchanging strokes. They may be short such as 'good morning' or long and complex such as a religious ceremony. They provide important maintenance strokes.

3. Pastimes – This is when you are just talking – not taking action. This way of structuring time does not usually involve real closeness. Examples of this would be when you are chatting about cars, cooking, sport, and future holidays. They are safe ways of being with people. When you are unable to pass time with others you can be experienced as having few social skills.

4. Activities – This is usually where you spend most of your time, doing work and chores. Activities produce strokes for doing something well, or negative ones for doing something poorly. Financial rewards or trophies are also ways in which you receive strokes for this way of time structuring.

5. Games and Substitute Feelings – These are familiar ways of operating that have a predictable outcome, and result in a bad feeling at the end of a game – the substitute feeling. This has a high stroke-yield but with negative outcomes for all parties and is not a healthy way to structure time. You do this outside of your awareness and need

to find ways to recognize the opening discount and your familiar patterns in order that you can change your behaviour. You also need to find ways to obtain strokes positively.

6. Play – this provides you with the opportunity to exchange strokes that are healthy rather than unhealthy. (Cowles-Boyd and Boyd, 1980). This is a very important part of the way in which you need to structure your time. You need to ensure that you have leisure time and find ways to protect it.

7. Intimacy – 'Intimate' in this context means being open with others and being prepared to trust and share vulnerability (whilst remaining in Integrating Adult Ego State or the Mindful Process). When you are being intimate with others there is no exploitation. This way of structuring time is the most rewarding but could also be the most risky as someone may be rejecting. However, when you are able to keep yourself and others OK you will be able to risk being open and intimate whatever the response from the other person.

If you spend too much time in (4) Activities, then you can avoid intimacy and this has a tendency to leave you 'stroke deprived'. Of course you will be achieving something from being a workaholic, such as wanting to avoid intimacy, or obtaining strokes for doing rather than for being and doing. In this way you will be addressing your need for stimulus but not considering your need for play and rest.

We have some basic biological needs and in TA these are called 'hungers' (see Chapter 5 on Recognition). We have hunger for *stimulus*, *belonging* and *structure*, with their associated sub-sets of leadership, incident, and sexual hunger.

When one or more of these needs are not met then there may be an overload on other hungers. For example, if you obtain insufficient structure you are likely to try to get your needs met through some other means, possibly by increasing the risks you take in your life. This way you satisfy 'incident' hunger. This is shown most clearly by young people who get into trouble with the police. Very often they have insufficient structure and belonging, so they go for incident as a way to meet their needs. An example of this in the workplace might be that you have a need to belong but have not developed the skills to make relationships. By becoming a 'workaholic' you can avoid intimacy and discount your real need to belong. Work then takes priority and you can rationalize your over-work as necessary, rather than as avoidance. This in turn will eventually cause you stress as your life is out of balance and your real need is ignored.

Your beliefs about time, your Driver or Working Styles and your injunctions (the messages you received, interpreted decided upon and incorporated) affect how you use time. For example, the Be Perfect Driver behaviour has an associated message of 'Don't make mistakes'. If you have incorporated this message you need to hear, and tell yourself, that it is OK to make mistakes and to learn from them.

If you only encourage someone to change their negative Driver behaviour they will be left with the injunctions (the 'don't' messages), which could have serious consequences. You need to consider your injunctions and then give yourself the permission you need to heal the Child Ego State, rather than going into the defensive Driver behaviour. You can then use the positive aspects of what was originally a defensive reaction to the injunction.

These positive aspects form what Developmental Transactional Analysts call the Working Style, a term coined by Hay (1993). Whilst you developed the Driver behaviour from a defensive position this action also helped to form your personality. If in adulthood you have a level of self awareness you always have the option to use the *strengths* of your Driver behaviour. In this instance we would describe it as a Working Style since you are using these qualities in a positive way.

You can also change by altering your behaviour rather than the messages you incorporated. By changing your behaviour you are likely to receive different responses from others that are favourable. As you start to experience life as easier you are then likely to be motivated to make any necessary changes.

When you are stressed, panicky, overwhelmed and your energy is not directed it can appear that you are not in control. If this happens then you will move out of the Mindful Process and will do less thinking. At these times it is helpful to make a shift in what you are doing – for instance, by taking a walk, phoning a friend or meditating, so that you can intentionally direct your actions. When you are directing your energy then your levels of motivation will be maintained, and even increased.

Contracting is an example of how organizations can channel this positive energy. The process of contracting frees potential energy, by clearly setting mutually agreed goals. By ensuring that there is a contract, and that the contract is measurable, manageable and motivational, the potential for games (see Chapter 9) will be reduced. There will be less stress as you experience yourself moving toward a common goal.

Decisions for Life

Your actions will be coherent and congruent if they are part of a greater plan. If you have dreams which you translate into goals and then transform these into tasks this will enable you to make decisions about whether a particular action will get you closer to your dream or further away. In an ideal world you would then only take work that gets you closer to your dream. Of course, eliminating all work which does not get you closer may not be possible straight away; however, you can minimize it. You just need to take one small step each day toward your dream. Part of this will be to consider who is best to do a particular piece of work, and delegate accordingly.

It is helpful to question the way you wish to spend your life. For some the drive is for acquisitions and material wealth, whereas for others it is about having enough money to relax and enjoy themselves, meet friends and spend time with the family. What you want to create in your life is a fundamental question. Having answered this you can then make other congruent decisions that support this.

For example, if you make the decision to be healthy, then how you structure your time needs to be congruent. Your time management will then also be about allowing time for, for instance:

- exercise
- having a massage
- meeting friends
- meeting colleagues for mutual support time, and so on

These tend to get squeezed out, but are necessary to obtain balance.

Trusting Yourself

If you trust your body as well as your thoughts and feelings you are more likely to be in tune with yourself. It is easy to discount physical signs and rationalize your way into situations rather than listen and consider what your feelings – emotional and physical – are telling you. In this way you will know if the next piece of work would push you over the top.

Worrying tends to affect life-balance. Most people worry about where they might find the money to meet financial commitments or what they will do if they get ill and cannot work. To worry is to be consumed and obsessed by the question, whereas, if you are worried about something and consider it attentively, rather than obsessively, you are likely to obtain options and keep your perspective. There is an exercise at the end of this chapter that addresses this issue.

A questioning, rather than a worrying, mind enables life-balance. Further, many of the things you worry about never happen. If they do happen and you have worried obsessively rather than attentively, you are likely to be too tired to deal with it.

Meditation is one of the practices that enable you to take time and space for yourself and get to know yourself. As you get to know yourself you are likely to be more relaxed about getting to know others. Meditation can also offer a quiet space to listen to your inner core and learn what you want. However, the primary focus is about space to be rather than do.

Time structuring is a way of satisfying structure hunger. If the way you structure time is unhealthy you will be avoiding, rather than dealing with conflict. When you are doing this you are being passive rather than active and are likely to be stressed as you turn away from what needs to be looked at. This turning away uses energy and, in the long run, is detrimental.

The way in which you structure time will be affected by your beliefs about yourself, others and life. Below are some ideas about how different beliefs might affect your actions.

Table 15.1   Beliefs and Stress

Belief	How this belief might contribute to stress	Revised belief
I must do this job perfectly.	Often results in overwork.	Some jobs need more care than others. I will pay attention to what I do and do them well enough.
I should do this job myself.	Too much work taken on.	Other people can do as well as I can. I can support others to develop their skills.
I must accept every task I am given.	Overwork.	There is a limit to what I can do and sometimes I need to say 'No'.
I messed up that meeting – I am a failure.	Meetings are dreaded.	Some things went right. I can learn from that experience.

Table 15.1 Continued

Belief	How this belief might contribute to stress	Revised belief
I can't ask for help or they'll think I am useless.	Something goes wrong and criticism results.	I can't be expected to know everything. I can ask for what I need.
I won't know the right thing to say to this person if they get distressed.	Avoiding difficult situations often increases feelings of powerlessness.	Listening and understanding is just as important as taking visible action.
I ought to be 'top dog'.	Fear of being overtaken.	It is healthy to have equal relationships.
I'm no good as a manager, that's why I'm not in that role.	Low self-esteem and lack of confidence.	I am as valuable as other people no matter what my role.

In order to maintain life balance you need to:

- Check your beliefs about time and work
- Develop an awareness of your feelings as well as your thoughts so that you can take the appropriate actions
- Take into account your social needs and how much imagination you have, without which life can be dull and you are likely to experience difficulty in amusing yourself
- Keep a check on reality as well as what action you need to take in any given context

Attachment in Organizations

Stress can be eased by the development of good relationships within the organization. As mentioned earlier there is a human need to belong and therefore part of the skills of good leadership is to promote a culture where there is positive recognition and space for constructive feedback, with an open-door policy from management. This process offers a secure base from which to operate.

When there is a culture of good relationships in an organization:

1. People want to belong.
2. There is a commitment to goals.
3. There is dialogue with mutual respect.
4. There is creative leadership.
5. There is maximum self-regulation.

When this culture is broken or not developed in an organization there is an increase in:

- absenteeism
- psychosomatic problems
- sabotage

- lack of loyalty
- low motivation
- human error
- burn-out
- low productivity
- lack of commitment
- aggression and violence (Kohlrieser, 2006)

Summary

In summary, when considering stress you need to take both the personal and the organizational issues into account and how these two areas interact with each other. Once you have decided what your own part is in this and which organizational processes, structures, systems and culture have an impact on you then you can consider the appropriate action to take. In order to do this you need to trust yourself, and ensure that you expect the best of yourself and your workplace.

EXERCISES

EXERCISE 1

What happens when you get stressed? What role does blame play in your responses? The blame diagram can be seen as the way in which you manage strokes when you are stressed – giving yourself or others (or both!) negative strokes because something has gone wrong. Consider what you do when you feel stressed:

- Do you blame yourself when mistakes happen, blame someone else, blame everyone, or not blame anyone and just get on and sort out any difficulties there may be?
- If you do go into one of the ineffective Modes (see Chapter 3), what is the usual outcome from doing so?
- Is this a repeating pattern?
- Is it helpful?
- Are other people affected negatively by your blaming attitude and actions?
- Is this helpful?
- If you realize that none of this is helpful or effective what will you change?

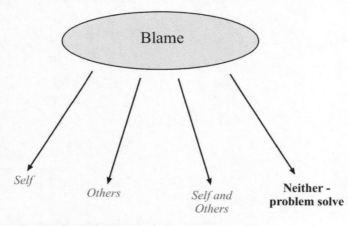

There is a difference between taking responsibility and blaming. Blaming is punitive and often not related to problem-solving. The process of blaming can also detract from learning lessons from mistakes as people become scared and do what they can to cover up errors. When you avoid blaming anyone you can use your energy to solve the problem.

Figure 15.1 The Blame Model
Source: Davis (unpublished).

EXERCISE 2

Take some time to ask yourself these fundamental questions. It is a good idea to write down the answers as you go:

- What do I want to create in my life?
- If I continue as I am will I achieve the life that I want to create?
- What would I be doing if I weren't working such long hours, with such intensity?
- What am I avoiding by working such long hours?
- What does each of my OK Modes say about the way I am spending my life? (Consider the answer from each of the Modes in turn and write down the responses so that you can really see what you are doing)

- How will I update the negative perspectives that are unhelpful to me so that I do achieve my dreams and visions?

EXERCISE 3

Saying 'no' to work opportunities is an important factor in managing our time. We often say 'yes' to work opportunities even when we are too busy and the reasons for this are numerous. Consider which of the following may be yours and if your particular reason is not listed then write it down for yourself:

- 'I can't afford not to.'
- 'I'm flattered to be asked.'
- 'They won't call me again if I say no.'
- 'I like doing this kind of work so much.'
- 'I don't like saying no it might offend them.'
- 'If I get my life in balance I will be faced with problems I don't want to acknowledge.'

What do you need to do or to tell yourself in order to become how you want to be? Who do you need to ask to support you with the changes you are going to make?

EXERCISE 4

If you are worrying about something then ask yourself:

- What am I worrying about?
- Be prepared to keep asking the question. You can do this whilst you are walking, or for instance doing the garden.
- Follow where the question leads you. If the question changes or another arises go with that one. Keep following the process as this will usually lead on to more and more fundamental issues that you need to address rather than avoid.

EXERCISE 5

Dissect the circle below according to the amount of time you think that you spend in, withdrawing, ritual, pastiming, activities, games, play and intimacy. If there are any areas that you believe to be too large or too small, consider what action you will take to remedy this. Are you wary about the consequences of these changes? What might you have to do, change, continue doing, stop doing and how would this be for you? Who might you need support or encouragement from to change this?

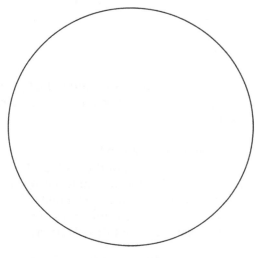

Figure 15.2 Time Structuring Circle

EXERCISE 6

This exercise is about beliefs and how they contribute to stress. There are examples of this in the table within the text above.

Consider your own beliefs and their effect and then revise these beliefs based on you current situation. If you struggle with this you might want to check out your thinking with others.

Table 15.2 Beliefs and Stress (blank)

Belief	How this belief might or has contribute to stress	Revised belief

EXERCISE 7

This is a useful exercise for individuals, teams, management teams and committees.

If you have a problem and are becoming stressed about it then consider the following questions:

1. What is the problem?
2. What is the cause of the problem?
3. What are the possible solutions to the problem?
4. What solution is recommended?
5. What are the likely outcomes of that solution?
6. Will you still adopt this solution?

These questions keep you to the point and enable you to focus.

16 *Concepts for Thriving*

Introduction

This chapter is based on a model called Concepts for Thriving. These concepts can be used by individuals, teams and organizations to assess what needs to change and where an intervention needs to be made. Very often interventions are directed at an inappropriate level and therefore do not actually address the issue. Because of this time and money can be wasted without a remedy being found.

These concepts are even more usefully applied as an underpinning to the development of an organization, department or team as they will enable the development of a healthy culture.

Whilst not directly TA, the model fits with the TA philosophy and the belief that safety and security are of paramount importance for a productive and harmonious workforce. The model takes into account both the individual and the organization and can be used as a diagnostic tool and a way to structure action. It is based on the assumption that there are seven basic components that promote a thriving individual, group, team and organization. These components are emotional safety, positive reinforcement, belonging, clear communication, productive activity, integration, and celebration. Celebration needs to run implicitly, if not explicitly, throughout these different components.

These seven components are built upon each other; that is, one must be in place before going on to the next. When they are established, nourished and applied in an organization that is the degree to which the organization, and the relationships within it, is functional. When these basic components are not established, nourished or applied, that will represent the extent to which the organization is dysfunctional.

EXAMPLE

The different members in a multidisciplinary team compete for the best way to do something. They are disparaging about those from agencies different to theirs (for example, designers have greater skills than those in marketing and sales) believing that their own particular profession is the most important. This includes having the best processes, structures and systems. Each team member believes that their way is the right way and that others should adopt it.	*Unless ways are found to bring team members together this competitive process will persist and be damaging to individuals and the team as a whole. Within such a competitive culture the workforce does not feel emotionally safe and trust is unlikely to develop. Factions will develop as people seek out someone else to align with as an attempt to feel a sense of connection and worth.*

The process that the team went through can be explained through three models. The first of these is Concepts for Thriving (Mountain, 2004), the second is aspiration and the third is the competence curve, which will be dealt with later. As the Concepts for Thriving model is the major theoretical model in this chapter this will be addressed first. This is an amended version of Roberts' Hierarchy of Functionality (1992).

Concepts for Thriving

Outlined below are the definitions of the concepts:

Table 16.1   Concepts for Thriving Definitions

Safety	When I have this my primary needs are taken care of, I am comfortable with myself, and boundaries are maintained.
Positive reinforcement	I am given positive strokes and there is mutual exchange.
Belonging	I start to develop a positive sense of who I am in this team or this particular situation.
Clear communication	I know I am being heard, and I am therefore more willing to hear others.
Productive activity	I am in the present moment and collaboratively solve problems. I recognize and am recognized for my competence, and I have a sense of who I am. I am able to balance giving and receiving.
Integration	I can be spontaneous. I make positive things happen in my life. I recognize my achievements. I enjoy who I am and what I do.
Celebration	My achievements are acknowledged. I accept myself, who I am, what I do and who I am in relation to others and the world. (This runs through every level).

These components are implicit in TA theory and these statements express an interest in thriving rather than stagnation.

In order to thrive we need:

- acceptance and protection which nurtures emotional safety
- praise which enables positive reinforcement
- acknowledgement of who and how I am in this group, which leads to a developing sense of belonging
- appreciation and respect which develops clear communication
- realistic expectations so that productive activity is more likely to take place
- facilitation to enable integration of learning and experiences
- celebration to enable acceptance at every stage – this may sound rather grandiose but that is generally because there is insufficient acknowledgement of people and achievements. However, the word 'acknowledgement' may work better in some contexts

If some aspects are not present in the work place then a negative environment is more likely to flourish. In place of the positive aspects, negative ones will create a culture of:

- blame
- ridicule
- humiliation
- unrealistic expectations
- alienation

When safety is weak or absent you might feel threatened and this will affect relationships. When this happens you may become defensive and give others negative strokes. This in turn is likely to lead to poor communication which leads to destructive actions with resultant conflicts. These lead back to the start of the process where the person feels threatened instead of safe.

Developing a Healthy Culture

All organizations need to provide a healthy environment for their employees. When you come into a new job, or are part of a team, you need to feel that who you are, where you are from, what you believe in, what skills you bring, and the experience you have to offer, are accepted in this new situation. Establishing Emotional Safety starts the process of attachment for team members. At this point effective contracting and clear expectations with a sense of welcome for everyone is an important part of the process. Boundaries need to be set and maintained and questions need to be welcomed and answered. Only then will Positive Reinforcement for the new person or team be heard. It is difficult to hear positive feedback for work well done if, at the same time, you feel that other team members are negatively competitive, hence the need for safety to be in place first.

Positive Reinforcement enables attachment and leads to engagement. These two components lead to a developing sense of belonging, and energy can start to be released for other things including greater interaction with each other and enhanced

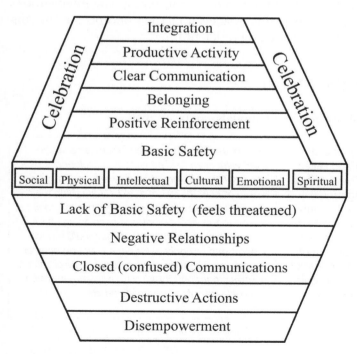

Figure 16.1 Concepts for Thriving

communication. As trust develops productivity will improve as less time is expended on tensions and conflict. Good supervision and coaching enable you to integrate your learning and experience so that there is continual professional growth and development. This enables you to experience yourself as 'resource-full'.

Physis

The Concepts for Thriving model can be linked with the TA concept of physis. Physis is the natural drive to health, it is the thrust of life itself. Human beings are self-actualizing and have an innate desire to pursue personal growth and well-being. This idea comes from the Greek philosopher Heraclitus and means change or growth.

In organizations you need to be encouraged and supported to learn and grow. In organizations that are over-structured, authoritarian and rule-bound then growth will be hampered, both for the organization and for the individual. This will prevent thriving and leads to stagnation instead.

Where there is little recognition, or recognition is manipulative, aspiration will be hampered as competition takes the place of cooperation.

The Competence Curve

The competence curve also relates to Concepts for Thriving. If you take a look at this curve you can see that it is natural for people to go through a range of emotions when there is change. (For further explanation of the curve and the appropriate interventions at each stage see also Chapter 12 on Integrative Leadership.) The Concepts for Thriving model is one way of addressing different needs at different times.

Examples of Applying the Model

The following case examples show how these models can be applied.

1) A multidisciplinary team experienced difficulties with communication and called in a consultant to assist them. They were shown the Concepts for Thriving model and asked to go into smaller groups to identify where they experienced the difficulty. Each of the groups identified the same concept and, rather than this being the concept of Clear Communication they all chose that of Safety. Having diagnosed their own problem they then discussed what they needed to do to change this.	*Having identified that none of them felt safe this team were open to identifying and exploring options. No one blamed anyone else; instead they looked at how they wanted to be. One thing they did was to make time in team meetings for small groups to talk about what had been going on for them in the last month so that they could receive support and recognition for what they had done or were doing. This led to an increased sense of safety, positive regard and thus improved communication as people felt safe to approach others.*

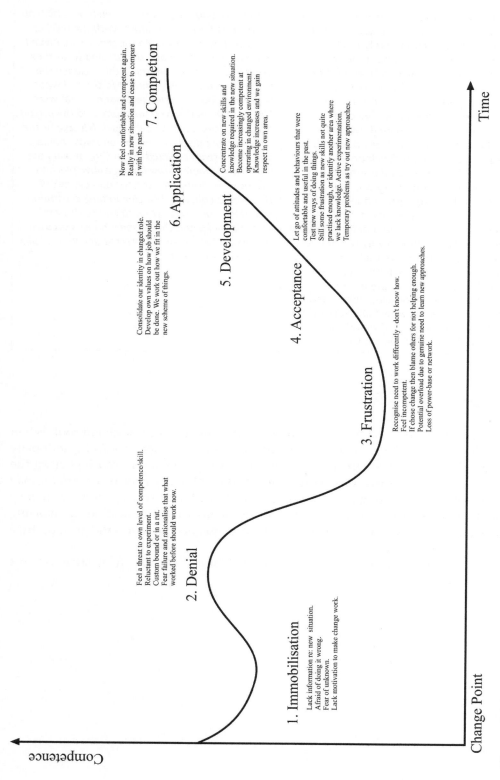

Figure 16.2 Competence Curve

Source: Hay, 1992.

Competence

Change Point

Time

1. Immobilisation

Lack information re: new situation.
Afraid of doing it wrong.
Fear of unknown.
Lack motivation to make change work.

2. Denial

Feel a threat to own level of competence/skill.
Reluctant to experiment.
Custom bound or in a rut.
Fear failure and rationalise that what
worked before should work now.

3. Frustration

Recognise need to work differently - don't know how.
Feel incompetent.
If chose change then blame others for not helping enough.
Potential overload due to genuine need to learn new approaches.
Loss of power-base or network.

4. Acceptance

Let go of attitudes and behaviours that were
comfortable and useful in the past.
Test new ways of doing things.
Still some frustration as new skills not quite
practised enough, or identify another area where
we lack knowledge. Active experimentation.
Temporary problems as try out new approaches.

5. Development

Consolidate our identity in changed role.
Develop own values on how job should
be done. We work out how we fit in the
new scheme of things.

6. Application

Concentrate on new skills and
knowledge required in the new situation.
Become increasingly competent at
operating in changed environment.
Knowledge increases and we gain
respect in own area.

7. Completion

Now feel comfortable and competent again.
Really in new situation and cease to compare
it with the past.

2) A team leader had experienced bullying from one of the senior managers and had taken disciplinary action in relation to this. The panel did not uphold the team leader's complaint. She had been off sick, and eventually returned to work within the same department. Even though her team members were supportive of her, relationships became strained, since the original problem had not been resolved. During a two-day team development process the reticence and tension were almost tangible but nothing was being expressed in the large group due to a lack of a sense of safety. This presented the consultant with the dilemma of the issue not being raised and finding a way to name the issue without blaming. Eventually, without naming the individual who was allegedly using bullying behaviour, the issue was raised by the consultant, who also stated that those who were passive about bullying were also condoning it and therefore responsible for it being perpetuated.	*In this situation the concept of Safety was high on the agenda for the consultant. With the relief of the issue being in the open the team were invited to decide how they wanted to be and what they needed to do to achieve this – this included the type of behaviour they wanted to see and what they would do to challenge situations that were Not OK–OK. In this way the team, and the person allegedly using bullying behaviour, felt safe as the issue was not dwelt on and no one was shamed. The whole team explored options for making the workplace a more relaxed and positive place to be, including listing the actions and behaviour that would enhance this. Due to time constraints a working party was set up to ensure this work was continued and the person who was accused of bullying behaviour volunteered and was readily accepted as a member.*

Summary

In summary, the Concepts for Thriving model can be used as an assessment tool. When communication is dysfunctional it may be that the workforce does not feel emotionally safe. Therefore, even when the initial request for assistance comes from higher up the Concepts model, it is worth considering whether this is the key issue or whether it may be a symptom of something else. The people concerned are likely to know what they need to do to develop a healthy environment and improve communication so involving the workforce in the assessment, analysis and any subsequent action is the most positive way to enable change.

The use of this model as a foundation for development enables an effective way to a healthy culture.

EXERCISES

EXERCISE 1

Team Solutions

This exercise is useful when there are difficulties with productivity, morale, competitiveness or communication. Concepts for Thriving is a good way to enable the team to diagnose where their difficulties lie. They can then discuss their options and any consequent actions they will take to improve the situation. The team can discuss where their interactions fit on the model. Very often the perceived problem area may be higher on the model than the one that in fact needs to be addressed.

1.   Put up and explain the Concepts for Thriving to your team.
2.   Break down into small groups asking the following questions:
     –   Where do they believe that there is room for improvement?
     –   How would they like the team to be?
     –   What do they need to change to achieve this?
     –   What will they do to ensure this is achieved?
     –   By when?
     –   Who is responsible for any particular action?
     –   How will they know when they have achieved their goals?
     –   How will they celebrate?

EXERCISE 2

Developing Leadership Awareness

Here are some questions to ask about leadership to ensure that the positive aspects of the Concepts for Thriving model are in place:
    Does the leader:

* Bring together individual contributions?
* Ensure that decisions are finalized and carried out?
* Maintain a check on whether objectives are set and achieved?
* Bring in information from outside to help the work remain relevant?
* Positively represent the team in other arenas?
* Summarize and clarify discussions?
* Support members in difficult situations?
* Relate to all levels of the organization?
* Operate in consistent ways that are congruent for them as an individual and congruent with the organizational values?
* Work in ways that are OK–OK?
* Operate largely within the Mindful Process of the OK Modes Model – for instance showing flexibility and choosing the most appropriate Mode to be in at any given time.

17 *Countering Anger and Conflict*

Introduction

Since we are human beings rather than machines it is likely that conflict or tension will occur sooner or later. Energy spent on tensions and relationship difficulties in the workplace cannot be spent on productivity so you need to develop a healthy environment in which to work and find ways to resolve issues. This chapter explores ways to deal with, and reduce, anger and conflict.

You don't have to be malicious for conflict to develop. A simple misunderstanding can create tensions until you check out what the difficulty is. Whilst conflict does not necessarily mean being angry, the way you think about anger will have an effect on the way you experience conflict situations. If anger is viewed as something to be avoided, is negative, means you or others do not care or that anger needs to be met with anger, this will influence how you behave and whether or not you avoid it, become aggressive, or are assertive.

Conflict can be between people or internally between different parts of the self. The latter occurs when you experience yourself in a dilemma and are not sure which way to go. However, the focus of this chapter is on conflict between people – individuals, teams, and departments.

EXAMPLE

The manager, Janet, firmly tells Mark that she wants him to staff the enquiry desk over lunch. However, he says that he is inundated with work and does not wish to break off from what he is doing. He says that it is not his problem that they are short-staffed and he does not see it as his job. Janet reminds him that they offer a service to their clients and part of this is being available on the enquiry desk when necessary. Mark thumps the table and escalates his frustration into anger. Janet says not to bother himself, she will find someone else to do it and marches off. In the end she sits on the enquiry desk herself.	*Janet has given in to a threatening employee. Mark has learnt that if he gets angry he can do as he likes, and he hates being on the enquiry desk. His response to Janet could be seen as coming from Oppositional Mode (see Chapter 3). His angry outbursts work for him as Janet is wary of angry feelings. Other staff members lose respect for her as a result of this. In this instance Janet comes across as operating from Inconsistent Mode (see Chapter 3).*

How different it would have been if Janet had stayed in Mindful Process and moved into the Structuring Mode. Had she been involved in developing a team which experienced themselves as offering a service to its customers then the culture could have been developed that had clear expectations of employees about helping out. Had this been the case she might have said something like:

Mark, I realize that you are busy and in the middle of something. However, everyone did agree that they would help out when and where necessary so that we give the best service to our clients. You also agreed to this. You may not like doing it and I do need you to go on the enquiry desk this lunchtime. So please save the work you are doing and go with good grace.

If she stays in the Mindful Process, Janet will be able to find other options for responding should Mark escalate his anger further. For example:

Mark, when you speak to me like that I feel angry. I have supported you on different occasions but this time you are out of order. I suggest you take time out to calm down. You are due to go on the enquiry desk in an hour, when you have completed your shift please come to my office where we can discuss these frequent emotional outbursts.

Causes of Anger and Aggression

There are many schools of thought about the causes of anger, aggression and violence. Some say it is instinctive and others say it is learned. Whichever theory is favoured these feelings and actions need to be dealt with. How we respond today will depend on how we were encouraged to respond in childhood in our family of origin, our neighbourhood and in our culture. For example, shyness and tenderness are often approved of in women, anger is not. Yet in many situations, anger or indignation is the most authentic response. Whether male or female, if we have been taught to repress anger then internalization will occur. Internalized anger brings on depression and self-deprecation.

Anger involves the mind, body and the behavioural habits that people have developed. In order to resolve anger, we need to change not only our thinking, but also our pulse rates. Emotional release is insufficient as it is only half the problem. To shout at someone may be helpful, but rarely is if it does nothing about the person who you feel has wronged you. Undertaking relaxation by, for instance, deep breathing is unlikely to be of assistance on its own if the person who is bothering you still has to be faced.

> Successful anger management deals with *thoughts* – the attitudes, perceptions and interpretations that generate anger; *the body* – teaching personal control; and *behaviour* – teaching new skills.

Often anger is the cover, or substitute, for other feelings (see Chapter 10) which you find it difficult to express:

I'm hurt. I'm worried. I don't know how to talk about my feelings. I don't know how to get my way. No one listens to me. I can't forgive what they did.

It is a myth that we all become angry at the same thing, or the same situation. You need to work out what triggers your own angry feelings and whether you want to change this, or whether you are happy with the way you express or repress these feelings. In short – does the way you manage your own anger enable you to feel safe, and are others safe from you?

In effective anger management both the individual and relationships with others benefit. The spontaneous outpouring of angry feelings may help an individual in the short-term but may not resolve the problem. To think twice about anger is to enhance the long-term benefit of the relationship and is more likely to solve the problem. When dealing with conflict situations you also need to decide what you are thinking and feeling. For example, there may be another feeling underneath your angry feeling. You might cover your anger with hurt feelings because you do not feel safe in expressing anger, or you might believe that expressing anger is bad. When this occurs it is likely that there is no resolution of the conflict. This is because you are expressing hurt but not the authentic feeling of anger. In this way the authentic feeling does not get heard and you do not feel able to let go of the issue. The difficulty is that all of this can happen outside your awareness. You need to develop your skills in learning what substitute feelings you have developed to cover your authentic feelings.

Culture plays a part in how conflict is managed. For example the white British culture is often portrayed as having a 'stiff upper lip' mentality that is, holding on to angry feelings. Other cultures, such as the Greek culture, tend to express their feelings and then move on. Therefore you need to be aware of your own and other's culture and how feelings are expressed.

Dealing with Anger

Many people have a negative view of anger and may confuse it with rage, which is much more violent and developmentally earlier. You can change your attitude about anger, develop a different perspective and in so doing empower yourself to deal more effectively with conflict. Rage on the other hand needs to be socially controlled and different skills established. In this chapter the focus is more on anger as this is the more usual emotion.

You need to know that anger:

- can be positive
- needs to be heard
- is about contact
- can show that you care
- needs to be dealt with as the situation happens
- should lead to positive negotiation and options to complete and end the difficulty
- does not necessarily need to be met with anger

When other people are angry with you, you need to ensure that you:

- share feelings, if appropriate, and take control of the situation calmly
- use humour to defuse situations if appropriate
- respond differently to someone, rather then predictably

- take time to learn where things went wrong so that you do it differently next time; this might mean working out which Mode of behaviour everyone adopted and which Mode you could have come from to positively change the situation
- are prepared to listen to the other person (seek first to understand before being understood)
- are aware that the angry feelings may cover some other feeling
- are willing to take control and set boundaries when necessary
- stay in the Mindful Process
- build relationships
- ask the person what they want from you to resolve the situation
- consider this answer and decide how you will respond
- ask the other person for what you want from them

Responding to Group Conflict

Group conflict may occur when a threat to safety is experienced. Conflict also occurs when groups need to problem-solve but technical solutions are given precedence over what is actually going on between people. Where the solution is technically good, but the group is not committed this could lead to a poor outcome. All group members need an eye to the process and need to stay in touch with how they feel about agreements and decisions.

EXAMPLE

A team had become split. There was great animosity between the two different groupings. One group saw themselves as more experienced, whilst the others believed that they got the worst jobs and were being held back by the other group. They also experienced the other group as bullying them. Team development was seen as the way forward. Communication had completely broken down between the team and grievance procedures were being initiated. After a two-day team development process both groups were beginning to talk to each other. One who had been experienced as a bully shared that he really wanted to understand what he could do as he was upset that there was so much bad feeling. Another person said that he realized that he personally, had demonized other group members believing that they did not have any feelings. He now realized that they were all feeling hurt.	*This can be considered using group imagoes (see Chapter 11). Each group experienced the others as an undifferentiated group that lacked feelings, rather than as individuals who may have different responses. As the others were objectified, rather than personalized, projection was easier. In such circumstances ways need to be found for people to be seen as individuals. Of course, some people are so damaged that working with others is very hard for them and it is not always possible to enable change – despite the use of a range of skills and techniques.*

Conflict may have come about between groups and departments because goals are incompatible. For example, the stock control department may not want so much capital lying around in stock, whilst the maintenance department may need surplus stock to ensure sufficient spares for machinery. Establishing goals which both can share will enable greater common ground. Once achieved it is more likely that there will be a sufficiently good relationship from which to gain an understanding of the other's perspective.

> Seeking to understand others and their perspective is a great starting point for developing a dialogue rather than a monologue.

People are often so busy trying to convert others to their way of thinking that they overlook the possibility that another person's perspective is of value. When this happens the message is likely to be that what others are saying is not important and, therefore, they are not important. You also know that when you feel heard you are more likely to be open to listening to others, and the same goes when the situation is reversed.

In conflict situations we tend to demonize other people and project onto them what we believe they are feeling, rather than asking them. Demonizing others leads to estrangement and polarization. As soon as something occurs that you find irritating, offensive, or difficult in some way you need to deal with it from the Mindful Process. You can do this by asking the other person questions about the situation to ascertain their perspective. It may be that, after hearing their perspective, you have no need to be angry after all.

Options

Problem-solving will depend upon what each party has to gain from the process. There are many different types of problem-solving and these will depend upon the levels of trust each party has of the other. You can solve problems through:

- trying to dominate or coerce the other person or people
- withdrawing from the situation so you just do not have to deal with it
- Over-Adaptation – for instance trying to second-guess what the other person wants and give it to them without checking it out; this also probably involves not considering your own needs and wants in this situation either
- allowing the one with the most power to win; this might be in relation to you or the other
- being cooperative and being assertive; this is true negotiation
- bringing in a third party to aid the resolution
- arbitration – and all parties agree to accept the decision of the arbitrator
- adjudication – where the adjudicator has the authority to impose the outcome

You also need to consider whether the situation is worth getting into conflict about. Some people try to fight every difficulty and get tired out. Sometimes it is worth letting go, though this will also entail letting go of any feelings of resentment.

The best way to obtain a positive outcome is to establish what each party wants to achieve. If you have a clear vision of your aims it may be that the very least the parties can agree on is the same vision. From this it is easier to work out how to achieve this vision or goal. Starting at the biggest picture you can all agree on is then, the first step toward achieving a positive outcome. You can think about this in terms of contracting. What is it each party wants to achieve, by when and is this measurable, manageable and motivational?

Of course it may be that some of the parties in the proceedings are keeping information back. For example, they may achieve a financial incentive if they don't compromise during the negotiations. By addressing possible hidden agendas discussions can be open and honest as hidden agendas will only serve to maintain a stalemate or achieve one of the more dominating or one-sided 'winning' positions. Those with a more Machiavellian frame of reference will find open and honest communication more threatening as it does little to maintain the dog-eat-dog process which they need to win.

If the conflict is between teams then the exchange of team members might allow for the development of understanding of each other's difficulties and needs and thus stereotyping of the other group can be diminished. Exploration of roles and relationships, the reciprocal demands and expectations and the possible conflict areas will create greater understanding. Conflict can then be addressed within this new awareness.

When conflict goes unacknowledged and unaddressed there is likely to be an increase in absenteeism, low motivation levels, human error, low productivity and lack of commitment. By remaining in the Mindful Process we can do just that – account the realities at all levels and from as many perspectives as possible. In this way we are more likely to make appropriate decisions and resolve conflicts and tensions.

Stay in the Mindful Process

When, in spite of using the effective Modes for communication, a situation of conflict arises, it is still important to remain in the Mindful Process and invite others to join you there. If you inadvertently slip into an ineffective Mode you will have less access to your ability to think and it will be necessary to take time out to re-establish the Mindful Process. This can be done in a number of ways. You can say that you need to take 15 minutes to calm down and then you will come back and talk about the situation, checking that the other person has the time for this. If they do not have the time to talk in 15 minutes then you need to check when they will be able to make the time.

When you are used to sensing what the here-and-now Mindful Process feels like it will be increasingly possible to remain in it. In addition when you realize that you might be shifting out of this Mode this realization in itself is likely to enable you to return to it.

Simple breathing techniques also help to regain the here-and-now Mode. By taking a couple of deep breaths you slow down your heart rate and are more likely to maintain your equilibrium. When you are stressed your body goes on alert. When you experience being threatened, the body prepares for action – often referred to as fight-flight (preparing for a battle or to run away). This is less likely to happen at work unless you work for instance for the rescue and support services and are frequently likely to encounter traumatic situations. However, when you are angry, or experience being threatened in some way, then these same systems can come into play. When you become hyper-aroused you are not as able to think clearly which is illustrated by the way that some people experience panic attacks. Breathing deeply allows you to slow down the process, integrate what is happening, so that more thinking is available to you to deal with the situation.

Once back in Mindful Process the aim is to get some sort of positive contact with the other person. You need to separate the person from the problem and look at how you can problem-solve. Identifying the needs of the other person as well as what you want yourself as this will help with getting to a resolution. Once you are in dialogue you can create a common goal with options and proposals of how to get there.

During the 'cold-war' President Reagan held summit meetings with President Gorbachev and, whilst neither man had a common set of beliefs, they kept talking. These summits actually kept the world safe. The learning in this is that talking does work. If it can work at the international level, with two presidents – Reagan and Gorbachev – then it can work at a local level with lower level issues.

Process not task

If you anticipate that someone will threaten you, or they have actually threatened you, then your behaviour will become defensive. In the work place any defensive behaviour takes up energy and detracts from the task in hand. Inevitably production will be hampered if you are:

- giving mental time to how you might win, dominate, impress
- avoiding someone finding out something
- worrying about how you might avoid being attacked

If you are concentrating on the process between you and others so much this is going to affect how much you hear. Therefore instructions may go haywire. When there is an unresolved difficulty you are likely to become more defensive. This defensiveness often results in not talking to the other person or people about what they think about a situation, and instead you can fill in the gaps in the information with your own negative imagination and then act on these projections. This is, of course, likely to lead to more and more difficulties between you and others. How much easier it would be to go and talk to those concerned as soon as a situation arises.

It is important to remember that the same thing can be said in different ways. The tone and inflection of your voice, the speed you say it and the audibility of it, will alter the content of what you say. In TA terms the OK Mode you use and the Life Position you come from will affect how you say something. The country and the region you come from will also affect these aspects and you need to consider the other person's culture as you may have very different ways of dealing with situations. In summary when dealing with conflict it is important to consider diversity and language and how these are influencing your thoughts, feelings and actions.

Developing Relationship and Understanding

In order to develop relationships it is useful for people to meet up face to face at least once for them to 'gel' as a group. Arguably there might need to be further face to face meetings from time to time to reinforce this. Without this the development of understanding is likely to be hampered and tasks can take longer to complete. An example of how this is useful is highlighted below:

A group of engineers living in various parts of the UK were given a task to do together. One of the group, Phil, suggested that they all meet up at least once so that they could get to know each other and develop a way of working together. He also explained that he had worked internationally in virtual teams and meeting up at least once made the work easier and quicker. The rest of the engineers could not understand this request and Phil was out-voted and they did not meet up. When conflict ensued it could not be resolved and resentment and animosity abounded.	*Because the group had not properly formed trust could not develop. When decisions had to be made and there were differences of opinion, it was difficult to resolve these by just using email and telephone conferencing.*

Beliefs and Difference

Managing a diverse work force is a difficult task because of the differences we believe exist. These beliefs develop into stereotyping behaviours that are more pervasive than prejudice because they set standards by which people are judged. These different frames of reference were termed 'assumptive worlds' by Frank (1974). In an attempt to create order and to make sense of the world we make assumptions. Some examples of these are:

- western assumptions about other races and cultures (and vice versa)
- men's assumptions about women (and vice versa)
- different professions' assumptions about each other

When observations are made about other groups, the differences between us and them tend to be exaggerated and similarities between ourselves and them tend to be ignored. ('They are all the same anyway,' 'They are not like us.')

In Structural Ego State terms assumptions and prejudices involve Parent and Child contaminations of the Adult, and are experienced as Adult Ego syntonic, that is, synonymous with the Adult. That is, they are experienced as facts, rather than beliefs. These different observations, beliefs and values are handed down through the culture and, as previously mentioned, embedded in our institutions, which create the cultural script.

You need to make the time to really *meet* each other. In this instance 'meet' means to experience who is really there with you, rather than who you might assume is there due to your expectations and assumptions. Scott Peck (1987) talks about getting to the stage of Community through dropping your prejudices and assumptions and seeing who is really in front of you. Only then can you be conflict resolving rather than conflict avoiding.

Summary

In summary, the only way to deal effectively with conflict is to seek to understand others and be willing to put down your prejudices and assumptions. In this way you are more likely to develop and maintain the relationship, keep boundaries and contract clearly for outcomes. The Winners' Pyramid is one of the concepts to keep in mind (see Chapter 9).

You need to be clear about the frames of reference that are being used so that you ensure you are all talking about the same thing. By testing out new ways of behaving during potential conflict situations you are more likely to be able to get to a conflict resolving process. The steps below outline how to get to new behaviours. First you need to be able to envisage new possibilities, consider the options and choices, take action, reflect on the outcome, consider if your previous frame of reference was helpful and, if not, decide on how you will update yourself.

You will have made fundamental choices about how to live life. If you believe that everyone is against you, or that it is a dog-eat-dog world, that everything and everyone is useless or, that we are all OK we just need to learn about each other, then this will affect how you communicate and what you communicate. You, therefore, need to decide how you want to be in life and how you want to be with others; this will then affect your behaviour as you move toward congruency.

Finally, a story that sums up how you need to be, whether in conflict or not:

Once there was a dog that found his way into a hall of mirrors. He found himself surrounded by dogs and snapped and snarled at them. They of course snapped and snarled back at him. Eventually he lay on the ground, still growling as no amount of snapping and snarling could stop the other dogs doing the same back and he felt he was fighting for his life.

Another day, a different dog came into the hall of mirrors. Seeing the other dogs surrounding him he wagged his tail and he was so pleased that they all wagged their tails back at him. This dog stayed quite some time enjoying the experience before deciding to find his way home, very happy and contented with his day. (Author unknown)

A diagram illustrates the benefits of positive self-talk in contrast to negative self-talk:

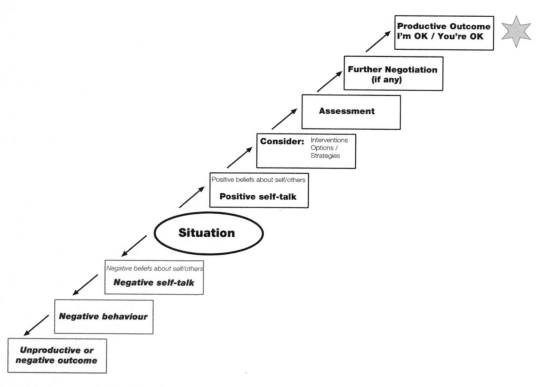

Figure 17.1 Assertive Responses

Finally, a diagram showing the six steps towards new ways of dealing with anger and conflict:

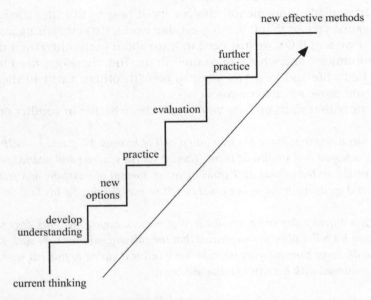

Figure 17.2 Six Steps to Anger Management

EXERCISES

EXERCISE 1

Changing Modes

Think of a time when you were in conflict with someone:

- Did you come from the ineffective or effective Modes?
- Which Mode do you think they came from?
- On reflection do you think you made any assumptions about someone or about the situation?
- What challenges would you now make to your own beliefs about self, others and life?
- How could you have said what you did say in a different way?
- What could you have said that would have improved the situation?
- What could you have said to yourself to help you in the situation?
- What will you do differently in future?

EXERCISE 2

Team Changes

When teams are in conflict it is necessary for everyone to realize that negative processes affect performance through low energy levels or energy expended on difficult relationships rather than on the task. Teams can be involved in solving these difficulties through consideration of the following questions:

- How would you like relationships to be at work? (Be specific – making your goals measurable, manageable and motivational.)
- How do you experience the relationships at work?
- What changes need to be made to bridge the gap between how you would like relationships to be and how they are?
- What is your responsibility in this process?
- What are the risks involved?
- Are they worth it?
- Do you have the formal or informal power to make these changes?
- What action needs to be taken next to achieve your own and team goals?
- What will you do?
- By when?
- Whose support will you seek to achieve these changes?

How will you celebrate when you have made the changes necessary to make the workplace an easier place to be?

18 *Conclusion*

Introduction

The aim of this chapter is to pull this comprehensive overview of Organizational Transactional Analysis together. To do so we share two additional models that we have developed to enable organizational assessment. As part of this overview we highlight the need for congruence between philosophy, values, goals and behaviour, without which trust will not develop.

One way we, the authors, like to consider organizations is by using the following model with its associated questions.

The Dynamic Diagnostic Diagram (The 3-D Model)

A MODEL FOR DIAGNOSIS AND INTERVENTION

The following model can be used to assess where the focus of an intervention needs to be – at a structural level in the organization. Each aspect is interrelated to so change in one area will have an effect on another. The diagram and associated questions were inspired by Jardine's work (1987). What follows is a summary of each area following which each aspect will be expanded so that a fuller picture and theoretical context is provided. In this way it is hoped that in-depth assessments will be made that are based on knowledge and awareness.

(1) PURPOSE AND IDENTITY

The area of purpose and identity is put in the centre of the model as this is the first area of concern when you decide to go into business and during its development. In this sector you need to consider whether all departments are clear about what they are aiming to achieve. There are some organizations whose purpose may seem to be clear. For example, a car manufacturer may see their purpose and identity at its simplest as 'To make cars'. However, if the purpose were 'To develop safe transport systems with both people and the environment in mind' this would have very different effect on the purpose and identity.

In order to ensure that the purpose can be carried out the organization requires the optimum mix of skills and abilities. They also need to ensure that this mix is in the right place at the right time, and that departments, teams and individuals are clear about what they want to achieve, and the processes and practices to fit with the espoused values. Within this area you might also consider whether there are celebrations of achievements (see Concepts for Thriving, Chapter 18). Where goals and priorities are set, achieved and then celebrated the purpose and identity are reinforced, and this feeds into the overall organizational, department and team culture.

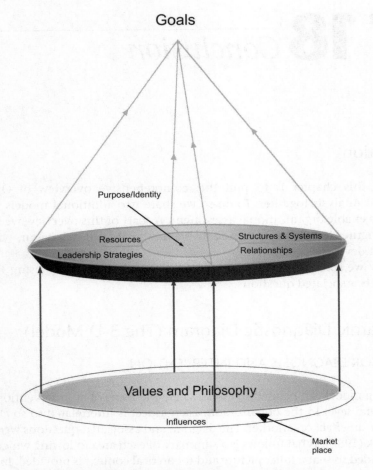

Figure 18.1 The 3-D model: Dynamic Diagnostic Diagram

Questions to ask here include:

- What are we here to do?
- With whom?
- What are we trying to achieve?
- Is our purpose and identity clear?
- Do all areas of the organization add value to the purpose and identity?
- Do all aspects of the structure have shared goals?
- If not, what are the leadership strategies to ensure everyone is pulling in the same direction?

(2) VALUES

The organizational values clearly affect the culture. The way in which business is undertaken and the conduct of the employees including styles of leadership will all be influenced by the underpinning values. Business ethics will also be involved here.

Some questions to ask when attempting to ascertain congruency between values and behaviour are:

- Are there clear values and a philosophy?
- Who originally set up the value base?
- Are those values still appropriate and relevant today?
- If so, are these values expressed and widely shared?
- Are all aspects of the structure congruent with these?
- Is the behaviour in all departments congruent with these values?

(3) STRUCTURE AND SYSTEMS

All organizations have a structure and have set up a set of systems to support the work being undertaken. Staff roles need to be clear and make sense as a whole and the structures and systems need to reflect the values and purpose. The developed systems need to support both the overall purpose and the day-to-day management. This includes the decision-making processes.

As an example of this area of the model we will highlight a very simple systems problem, which, if resolved, could save the organization time and money, and develop a greater sense of achievement for the employees, rather than the frustration that did occur.

A multinational organization wanted to ascertain the views of its leadership. One hundred leaders across the world were asked to complete a questionnaire online. The forms being used were not all in the same format. This meant that those collating the information were expected to reformat them so that they were all uniform. Therefore the 100 forms were reformatted by two more people who then sent them on to the administrator who typed out the responses again into a brochure.	*The middle part of the process, the reformatting, could have been avoided if the original group who devised the questionnaire had considered whether the system they were using fitted their structure and requirements.*

Questions to ask with regard to structure and systems include:

- Do our structures support what is being undertaken?
- Do the structures and systems reflect the organization's values and purpose?
- Are staff roles clear and do they make sense as a whole?
- Do the systems permit effective day-to-day management?
- Are decision-making procedures sound?
- Are there regular reviews of individual/team development needs?

(4) RELATIONSHIPS

In this context 'relationships' include all the different formal and informal relationships that exist in the organization. There may be ongoing disagreements or conflicts in the organization, which may not be openly acknowledged, and this will have an effect on the way the organization functions. For example, emails, memos and seminars will have little impact if there is a significant person or group of people who disagree with decisions or interventions. This means that a person, or group of people, is informally influential in the decision-making processes, which can be either negative or positive to the process. In TA this type of leadership is called psychological leadership (see Chapter 12) and, as previously stated, it can have both positive and detrimental effects upon the progress of the department, team, and wider organization. For example, the psychological leader of a group has the potential to sabotage any action or behaviour that the formal or responsible leader may suggest.

This context also includes how psychologically distant or close different people feel in relation to each other. Micholt refers to this as psychological distance and highlights the importance of this for the organization. We developed this further in Chapter 4, on relationships. By the assessment of the psychological distance between leaders and team members, between leaders and the senior management group, and between team members themselves it is possible to design interventions that will address the situation and create harmony.

Questions to ask here include:

- What formal and informal relationships exist in the organization?
- Where can good relationships be built on and poor ones improved?
- Do the relationships reflect the organizational values?
- Is there openness and willingness to confront difficulties?
- Is there trust and support between employees/team members?
- Are internal and external communications good?
- Are conflicts resolved?
- Are relationships with other groups, teams, and departments sound?
- Are people prepared to review the way they operate?
- Do efforts match values and purpose?

(5) RESOURCES

Most organizations would value extra resources, including buildings, equipment, finances and people. However, some organizations lack the strategic planning through which to organize the best use of the resources they have (see the above example about re-formatting questionnaires). Often there is staff overlap on tasks, or departments are situated inappropriately causing difficulties with communication and liaison.

Resources can be used ineffectively due to poor use of time by management, by workers, by defects in design or defects in manufacturing or in the specifications. The same too goes for consultants who contract ineffectively with the commissioning agent of the organization. When this happens the consultant is likely to design inappropriate or ineffective interventions.

Questions to ask about resources include:

- Are there sufficient resources, human, material and financial?
- Is there an appropriate mix of these?
- Are the resources well used and do they fit with the purpose and priorities?
- Are the resources regularly evaluated and the need for additional ones assessed?
- Could the resources be better utilized?
- Have all aspects been taken into account?

- Are contracts sufficiently detailed to ensure success?
- Are the consequences of organizational interventions considered from a range of perspectives?

(6) LEADERSHIP

The nature of the leadership role is an important part of the assessment, as is the way people follow. For example, autocratic leadership encourages passivity and resentment. This in turn will affect organizational loyalty and therefore levels of production.

Questions to ask here include:

- Does the leader bring together individual contributions?
- Does the leader ensure that decisions are finalized and carried out?
- Does the leader maintain a check on whether objectives are set and achieved?
- Does the leader bring in external information to help the work remain relevant?
- Does the leader represent the team in other arenas?
- Does the leader summarize and clarify discussions?
- Does the leader support members in difficult situations?
- Does the leadership relate to all levels of the organization?
- Is the leadership style consistent and congruent with the values?

(7) GOALS

Clarity of goal setting is important. It is the leader's role to ensure that all departments are heading in the same direction with an overall view of the relevant steps along the way. Regular reviews of the organizational goals are necessary in order to ensure they are still current and relevant to the present day. Keeping abreast of current realities may mean amending the goals.

ASPIRATION

Berne talked about the 'thrust of life' which he called the aspiration arrow or physis, which indicates the natural desire to be autonomous and free. The arrows toward the goals on the 3-D model indicate physis energy and there is also an implied central core of the organization that is healthy and which therefore affects all other parts of the organization to aspire to health.

The terminology 'thrust of life' indicates an energetic dimension. When this energy is blocked we either try to find ways to adapt and compromise, give up trying, get angry and rebel, or find ways to do it our way and remove the block. This is particularly relevant in terms of the effects on the work force.

Questions to be asking here include:

- Are the goals clear and widely shared?
- Do the goals fit with the values?
- Does the workforce have sufficient skills to match the goals set?
- Are the goals for each department congruent with the organizational goals?
- Are the leadership goals congruent with the organizational goals?

- Are the current goals relevant to the current market place?
- What external influences need to be accounted in relation to goals?
- Does any vision statement reflect the organizational goals?

When all sectors of the 3-D model are assessed, and the appropriate interventions made, production should increase and goals achieved. This process enables the energy that may previously have been used in negative or divergent ways to be harnessed for positive processes for the good of the workforce and for the organization as a whole. It is almost as if the physis arrow (the arrow of aspiration) goes right up through the centre of the diagram.

Congruence

In summary, the benefit of using Organizational Transactional Analysis as the method of approach is that, being a social psychology, it can look at individual as well as the organizational interventions and can enhance congruency between the organizational values and philosophy, processes and systems, and the behaviours of the people.

That an organization is congruent in all aspects of its operation is paramount, as this promotes trust within the workforce. All aspects of the organization need to be aligned with each other to ensure a cohesive approach. These areas include, but are not limited to: identity, beliefs and values; skills and knowledge; the environment; and behaviour.

Individually, when you are experienced as congruent your behaviour and verbal expression reflect your philosophy and value base. When this does not occur you can give off signals that you are not at ease with yourself and therefore not at ease with others and this will develop a sense of incongruity. Others are less likely to trust you, even if they don't understand why this is. The TA concepts of games, substitute feelings and ulterior messages are all related to incongruity.

When you engage in positive self-talk you increase your confidence and feelings of OKness about yourself and others are increasingly willing to give and receive positive recognition. When you believe that everyone is OK you will be congruent in thought, feelings and actions.

The following model outlines the organizational areas between which there needs to be congruence in terms of structures, policies and practice. It is similar to the 3-D model but has greater detail about the areas to be considered with a view to congruence.

Congruency is required between all levels of the organization.

Summary

Having considered the 3-D and Organizational Web models you can start to apply the Transactional Analysis concepts outlined in this book and decide which are relevant as interventions to develop the organization.

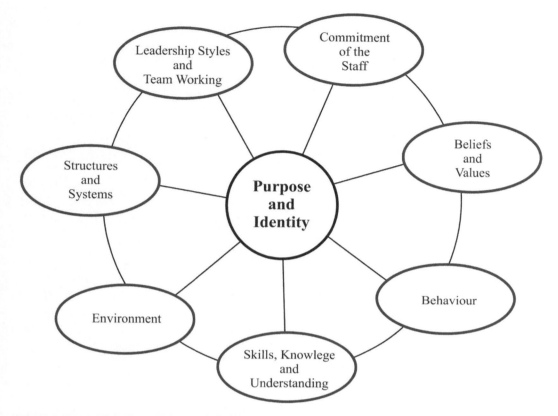

Figure 18.2 The Organizational Web Model

Source: Mountain, A. (2004).

And Finally

In the introductory chapter we said that our aims were to:

- Offer those in business an overall guide to increasing productivity through developing and enhancing workplace relationships
- Enable the reader to develop an understanding of themselves and others so that they can be aware of the processes involved in carrying out decisions and strategies
- Give some clear 'how-tos' for those who require extra tools for developing effective communication
- Offer a way of understanding the relationship between people, the processes and productivity

We hope that, having read the book, you will now have an understanding of the way in which Developmental Transactional Analysis, and Organizational TA in particular, can be used throughout an organization to enable the improvement of the organizational culture – promoting a healthy environment in which to work, where people feel respected and valued, with the space to be creative as well as the skills to set and maintain boundaries.

Appendix 1: TA Training

The Official Introduction to Transactional Analysis (the 'TA101') which is a general introduction to the TA field is a course which is available in many locations both in the UK and around the world.

There are various training courses in Organizational Transactional Analysis ranging from year-long Foundation Courses to advanced training with the option of leading to an internationally validated qualification in TA. A web search for 'Organizational TA Training' should list options local to your country. There is also a generic term 'Developmental TA' which covers all the non-psychotherapy applications of TA.

Transactional Analysis Journal

Many of the references in this book refer to the *Transactional Analysis Journal*, which is still the most productive source for articles and theory on Transactional Analysis. There is a CD-ROM available with almost all articles from the journal from 1971 to 2008. This can be ordered via: www.tajdisk.co.uk.

Becoming an Organizational Transactional Analyst

What does it take to become an Organizational Transactional Analyst?

The experience and training required for qualification in this field generally takes around four to five years. To develop this expertise Organizational Transactional Analysts need to have satisfied the competencies for this field and have:

- Experience in organizations in the public, charitable and private sectors.
- Undertaken in-depth training programmes in Transactional Analysis. (It takes 5–6 years to reach Certified Transactional Analyst level including 750 hours of documented practical experience, 150 hours of supervision of our work, and 600 hours of training.)

Once the sponsor agrees that the candidate is personally and professionally ready to go for examination the candidate writes a 24,000 word dissertation. This includes an in-depth case study on a piece of work undertaken. Once this dissertation has been passed there follows an oral examination and, if successful, the candidate becomes a Certified Transactional Analyst in the field of specialization.

If they wish to, the CTA can then continue on to become a Teaching and Supervising Transactional Analyst. They need to wait for one year to elapse, during which time they are preparing for an endorsement process where they need to:

- Take part in an assessment process designed to assess training and supervision skills. Once passed then candidates become Provisional Teaching and Supervising Transactional Analysts. (It then takes another 5–7 years to build up the required hours before being eligible for the TSTA examination.)
- Accrue 500 hours of supervision experience.
- A Teaching Transactional Analyst candidate must also accrue 300 hours of experience teaching TA, plus 100 hours of continuous professional development, and complete 12 hours of presentations at conferences and professional meetings.
- Once these hours have been completed, and the sponsor believes that the PTSTA is personally and professionally ready, they can put in for the TSTA exam. This involves three different boards, one on theory, one on training or teaching, and the other on supervision. The teaching and supervision boards include practical live teaching and supervision in front of the board, and the candidate is asked questions about their philosophy and practice.

Both the Certified Transactional Analyst and the Teaching and Supervising Transactional Analyst levels are nationally and internationally accredited by a number of International Transactional Analysis Associations – see Appendix 2 for a list of these. It is the International Associations – ITAA and EATA – which have the responsibility of accreditation and endorsement.

Appendix 2: Information about TA Associations Nationally, Regionally and Internationally

In the UK

INSTITUTE OF DEVELOPMENTAL TRANSACTIONAL ANALYSIS
Wildhill
Broadoak End
Hertford
Herts
SG14 2JA
England
email: admin@instdta.org
website: www.instdta.org

The IDTA is the UK association for the non-psychotherapy applications of TA – for which Julie Hay coined the term 'developmental' – to reflect that in organizations and education the focus is on people developing, rather than on 'therapy' per se – though of course these interventions can be therapeutic.

INSTITUTE OF TRANSACTIONAL ANALYSIS
Broadway House
149–151 St Neots Road
Hardwick
Cambridge
CB23 7QJ
Tel/Fax: 01954 212468
email: admin@ita.org.uk
website: http://www.ita.org.uk/

The ITA, whilst being open to membership for people from any of the four fields of application, has a membership largely consisting of people specializing in psychotherapy.

In Europe

EUROPEAN ASSOCIATION OF TRANSACTIONAL ANALYSIS
website: http://www.eatanews.org/

EATA is the Europe-wide regional TA association. It is not possible to be a member other than through one of the national Associations (such as IDTA or ITA or any of the other national associations listed on pages 257–8).
EATA is affiliated to ITAA and WAPATA.

Internationally

INTERNATIONAL TRANSACTIONAL ANALYSIS ASSOCIATION
website: http://www.itaa-net.org/

The ITAA has members in over 65 countries. It is possible to join the ITAA as an individual member. It was the founding TA association – having its beginnings in the San Francisco seminars that Eric Berne ran in the 1960s.

WESTERN PACIFIC ASSOCIATION OF TRANSACTIONAL ANALYSIS
website: http://www.wpata.com.au/

This body, formed in 1985, encompasses Australia and New Zealand.

National TA Associations in Europe[1]

Armenia	(no website)	AATA
Austria	http://www.itap.at/	Institut für transaktionsanalytische Psychotherapie ITAP
Austria	http://www.transaktionsanalyse.at/	Österreichisches transaktionsanalytisches Institut im Sozial-Pädagogik und Organisationsbereich (ÖTISO)
Belgium	http://www.assobat.be/accueil/	Association Belge pour l'Analyse Transactionnelle
Bosnia-Herzegovina	http//bihota.com/	BIHOTA
Croatia	http://www.uta.hr/	Udruga Transakcijske Analize (UTA)
Czech Republic	http://www.ta-cata.cz/	Ceska asociace transakcni analyzy CATA
Denmark	(no website)	DTA
Finland	http://www.finta.net/	The Transactional Analysis Association of Finland (FINTA)
France	http://www.ifat.net/	Institute Francaise d'Analyse Transactionnelle (IFAT)
Germany	http://www.dgta.de/	Deutsche Gesellschaft für Transaktionsanalyse (DGTA)
Hungary	http://www.hata.hu/	HATA Hungarian Association for Transactional Analysis
Italy	http://www.aiat.it/	Associazione Italiana di Analisi Transazionale
Italy	http://www.centropsi.it/	Centro di Psicologia e analisi Transazionale (CPAT)
Italy	http://www.sieb96.org/iat/iat.htm	Istituto Analisi Transazionale (IAT)
Italy	http://www.formazionepoiesis.it/	Istituto di Formazione in Analisi Transazionale (AUXIMON)
Italy	http://www.ianti.it/	IANTI – TA Integrative Institute
Italy	http://www.irpir.it/	Istituto di Ricerca sui Processi Intrapsichici e Relazionali (IRPIR)
Italy	http://www.simpat.org/	Società Italiana di Metodologie Psicoterapeutiche ed Analisi Transazionale (SIMPAT)

---

1   ITA and IDTA are already listed above.

Lithuania	(no website)	LTAA
Macedonia	(no website)	MATA
Netherlands	http://www.nvta.nl/	The TA Association of the Netherlands
Norway	http://www.transaksjonsanalyse.com/	Norsk Transaksjonsanalytisk Forening (NTAF)
Romania	http://www.arat.ro/	ARAT
Russia	(no website)	(Ryazan) RATA
Russia	(no website)	(St. Petersburg) SITA
Serbia	http://www.sata.co.yu/	Srpske Asocijacije za Transakcionu Analizu (SATA)
Slovenia	http://www.sloventa.si/	SLOVENTA
Spain	http://www.apphat.org/	APPHAT
Spain	http://www.atainfo.org/	La ATA-Asociación de Análisis? Transaccional
Sweden	http://www.transaktionsanalys.se/	Svenska Transaktionsanalytiska Föreningen
Switzerland	http://www.asat-sr.ch/	ASAT-SR Association Suisse d'Analyse Transactionnelle
Switzerland	http://www.dsgta.ch/	Deutschschweizer Gesellschaft für Transaktionsanalyse DSGTA
Ukraine	http://www.uata.org.ua/	UATA UATA-Associazione Ucraina di AT

References

Adams, A. (1992). *Bullying at Work – How to Confront and Overcome It*, London: Virago.

Ainsworth, M., Blehar, M., Waters, E. and Wall, S. (1978). *Patterns of Attachment*, Hillsdale, NJ: Erlbaum.

Allen, J.R. and Allen, B.A. (1989). Stroking: Biological Underpinnings and Direct Observations, *Transactional Analysis Journal*, 19:1, pp. 26–31, San Francisco, USA: ITAA.

Altorfer, O. (1977). Authentic Courtesy and Personal Power: Two Aims of Emotional Job Fitness, *Transactional Analysis Journal*, 7:4, pp. 339–341, San Francisco, USA: ITAA.

Argyris, C. (1999). *On Organizational Learning*, Oxford: Blackwell Business.

Barnes, G. (1981). On Saying Hello, *Transactional Analysis Journal*, 11:1, pp. 22–32, San Francisco, USA: ITAA.

Batts, V.A. (1982). Modern Racism: A TA Perspective, *Transactional Analysis Journal*, 12:3, pp. 207–209, San Francisco, USA: ITAA.

Baumard, P. (1999). *Tacit Knowledge in Organizations*, London, England: Sage.

Bellman, G.M. (1990). *The Consultant's Calling, Bringing Who You Are to What You Do*, San Francisco: Jossey-Bass Inc.

Berne, E. (1961). *Transactional Analysis in Psychotherapy*, London: Souvenir Press.

Berne, E. (1962). Classification of Positions, *Transactional Analysis Bulletin*, 62:3 p. 23, San Francisco, USA: ITAA.

Berne, E. (1963). *The Structure and Dynamics of Organizations and Groups*, New York: Ballantine Books.

Berne, E. (1964). *Games People Play*, Harmondsworth: Penguin.

Berne, E. (1966). *Principles of Group Treatment*, New York: Grove Press.

Berne, E. (1970). *Sex in Human Loving*, Harmondsworth: Penguin.

Berne, E. (1975). *What Do You Say After You say Hello?* London: Corgi.

Branson, R. (2000). *Losing My Virginity – The Autobiography*, London: Virgin Publishing.

Campos, L.P. (1971). Transactional Analysis Group Leadership Operations, *Transactional Analysis Journal*, 1:4, pp. 219–222, San Francisco, USA: ITAA.

Carter, R. (1999). *Mapping the Mind*, London: Seven Dials.

Chaleff, I. (2003). *The Courageous Follower: Standing Up To and For our Leaders*, Berrett–Koehler, 2nd revised edition.

Clarkson, P. (1992). *Transactional Analysis Psychotherapy: An Integrated Approach*, London: Routledge.

Clavier, D.E., Timm, P.R. and Wilkens, P.L. (1978). Effects of Salient Communicative Strokes on Subordinate Employees in a Health Care Organization, *Transactional Analysis Journal*, 8:4, pp. 300–305, San Francisco, USA: ITAA.

Collinson, D. (1994). Strategies of Resistance: Power, knowledge and subjectivity in the workplace, in Jermier, J.M. et al. (eds), *Resistance and Power in Organizations*, London, England: Routledge, pp. 25–68.

Conner, D. (1998). *Managing at the Speed of Change*, Chichester, England: Wiley.

Cowles-Boyd, L. and Boyd, H. (1980). Play as a Time Structure, *Transactional Analysis Journal*, 10:1, pp. 5–7, San Francisco, USA: ITAA.

Crossman, P. (1966). Permission and Protection, *Transactional Analysis Bulletin*, 66:19, San Francisco, USA: ITAA.

Crossman, P. (1977). Acceptance Speech, Eric Berne Memorial Award, *Transactional Analysis Journal*, 7:1, pp. 104–106, San Francisco, USA: ITAA.

D'Amore, I. (1997). The Source of Motivation and Stroke Theory, *Transactional Analysis Journal*, 27:3, pp. 181–191, San Francisco, USA: ITAA.

Davidson, C. (1999). I'm Polygonal, OK. *INTAND Newsletter*, 7:1, pp. 6–9, Watford, England.

Davis, J. (unpublished). 'The Blame Model'.

Dusay, J. (1972). Egogram and the Constancy Hypothesis, *Transactional Analysis Journal*, 2:3, pp. 37–41, San Francisco, USA: ITAA.

Edmunds, G. (2003). Investment Games, San Francisco: *Transactional Analysis Journal*, 33:1, pp. 68–75, San Francisco, USA: ITAA.

English, F. (1975). The Three-Cornered Contract, *Transactional Analysis Journal*, 5:4, pp. 383–384 ITAA, San Francisco, San Francisco, USA: ITAA.

English, F. (1987). Power, Mental Energy and Inertia, *Transactional Analysis Journal*, 17:3, pp. 91–98, San Francisco, USA: ITAA.

Ernst, F. (1971). OK Corral, The grid to get on with, *Transactional Analysis Journal*, 1(4), pp. 231–240, San Francisco, USA: ITAA.

Erskine, R. and Zalcman, M. (1979). The Racket System: A Model for Racket Analysis, *Transactional Analysis Journal*, 9:1, pp. 51–59, San Francisco, USA: ITAA.

Fox, E.M. (1975). Eric Berne's Theory of Organizations, *Transactional Analysis Journal*, 5:4, pp. 345–353, San Francisco, USA: ITAA.

Freedman, L. (1993). TA Tools for Self–Managed Work Teams, *Transactional Analysis Journal*, 23:2, pp. 104–109, San Francisco, USA: ITAA.

Gallagher, K. et al. (1997). *People in Organisations, an active learning approach*, Gateshead, Tyne and Wear, England: Blackwell Business.

Garfield, V. (1993). Ethical Principles for Work in Organizations, *Transactional Analysis Journal*, 23:2, pp. 60–65, San Francisco, USA: ITAA.

Gibb, J.R. (2001). Defensive Communication, in Osland, J.S. Kolb, D.A. and Rubin, I.M. (eds), *The Organizational Behaviour Reader*, 7th edition, New Jersey, USA: Prentice Hall, pp. 195–200.

Goulding, R. and Goulding, M. (1976). Injunctions, Decisions and Redecisions, *Transactional Analysis Journal*, 6:1, pp. 41–48, San Francisco, USA: ITAA.

Gowell, E. (1975). Transactional Analysis and the Body: Sensory Stimulation Techniques, *Transactional Analysis Journal*, 5:2, pp. 148–151, San Francisco, USA: ITAA.

Gregory, R.L. (1970). *The Intelligent Eye*, London, England: Weidenfeld and Nicolson.

Hay, J. (1993). *Working it out at Work*, Hertford, England: Sherwood Publishing.

Hay, J. (2009). *Transactional Analysis for Consultants*, Hertford England: Sherwood Publishing.

Health and Safety Executive (2010). website: www.hse.gov.uk.

Herrman, N. (1995). *The Creative Brain*, North Carolina: Brain Books.

Hine, J. (1990). The Bilateral and Ongoing Nature of Games, *Transactional Analysis Journal*, 20:1, pp. 28–39, San Francisco, USA: ITAA.

Hondelink, E.R. (1965). *Review of Dr Beeching's Report – The Reshaping of British Railways*, Northwood, Middlesex, England: The Great Central Association.

Ishmael, A. with Alemoru, B. (1999). *Harassment, Bullying and Violence at Work*, London, England: The Industrial Society.

Jacobs, A. (1987). Autocratic Power, *Transactional Analysis Journal*, 17:3, pp. 59–71, San Francisco, USA: ITAA.

James, J. (1973). Game Plan, *Transactional Analysis Journal*, 3:4, pp. 14–17, San Francisco, USA: ITAA.

James, M. and Jongeward, D. (1985). *Born to Win*, Reading Massachusetts: Addison Wesley.

Janis, I. (1972). *Victims of Groupthink*, New York: Houghton Mifflin.

Jaworski, J. (1998). *Synchronicity, The Inner Path of Leadership*, San Francisco, USA: Berrett-Koehler.

Jermier, J.M., Knights, D. and Nord, W.R. (eds) (1994). *Resistance and Power in Organizations*, London, England: Routledge.

Johnson, G. and Scholes, K. (1997). *Exploring Corporate Strategy: Text and Cases*, Harlow, Essex, England: Prentice Hall.

Karpman, S. (1968). Fairy Tales and Script Drama Analysis, *Transactional Analysis Bulletin*, 7:26, pp. 39–44, San Francisco, USA: ITAA.

Karpman, S. (1971). Options San Francisco: *Transactional Analysis Journal*, 1:1, pp. 79–87, San Francisco, USA: ITAA.

Koch, R. (1998). *The 80–20 Principle, The secret of achieving more with less*, London, England: Nicholas Brealey Publishing Ltd.

Kohlreiser, G. (2006). *Hostage at the Table: How Leaders Can Overcome Conflict, Influence Others, and Raise Performance*, San Francisco: Jossey–Bass.

Kolb, D. (1984). *Experiential Learning: Experience as the Source of Learning and Development*, Englewood Cliffs, New Jersey, USA: Prentice Hall.

Krausz, R. (1980). TA and Management Effectiveness, *Transactional Analysis Journal*, 80:1, pp. 21–24, San Francisco, USA: ITAA.

Krausz, R. (1986). Power and Leadership in Organizations, *Transactional Analysis Journal*, 16:2, pp. 85–94, San Francisco, USA: ITAA.

Lankton, S.R., Lankton, C.H. and Brown, M. (1981). Psychological Level Communication in Transactional Analysis, *Transactional Analysis Journal*, 11:4, pp. 287–299, San Francisco, USA: ITAA.

Lapworth, P., Sills, C. and Fish, S. (1997). *Transactional Analysis Counselling*, Bicester, Oxon: Winslow Press Ltd.

Lewis, T., Armini, F. and Lannon, R. (2001). *A General Theory of Love*, New York: Vintage Books.

Macefield, R. and Mellor, K. (2006). Awareness and Discounting: New Tools for Task/Option–Oriented Settings, *Transactional Analysis Journal*, 36:1, pp. 44–58, San Francisco, USA: ITAA.

MacKay, C.J. et al. (2004). Health and Safety Executive in Management Standards and Work Related Stress in the UK: Policy background and Science, *Work and Stress*, 18:2, pp. 91–112, London, England: Taylor Francis Group.

Makin, P., Cooper, C. and Cox, C. (1996). *Organizations and the Psychological Contract*, Leicester, England: BPS Books.

Manning, S. (2001). Bad Men: A social theory relating to the antisocial process, the FU defence pattern, and script formation in violent men in New Zealand, unpublished manuscript for Masters Degree.

Maslow, A. (1943). A Theory of Human Motivation, *Psychological Review*, 50, 370–96, Washington, USA.

Massey, R.F. (1996). Transactional Analysis as a Social Psychology, *Transactional Analysis Journal*, 26:1, pp. 91–99, San Francisco, USA: ITAA.

Mayo, E. (1949). Hawthorne and the Western Electric Company, in Gallagher, K. et al.(1997), *People in Organisations: An Active Learning Approach*, Gateshead, Tyne and Wear, England: Blackwell Business.

McGregor, D. (1960). *The Human Side of Enterprise*, London, England: McGraw-Hill Book Company.

Mellor, K. and Sigmund, E. (1975). Discounting, *Transactional Analysis Journal*, 5:3, pp. 295–302, San Francisco, USA: ITAA.

Mescavage, A. and Silver, C. (1977). 'Try Hard' and 'Please Me' in Psychological Development, *Transactional Analysis Journal*, 7:4, pp. 331–334, San Francisco, USA: ITAA.

Micholt, N. (1992). Psychological Distance and Group Interventions, *Transactional Analysis Journal*, 22:4, pp. 228–233, ITAA, San Francisco.

Mountain, A. (2004). *The Space Between: Bridging the Gap between Workers and Young People*, UK: Russell House Publishing.

Mountain, A. and Davidson, C. (2005). Assessing Systems and Processes in Organizations, *Transactional Analysis Journal*, 35:4, pp. 336–345, San Francisco, USA: ITAA.

Nabudere, D.W. (accessed January 2010). Ubuntu Philosophy: Memory and Reconciliation, http://www.grandslacs.net/doc/3621.pdf.

Niemeier, D. and Douglas, H. (1975). Transactions and Self-Actualization, *Transactional Analysis Journal*, 5:2, pp. 152–157, San Francisco, USA: ITAA.

Nuttall, J. (2000). Intrapersonal and Interpersonal Relations in Management Organizations, *Transactional Analysis Journal*, 30:1, pp. 73–83, San Francisco, USA: ITAA.

Osland, J.S., Kolb, D. and Rubin, I.M. (eds) (2001). *The Organizational Behaviour Reader*, 7th edition, New Jersey, USA: Prentice Hall.

Peck, M. Scott (1987). *The Different Drum: Community Making and Peace*, New York: Simon and Shuster.

Perkins, D.N.T. (2000). *Leading at the Edge: Leadership Lessons from the Extraordinary Saga of Shackleton's Antarctic Expedition*, New York: Amacom – American Management Association.

Poelje, S. van (1994). 'Contracting for Organizational Change', in Poelje, S. van and Steinert, T. (eds) (1996), *Transactional Analysis in Organizations: First of selected articles 1974–1994*, ITAA, San Francisco, USA, pp. 102–108.

Poelje, S. van (1995). Development of Autocratic Structures, *Transactional Analysis Journal*, 25:3, pp. 265–270, San Francisco, USA: ITAA.

Poelje, S. van and Steinert, T. (eds) (1996). *Transactional Analysis in Organizations: First of Selected Articles 1974–1994*, ITAA, San Francisco, USA.

Poindexter, W.R. (1975). Organizational Games, *Transactional Analysis Journal*, 5:4, pp. 379–382, San Francisco, USA: ITAA.

Poindexter, W.R. (1977). *The Poindexter Organization*, Agoura: Transan Publications.

Porter, N. (1975). Functional Analysis, *Transactional Analysis Journal*, 5:3, San Francisco, USA: ITAA.

Raynor, C., Hoel, H. and Cooper, C.L. (2002). *Workplace Bullying: What We Know, Who is to Blame, and What Can We Do?* London, England: Taylor and Francis.

Remland, M.S. (2000). *Nonverbal Communication in Everyday Life*, Boston, USA: Houghton Mifflin Company.

Research on Language and Social Interaction, 1990/91, vol. 24, Taylor and Francis.

Rissman, A. (1975). Trilog, *Transactional Analysis Journal*, 5:2, pp. 170–177, San Francisco, USA: ITAA.

Roberts, D. (1992). 'Hierarchy of Functionality', workshop notes from ITAA Conference, New Zealand.

Roberts, D. (1997). Find Purpose, Find Power, Los Angeles, California: Human Esteem Publishing.

Schiff, J. et al. (1975). *The Cathexis Reader*, Harper and Row (out of print).

Shaffer, T.L. (1970). The Law and Order, Game *Transactional Analysis Bulletin*, 70:34, San Francisco, USA: ITAA.

Siebert, A. (2005). *The Resiliency Advantage*, San Francisco, USA: Berrett–Koelher Publishers.

Siegel, B. (1999). *The Developing Mind*, New York, London: Guilford Press.

Silberman, M. (1999). *Team and Organization Development Sourcebook*, New York, USA: McGraw-Hill.

Sills, C. (ed.) (1997). *Contracts in Counselling*, London: Sage.

Sills, C. and Hargaden, H. (eds) (2003). *Key Concepts in Transactional Analysis: Contemporary Views: Ego States*, London: Worth Publishing.

Spitz, R. (1946). *Hospitalism, The Psychoanalytic Study of the Child*, vol. 2, New York, NY: International Universities Press, pp. 113–117.

Steiner, C. (1971). The Stroke Economy, *Transactional Analysis Journal*, 1:3, San Francisco, USA: ITAA.

Steiner, C. (1974). *Scripts People Live*, Toronto: Bantam Books.

Steiner, C. (1984). Emotional Literacy, *Transactional Analysis Journal*, 14:3, pp. 162–173, San Francisco, USA: ITAA.

Steiner, C.M. (1987). The Seven Sources of Power: An Alternative to Authority, *Transactional Analysis Journal*, 17:3, pp. 102–104, San Francisco, USA: ITAA.

Stern, C. (1978). Congruent and Incongruent Transactions, *Transactional Analysis Journal*, 8:4, pp. 312–315, San Francisco, USA: ITAA.

Stern, E. (ed.) (1984). *TA The State of the Art*, Dordrecht, the Netherlands: Foris Publications.

Stewart, I. and Joines, V. (1987). *TA Today*, Nottingham, England: Lifespace Publishing.

Summers, G. and Tudor, K. (2000). Co-creative Transactional Analysis, *Transactional Analysis Journal*, 30:1, pp. 23–40, San Francisco, USA: ITAA.

Summerton, O. (1979). RANI: A New Approach to Relationship Analysis, *Transactional Analysis Journal*, 9:2, pp. 115–118, San Francisco, USA: ITAA.

Tannen, D. (2001). The Power of Talk: Who Gets Heard and Why in Osland, J.S., Kolb, D. and Rubin, I.M. (eds), *The Organizational Behaviour Reader*, 7th edition, New Jersey, USA: Prentice Hall.

Taylor, F. (1912). *Scientific Management*, republished (2003) London: Routledge.

Temple, S. (1999) Functional Fluency for Educational Transactional Analysts, *Transactional Analysis Journal* 29:3.

Temple, S. (2004). Update on the Functional Fluency Model in Education, *Transactional Analysis Journal* 34:3.

Tudor, K. (1997). A Complexity of Contracts, in Sills, C. (ed.), *Contracts in Counselling*, London: Sage, pp. 157–172.

Wenger, E. (1998). *Communities of Practice: Learning, Meaning and Identity*, Cambridge: Cambridge University Press.

Wenger, E. and Snyder, W. (2000). Communities of Practice: The Organizational Frontier, *Harvard Business Review*, 78:1, Jan–Feb, pp. 139–145.

White, J.D. and White, T. (1975). Cultural Scripting, *Transactional Analysis Journal*, 5:1, pp. 12–23, San Francisco, USA: ITAA.

White, T. (1994). Life positions, *Transactional Analysis Journal*, 24:4, pp. 269–276, San Francisco, USA: ITAA.

White, T. (1995). I'm OK You're OK. Further considerations. *Transactional Analysis Journal*, 25:3, pp. 236–244, San Francisco, USA: ITAA.

Wickens, P. (1995). *The Ascendant Organization*, Basingstoke, England: Macmillan Business.

Woods, M.F. (1982). Personality and Learning: The Rissman Trilog and the Experiential Learning Cycle, *Transactional Analysis Journal*, 12:2, pp. 153–158, San Francisco, USA: ITAA.

Woollams, S. and Brown, M. (1979). *The Total Handbook of Transactional Analysis*, New Jersey, USA: Prentice Hall.

Transactional Analysis Journal articles referred to above may not be easily available. However, please see our note on page 253 about a CD-ROM containing collected articles.

Index

If you have found this book useful you may be interested in other titles from Gower

Communicating Strategy
Phil Jones
Paperback: 978-0-566-08810-0
ebook: 978-0-7546-8288-2

Complex Adaptive Leadership:
Embracing Paradox and Uncertainty
Nick Obolensky
Hardback: 978-0-566-08932-9
ebook: 978-0-566-08933-6

Corporate DNA:
Using Organizational Memory
to Improve Poor Decision-Making
Arnold Kransdorff
Hardback: 978-0-566-08681-6

Cultural Differences and Improving Performance:
How Values and Beliefs Influence Organizational Performance
Bryan Hopkins
Hardback: 978-0-566-08907-7
ebook: 978-0-566-08908-4

Hoshin Kanri:
The Strategic Approach to Continuous Improvement
David Hutchins
Hardback: 978-0-566-08740-0
ebook: 978-0-7546-9098-6

Improving Learning Transfer:
A Guide to Getting More Out of What
You Put Into Your Training
Cyril Kirwan
Hardback: 978-0-566-08844-5
ebook: 978-0-566-08986-2

GOWER

Informal Learning:
A New Model for Making Sense of Experience
Lloyd Davies
Hardback: 978-0-566-08857-5

Managing the Psychological Contract:
Using the Personal Deal to Increase Business Performance
Michael Wellin
Hardback: 978-0-566-08726-4
ebook: 978-0-7546-8189-2

MisLeadership:
Prevalence, Causes and Consequences
John Rayment and Jonathan Smith
Hardback: 978-0-566-09226-8
ebook: 978-0-566-09227-5

Pattern Making, Pattern Breaking:
Using Past Experience and New Behaviour in
Training, Education and Change Management
Ann Alder
Hardback: 978-0-566-08853-7
ebook: 978-1-4094-1911-2

Systems Leadership:
Creating Positive Organisations
Ian Macdonald, Catherine Burke and Karl Stewart
Hardback: 978-0-566-08700-4
ebook: 978-0-7546-8313-1

Visit **www.gowerpublishing.com** and

- search the entire catalogue of Gower books in print
- order titles online at 10% discount
- take advantage of special offers
- sign up for our monthly e-mail update service
- download free sample chapters from all recent titles
- download or order our catalogue

T - #0029 - 230424 - C0 - 246/174/16 - PB - 9781472461599 - Gloss Lamination